A MANUAL OF FOREIGN EXCHANGE

A MANUAL OF
FOREIGN EXCHANGE

BY

H. E. EVITT

SEVENTH EDITION

BY

RAYMOND F. PITHER A.I.B., M.I.Ex.

Pitman Publishing

Seventh edition 1971

First paperback edition 1971

SIR ISAAC PITMAN AND SONS LTD.
Pitman House, Parker Street, Kingsway, London WC2B 5PB
P.O. Box 6038, Portal Street, Nairobi, Kenya

SIR ISAAC PITMAN (AUST.) PTY. LTD.
Pitman House, Bouverie Street, Carlton, Victoria 3053, Australia

PITMAN PUBLISHING COMPANY S.A. LTD.
P.O. Box 11231, Johannesburg, S. Africa

PITMAN PUBLISHING CORPORATION
6 East 43rd Street, New York, N.Y. 10017, U.S.A.

SIR ISAAC PITMAN (CANADA) LTD.
495 Wellington Street West, Toronto 135, Canada

THE COPP CLARK PUBLISHING COMPANY
517 Wellington Street West, Toronto 135, Canada

Cased edition   ISBN: 0 273 31460 2
Paperback edition   ISBN: 0 273 31459 9

PRINTED IN GREAT BRITAIN BY
UNWIN BROTHERS LIMITED
WOKING AND LONDON
G1(B.2100/1021:43)

PREFACE TO FOURTH EDITION

MORE years ago than I care to remember, I was inveigled into re-writing a book called *Practical Banking, Currency and Exchange*. Owing to the events of the early 1930s this book, like Topsy, just growed until it was decided to separate the banking section from those on currency and exchange. The result was a small (and now defunct) book called *Practical Banking* and a much larger and favourite child called A MANUAL OF FOREIGN EXCHANGE. This last, I am modestly proud to say, ran into several editions and reprints and has been one of the standard text-books on the subject recommended by the Institute of Bankers and other professional bodies since long before the last war.

That war, however, caused such profound changes to be made in the practice of Foreign Exchange in this country and elsewhere that I produced *Exchange and Trade Control in Theory and Practice* which, I think, is still of value, though now to an increasing extent mainly historical. In the meantime, the "Manual" retained its pre-war form, and I was repeatedly urged to rewrite it, as "gold points, foreign exchange dealings, arbitrage and all that as you knew them, old boy, will never return!"

Apart from funking the job, however, I stubbornly refused to believe that Exchange Control in its most rigid form and restrictions on exchange dealings would continue indefinitely, and my faith was at last justified with the reopening of the London Foreign Exchange Market on 17th December, 1951, and the subsequent steady series of relaxations in Exchange Control both at home and abroad. Still I hesitated because the "convertibility" question had by then come very much to the fore, and its ultimate shape and the conditions accompanying its introduction could affect greatly the remaining restrictions on the international exchange of sterling and on the complete freedom of action of the members of the London Foreign Exchange Market.

But at last I have succumbed and have almost entirely rewritten the old "Manual," though basic principles have not changed and some of the original material is still included. In order to avoid producing too cumbersome and too expensive a work, however, I decided to concentrate on practical foreign exchange and to omit the sections of the old book dealing with economic and historical matters and with the various forms and uses of bank and other credits. I have also touched but lightly on Exchange and Trade Control and such international bodies as the World Bank, the I.M.F., the O.E.E.C., E.P.U., etc., as these have been covered in detail in my book on Exchange Control. The result is, perhaps, technical, but foreign exchange bristles with technicalities which I have tried to explain in language understandable of the layman. I have been described (amongst other things) as a foreign exchange "expert," and an "expert" has been defined as a person who knows more and more about less and less. I am not at all sure about the "more and more," but I am dead certain about the "less and less"!

To all those sources from which I have drawn information, such as Deutsch, Hartley Withers, the original Clare, W. F. Spalding and other masters of the craft, to my banking friends and Lloyds Bank, Ltd. in particular who have so readily given me advice on modern practice in regard to foreign bills of exchange, with which I had got somewhat out of touch, and to my invaluable Secretary, I tender my warmest thanks and absolve them of all responsibility for the results of their help. I am also indebted to the Institute of Bankers for permission to use some material from a talk which I had the privilege of giving to their London Members on "The London Foreign Exchange Market" as one of the Spring Lectures of 1953. To my friends—the readers—be they bankers, traders, students, or just seekers after knowledge like myself, Greetings and Good Luck!

H.E.E.

Great Winchester St., E.C.2.
March, 1955.

PREFACE TO THE SEVENTH EDITION

It has been my intention during the revision to retain as much as possible of the original material whilst, at the same time, bringing it as up to date as is possible for a subject of this nature. Nevertheless, the advent of the decimalization of sterling prompted me to use decimal sterling throughout except in the Gold chapter. The Gold chapter itself presented a problem, but because of its inestimable value, if only in theory, it has been left complete with only a small addition. I have received very valuable assistance from many banks and individuals and I cannot record my thanks to them all separately, but I would like to make special mention of the aid from the Bank of England and Mr. Derek Tilson, A.C.I.S., A.I.B. In addition, I am most grateful to Mr. W. W. Syrett, who carried out the previous revision, for agreeing to allow me to consult him if I so desired.

R.F.P.

CONTENTS

CHAPTER I

DEFINITIONS

Barter; Money and Currency; Convertibility and Inconvertibility;
Foreign Exchange and Rate of Exchange; Mint Par of Ex-
change and Purchasing Power Parity; External Under- and
Over-valuation; Inflation, Deflation and Reflation;
Devaluation and Revaluation

AMONGST early communities and primitive tribes the only way in
which a man could satisfy a want which he could not himself supply
was by exchanging the products of his own personal efforts for those
of his neighbours'. For example, a potato grower who desired some
variation of his diet would exchange part of his product for meat
supplied by a trapper, who in turn would exchange pelts for some
rude garment made from skins by another member of the community. Such a cumbersome procedure, however, could not survive
with the development of social conditions. Imagine a fisherman,
who had a good catch of herring and wanted a new pair of trousers,
trying to find a tailor who was sufficiently fond of herrings to be
ready to make such an exchange! Even then the nice question would
arise of the precise quantity of herring which would represent an
acceptable value both to the fisherman and the tailor. It is to be
feared that on a hot day the fisherman would find himself with a
depreciated currency before he got his trousers!

Barter

This exchange of personal output is known as "barter" and is, of
course, still practised in very primitive communities. For centuries,
however, the exchange of products and services has been conducted
by an indirect method of barter involving some medium in terms of
which the values of all commodities can be expressed. Even where in
quite recent years transactions between Governments or between
residents of different countries have been described as "barter
trade," it has never been the case that a quantity of one product has
been directly exchanged for a quantity of another product. Each side
values its product in terms of some agreed denominator of value,
and thus the quantity of one product equivalent in value to a certain
quantity of the other product is ascertained. Under the modern,
highly-organized social system the means for the exchange of goods
and services must also be highly organized and planned, so that the

1

producers of primary products can be supplied with manufactured goods while such products flow into and are used in the course of the manufacturing process.

Aphorism: a seller deprived of his market is a buyer robbed of his purchasing power.

Money and Currency

Money is something which is accepted generally by a community as a measure of value and a medium for the exchange of goods and services. It gives the owner a command over the goods and services of other members of his community which he should be able to exercise at his option, and anyone who has exchanged his goods or his labour for money should have obtained something with which he can procure the goods or services of others to an extent which satisfies him that he has received a fair return.

The substance used as money must be one which is desired for its own sake as well as for its utility in facilitating the exchange of goods and services. Oxen amongst the ancient communities, tea in China, salt in India and Arabia, cowrie shells in Africa have all served as material money because they had in themselves a value in the eyes of the persons using them. The substance chosen as money must act as—

(*a*) A MEDIUM OF EXCHANGE in that it is freely accepted within the community in exchange for goods and services;

(*b*) A MEASURE OF VALUE in that the value of all other commodities and services can be measured or expressed in terms of the commodity used as money, i.e. it is a common denominator of value;

(*c*) A STORE OF VALUE in that the passage of time should not cause its power to command a given quantity of goods or services to change significantly;

(*d*) A STANDARD FOR DEFERRED PAYMENTS, which follows from its being a store of value and which means that where a creditor and debtor agree upon payment at some future date in terms of money, for goods or services rendered immediately, the money shall, when the future date arrives, still represent a command over a similar quantity of goods or services and that no hardship or loss is suffered by either party by reason of the debt having been expressed in terms of money; in other words, money must possess a purchasing power which remains basically stable even over lengthy periods.

The term "money" in the modern sense has a narrower meaning than the term "currency." The term "money" is now used to describe actual money in the form of coin or notes or in any other form which passes freely from hand to hand as the recognized medium of exchange within a country. Thus, if we speak of English "money" we should mean the Bank of England notes and the small change in the form of coins which are used for everyday payments. On the other hand, "currency" is a generic term and covers not only the actual coins and paper money in use in a country but also any credit instruments which convey the right to wealth in terms of any given unit, such as a cheque, a promissory note, a bill of exchange or any other instrument capable of transferring the property in a stated number of the units of account which are in use in any given country. Thus, dealings in British, French, Dutch or any other "currency" should mean the buying and selling of the right to a certain number of the units of account of that country, which *may* be in the form of actual coin or notes but is usually in the form of a credit instrument capable of transferring the property in the units of account concerned.

In this connexion it must be pointed out that, contrary to popular misconception, it is physically impossible to transfer or bring, for instance, dollars to London or to send sterling to New York. It is, of course, possible to carry a certain amount of currency on the person from one of these centres to the other or to remit substantial sums in coin and/or notes through the post, but when carried on the person and intended for use in the other country they must first be exchanged for local currency before they can be used as money in the other country. If a London banker arranges for a quantity of French franc notes to be remitted to him from France, he does not intend to use them to meet the cheques of his customers over the counter, but he requires them to meet the needs of customers who intend to visit France and therefore require French money to spend in that country. Useful possession of a currency can be had only in the country in which it passes current and this, as we shall see later, is the fundamental of foreign exchange.

Convertibility

With the growth of international relationships and the existence of differing units of account in the various countries of the world, the need arose for some common denominator of value which would be acceptable everywhere and in terms of which each separate unit of account could be expressed. From time immemorial the precious metals, gold and silver, have been almost universally acceptable and it was, therefore, only logical that these metals should become the international common denominators of value. Some countries would only regard gold as an international medium of value, while others, such as China and other Far Eastern countries, regarded silver as their common denominator. In a few cases, and for comparatively short periods, a dual standard of values based on fixed proportions of both metals and known as *bimetallism* was in operation, but by the beginning of the twentieth century the greater part of the world was basing the value of its currency units on gold, while the Far East and part of the Middle East based their currencies on silver. The various types of Gold Standard are discussed in a later chapter, and gold has now almost, if not entirely, displaced silver as a basic denominator of values and as a store of value in the former silver-using countries. The ultimate means of payment between countries is, therefore, gold and the status of any currency has come to be measured by the extent to which that currency is readily convertible into gold.

The term "convertibility" can therefore be defined, in relation to a currency, as the ability of any holder of that currency to exchange it at will and on demand into any other currency or into gold. It is also essential that there should be no restrictions on the free disposal of the other currency by the owner and that if he elects to exchange his original holding of a currency for gold he should be allowed freely to move that gold wherever he wishes. In the early discussions on the possible return to convertibility of the pound sterling which commenced in 1952, the term was given the narrow interpretation of merely the right of conversion of holdings of sterling into American dollars, owing to the world scarcity of that currency which had prevailed since the end of the 1939–1945 war. As events developed, however, the orthodox conception of convertibility was adopted, and "convertibility" is now taken to mean the right of conversion of a currency into any other currency or into gold, with the free disposal of either.

In this connexion two stages of convertibility have to be recognized. "Full" convertibility is regarded as the right given by a country in respect of its currency, to non-residents and residents alike, to convert their holdings of that currency into any other currency or gold at will and on demand. "Limited" convertibility is an intermediate stage under which the right of conversion is granted only to non-residents and only in respect of their holdings of the currency concerned which have arisen as a result of current commercial, financial and capital transactions, but not in respect of holdings which were in their ownership before the introduction of "limited" convertibility. To this should be added that "full" convertibility, in the complete sense of the term, would apply to *all* holdings of a currency whether acquired prior or subsequent to the introduction of convertibility and whether resulting from commercial, financial, capital or any other kind of transaction. At the time of writing this goal still remains to be attained.

Inconvertibility

This is, of course, the converse of convertibility and implies simply that any holder of a currency which is inconvertible has no statutory right to demand the conversion of that currency into any other currency or gold. Any such conversion is entirely at the discretion of the authorities in the country concerned, which will be exercised through some form of exchange control under which applications must be made to the authority for permits to convert the local currency into any other currency or into gold. The degree to which the authorities feel able to grant such permits and the types of currency into which they are prepared to allow conversion to take place mark stages of progress, first towards "limited" convertibility, and secondly towards "full" convertibility. The wide extension of the Transferable Sterling Account System by the British authorities in March, 1954, in effect made sterling convertible both for non-residents and residents (for permitted purposes) into the currencies of all the foreign countries which were made members of the system and, subject to any restrictions existing within any of those countries themselves, made sterling a bridge across which *inter*convertibility of currencies could pass.

Foreign Exchange

It has already been stated that money is a common denominator in which the relative values of goods and services can be expressed, that throughout history any community which forms itself into a nation for the purposes of self-government immediately introduces its own distinctive unit of account, and that useful possession of any currency can be had only within the country in which it passes current. In order, therefore, that the owner of one kind of money expressed as a particular currency unit should exchange it for another kind of money expressed as a different currency unit, some mechanism to effect such an exchange must exist and some designation be given to such operations.

The means and methods by which rights to wealth expressed in terms of the currency of one country are converted into rights to wealth in terms of the currency of another country are known as "foreign exchange." The term covers the methods by which the currency of one country is exchanged for that of another, the causes which render such exchanges necessary, the forms in which such exchanges are conducted, and the ratios or equivalent values at which they are effected.

The expression "foreign exchange" is also popularly used to denote a foreign currency, e.g. a bank is said to buy or sell "foreign exchange," meaning that it buys or sells rights to foreign currencies or the foreign moneys themselves. In addition, the expression "foreign exchanges" or "exchanges" is used particularly by the Press to describe the ratios or rates of exchange at which currencies exchange for one another.

Rate of Exchange

The rate of exchange is the price of one currency in terms of another or, in other words, the number of units of one currency which exchange for a given number of units of another currency. In a free world economy the price or rate of exchange of one currency in terms of others cannot be fixed but varies continuously with variations in the existing relation between the world demand for, and the supply of, that currency. Various bases or starting points for the calculation of a ratio between two currencies can be used, but under present conditions this starting point is set (at least for countries which are members of the International Monetary Fund) by a declared gold parity for the currency concerned which gives a parity with the U.S. dollar through the fixed price for gold current in the U.S.A.

As between two currencies, whether the rate of exchange is quoted as a price for a unit or a given number of units of the second currency in terms of units of the first currency, or vice versa, depends upon the circumstances and prestige attaching to the two currencies. Owing to the overwhelming importance of sterling in international trade during the nineteenth century and the comparatively large purchasing unit represented by the pound sterling, it was inevitable that rates of exchange for sterling should be quoted as so many foreign currency units for the unit of one pound sterling. In other cases, however, rates of exchange are quoted by each country in terms of so many home units for one of a given number of foreign units as, for instance, in the case of the U.S.A. and Canada where the U.S.A. quotation is in U.S. dollars and cents per Canadian dollar, while Canada quotes so many Canadian dollars and cents per U.S. dollar. The methods and meanings of exchange quotations are dealt with in detail in a later chapter.

Mint Par of Exchange

The most usual base or starting point for the calculation of the value of one currency in terms of another is the comparison of the quantity of precious metal contained in each of the two currency units. It is essential that the metallic content should be fixed by law in each case, even though it may be only theoretical. Such a method of comparison is known as the *Mint Par of Exchange* or the *Mint Parity* and may be defined thus: *where two countries use the same metal as the basis of their currencies, the Mint Par of Exchange between them is the number of units of the one currency which should legally contain the same amount of pure metal as does, legally, a given number of units of the other currency.* At the present moment only a few countries have given a legal gold content to their units of currency and even then such figures are entirely theoretical as there are hardly any gold coins in general circulation. If and when a fairly general return to currency convertibility is made, the countries concerned will be under the necessity of giving an actual legal gold content to their units of currency as distinct from the declarations of gold parities made by member countries to the International Monetary Fund, which are administrative only.

The calculation of a Mint Par of Exchange is merely one of Compound Proportion, but is more usually carried out by means of the arithmetical process known as the "Chain Rule," of which the method of working is described in a later chapter. For example, the United States dollar has a theoretical metallic content of 15·2381 grains of gold $\frac{9}{10}$ths fine. Assuming that the English sovereign (which is still the basic legal currency unit) were given a legal content of 32·9144 grains fine, it would then be possible to calculate a Mint Par of Exchange between Britain and the U.S.A., which would work out at $2·40 per £1. By similar comparisons the Mint Parities between any two countries *using the same metal* as their standard of value can be calculated, but it must be emphasized that the result gives merely a theoretical measurement of the value of one standard coin in terms of another standard coin. It takes no account of practical variations in the weight or fineness of actual coins due to abrasion or remedy allowance, nor of possible restrictions in either or both of the two countries concerned on the free import or export of gold coins. The "geographical factor," which also affects the physical transfer of gold coins or gold in bulk, is discussed in the chapter on Gold Points.

The Purchasing Power Parity Theory

This is another method of arriving at a starting point for the comparison of the values of any two currencies, but it is by no means reliable as it takes no account of variations in national tastes, habits, and standards of living. It was developed soon after the end of the

1914–1918 war by Professor Gustav Cassel of Stockholm, who advanced the theory that, under normal conditions, people do not buy a currency for the sake of owning it but because the possession of it enables them to satisfy some want to better advantage than if they owned some other currency. This led to the following enunciation of the theory—

The Purchasing Power Parity between any two countries is that amount of the currency of one country which endows the holder with the same amount of purchasing power, i.e. command over goods and services, as would a stated amount of the currency of the other country. While the value of the unit of one currency in terms of units of the other will vary over short periods, or at any particular time, in accordance with fluctuations in the market conditions of supply and demand, yet, in the long run, that value will be determined by the relative command over goods, services and securities of similar status, i.e. purchasing power, which each unit of currency possesses in its own country.

The theory may be illustrated by assuming that a bicycle costs £10 in England or $30 in America. If the current rate of exchange is $3–£1, the bicycle will cost the same in either country, and the exchange is at the Purchasing Power Parity. If, however, the exchange rate moved until £1 became worth only $2, it would be cheaper for an American to buy a bicycle in England because he could then buy £10 for $20. (For the purposes of this illustration transport and other costs are ignored.) The increased demand for bicycles inEngland and the falling off in demand in America would cause a rise in the price of the English machine and a fall in the price of the American machine, while, on the other hand, the demand in America for pounds against dollars would cause the exchange rate to move in favour of the pound. According to the theory, this process would continue until the price of bicycles in England rose to, say, £11 10s. and fell to $27 in America, while the rate of exchange rose to, say, $2·35 per £1. At this stage the exchange rate would once more represent the approximate Purchasing Power Parity, and it would be just as profitable for the American to buy his bicycle in his own country as in England.

As a further illustration of the theory, if the price of a similar type of coal were 50 zloty per ton in Poland and 10 D-marks per ton in Germany, and the relative exchange rates with Italy were 100 zloty or 25 D-marks per 100 lire, an Italian could buy 2½ tons of coal from Germany for 100 lire, as against only 2 tons from Poland, for the same outlay in his own currency. Theoretically, this should have a four-fold effect—

(a) The diversion of the Italian demand for coal from Poland to Germany would leave Polish producers with an evergrowing surplus which would induce them to offer supplies at a lower price in the hope of attracting buyers of this surplus.

(b) At the same time the falling-off in the demand for zloty against lire would force owners of zloty who wanted lire to offer a higher rate of exchange in the hope of attracting buyers, i.e. the zloty cheapens.

(c) The increase in the demand for German coal would reduce stocks there and lead producers to ask a higher price for further deliveries.

(d) The increase in demand for D-marks against lire would force those who had lire and wanted D-marks to offer a better rate of exchange in the hope of attracting sellers of D-marks, i.e. the D-mark becomes dearer.

The sum total of all these influences is that internal prices-cum-exchange rates adjust themselves until the price of either Polish or German coal to an Italian is roughly the same, e.g. if in Poland the exchange rate rises to 108 zloty per 100 lire and the price of coal falls to 48 zloty per ton, while in Germany the D-mark becomes dearer until only 24 can be purchased for 100 lire and coal rises to $10\frac{3}{4}$ D-marks per ton, then an expenditure of 100 lire would give an Italian roughly $2\frac{1}{4}$ tons of coal from either country. Neither exchange rate would, however, move beyond a point at which it became much dearer or much cheaper to buy any article in common demand in one or the other country because the process of equating prices and exchange rates would begin afresh.

Both these examples are, of course, impossibly simple as trade between two countries is not confined to one article only and price differences in one direction may be offset by other price differences in the opposite direction. While these factors might result in changes in the respective internal price levels, their opposite effects would leave the exchange rate unchanged. If due regard is paid, however, to the limitations of this theory, it can form a useful guide both in explaining and, to some extent, forecasting certain movements in the exchanges.

External Under- and Over-valuation

It is most important to appreciate that the external selling price of any commodity or service is its internal price combined with the rate of exchange between the selling and buying countries. For example, a British motor-car manufacturer produces a popular model for which the minimum selling price must be £400 in order to cover all costs of production and to show a small margin of profit.

Ignoring transport costs, if the rate of exchange between Britain and France is F.fcs.1,000 per £1, the manufacturer must sell his car in France for F.fcs.400,000 in order to produce the £400 which he requires in this country. If the value of the French franc appreciates until the rate becomes only F.fcs.900 per £1, he can afford to offer the car in France for F.fcs.360,000, as this sum will again produce the £400 which he requires. On the other hand, if the price of French francs cheapens and the rate moves to F.fcs.1,100 per £1, he will have to ask F.fcs.440,000 in order to receive the required £400. We saw in an earlier example how, in theory, internal prices and rates of exchange tend towards a mutual adjustment rather than one factor remaining constant while the other fluctuates but, even so, it can be seen clearly that the home producer requires a minimum sum in his own currency to cover costs incurred and profit required in that currency, and that his external price must therefore vary with variations in the rate of exchange between his own country and a buying country in order to secure the minimum amount of home currency which he requires and yet, at the same time, to make his external price as competitive as possible.

Where fluctuations in a rate of exchange are limited, either because a currency is on some form of gold standard or because it is arbitrarily and artificially controlled by the Government, it frequently happens that the resulting external sales prices of home products become out of line with world prices for similar products because of the current level of internal prices. As will be seen later, under any form of gold standard a certain number of currency units are made the legal equivalent of a specified quantity of fine gold. If, in fact, the purchasing power of the currency is such that the quantity of goods and services that could be purchased with a stated number of units of currency is less than the volume of goods and services that would be equivalent to the amount of fine gold theoretically represented by that number of currency units, then the currency is said to be over-valued. If, on the other hand, the purchasing power of the given number of currency units would provide a greater volume of goods and services than would be required to purchase the currency equivalent in fine gold, then the currency is said to be under-valued.

Similarly, if by Government decree a currency is given exchange values in terms of other currencies which do not represent the true purchasing power abroad of the home currency, then it is again either over- or under-valued externally. For example, if a group of commodities and services in common use both in this country and in Holland would cost £100 here or fl.1,000 in Holland, then the purchasing power parity would be fl.10 per £1. The arbitrary fixation by Government decree of a rate of exchange with Holland of fl.11 equals £1 would then over-value sterling, while a rate of fl.9 per £1 would under-value it. In either case the distortion of the true currency value would cause either an increase in purchases from and a falling off in sales to Holland in the first case, or a falling off in purchases from and an increase in sales to Holland in the second case. If no adjustment in internal prices in both countries took place, the pressure against sterling in the first case, and in favour of it in the second case, would eventually force the Authorities to adjust the official rate to a realistic level.

There have been many instances, however, of the deliberate fixation of exchange rates which did not represent the true exchange value of a currency. During the German occupation of Holland, the German Authorities fixed a rate of exchange between the mark and the guilder which greatly over-valued the former currency. In consequence, German purchases of Dutch agricultural and other products were made artificially cheap, while Dutch purchases of German products which were essential to them and which they could not obtain elsewhere under war conditions were made unnecessarily dear in order that a certain quantity of Dutch products could be purchased with a smaller quantity of German products than the relative purchasing powers of the two currencies justified. Again, after the liberation of France the French franc was given the artificial value of F.fcs.280 per £1, which within a short time had to be raised to F.fcs.480 per £1, but which, even then, grossly over-valued the French franc. The object was, however, to make it possible for France and her Empire to purchase cheaply the vast quantities of materials required for the reconstruction and rehabilitation of her devastated territories and to restart her industries in production. As soon as French productivity had reached the stage where exports were once more possible, however, the exchange rate had to be quickly adjusted by stages to a level more in accordance with the purchasing power of the French franc in order to make her external sales prices competitive with world prices. There are still instances of over-valuation of currencies disguised by export subsidies or concealed incentives. Obviously, if too high a value is placed on the home currency unit, it cheapens the cost of imports from abroad, but it also raises the external sales price of home products to foreign buyers and this handicap has to be removed by what can only be described as subterfuges. While stability of exchange rates, as well as of prices, is greatly to be desired, there must always be a degree of flexibility sufficient to allow any necessary adjustments to be made to keep internal prices in line with world prices.

Inflation

It has been aptly said that a country is suffering from inflation of the currency when there is too much money chasing too few goods. Money of itself is useless. You cannot eat it, or wear it, or live in it, and its utility lies only in its ability to act as a medium of exchange and a purchasing agent. Although it is not possible for a country to become bankrupt in the sense that a firm or individual is officially made bankrupt, it is under the same economic necessity as the firm or individual of endeavouring to make its income balance its expenditure. What is known as "deficit financing," i.e. a Government budget deliberately aiming at an excess of expenditure over income, is directly inflationary as regards the internal currency and credit system because it places in the hands of the community more purchasing power (deriving from credits raised by the Government) than it withdraws from the community in the shape of taxation. Unless this increase in the supply of money or spending power is offset by an increase in productivity, so that there are more goods on sale against the increase in the money supply, then those members of the community who are in possession of excess spending power will be prepared to use it by paying higher prices for the limited amount of goods offered for sale. This touches off a general rise in the price level, which inevitably causes a demand for higher wages by the lower-paid workers. So commences the vicious inflationary spiral in which wages are always chasing prices and each wage increase reflects itself in still higher prices. In a time of business depression a mild dose of inflation may prove beneficial to the body economic but, like all strong medicines, an overdose can reduce the patient to a state of prostration.

Deflation

When the total volume of money and credit available in a community is reduced, either fortuitously or deliberately, after a period during which that volume would appear to have been in excess of requirements, the process is said to be one of deflation. In other words, it is a process of adjusting the available volume of money and credit and the rapidity of its circulation to the amount of money work to be done in the shape of facilitating the exchange of available goods and services. Necessarily, a state of inflation must have existed before deflation can take place. The process usually requires "surplus financing" in the Government budget by a reduction in national expenditure and an increase in taxation, so that the national income exceeds expenditure and spending power is withdrawn from the community. If there has been over-creation of credit, interest rates must be raised to discourage borrowing and encourage saving, re-payment of loans must be required even if forced sales of goods and securities result, and the granting of further credit must be strictly limited. These conditions tend to create unemployment and falling wages, so that, as with inflation, the dose must be moderate and carefully graduated if hardship to the masses is to be avoided. It can be likened to a little blood-letting which, if effected wisely, relieves a state of congestion but which, if carried to excess, again prostrates the patient.

Reflation

This is a hybrid term coined to denote a condition of affairs where deflation has been carried out too fast or too far. If, after a period of deliberate deflation, it becomes apparent that a fall in prices and wages has been caused to an extent which is having serious effects on industry and trade, then the blood-letting process must be replaced by one of blood transfusion, and some resort to inflationary principles must be made. As, however, such a process does not result in inflation as such, but is merely retracing steps taken too far in the wrong direction, it is known as "reflation" so as to absolve it of any inflationary taint.

Devaluation

Where for any reason, such as external over-valuation, it is considered necessary to cheapen the exchange value of a currency in terms of others by giving it a lower exchange value, the process is known as "devaluation." If a currency is on a gold standard, devaluation is effected by raising the price of gold in terms of the currency concerned, and this automatically decreases the number of units of other gold standard currencies required to purchase a given number of units of the first currency. During the past half-century examples of currency devaluation are legion. The basic causes are usually over-spending by the Government and under-taxation of the community, or the inefficient collection of taxation. The resulting inflationary condition produces the spiral of price and wage increases until the internal price level, combined with the current rate of exchange, puts external prices far above world level. In place of the proper corrective of regaining internal economic stability by reduced Government expenditure, increased taxation, restriction of credit, higher interest rates, etc., it is too often the case that Governments take the line of least resistance and restore their external selling power by cheapening the exchange value of the currency. This is, however, merely a "shot in the arm," as the reduction in external selling prices can only be temporary because the increased internal cost of essential imports must, before long, reflect itself in increased internal prices and so nullify some, if not all, of the previous advantages of devaluation. The bad effects of such a step, and the possibility that currency devaluation by one country may lead to competitive devaluations by other countries, have been recognized by most leading world authorities, and provisions against such steps being taken, except to correct a fundamental disequilibrium, have been written into the constitution of the International Monetary Fund. Internal economic health is the great preventive against the external virus of currency devaluation.

Revaluation

This again is a somewhat hybrid term which can mean either a retraction from too great a devaluation of a currency, or the adjustment of a condition in which a currency has been under-valued externally. There are, unfortunately, all too few instances of this disciplinary process having been used. In September, 1949, when an enforced devaluation of the pound sterling took place and its dollar parity was reduced from 4·03 to 2·80, most of the Continental countries effected currency devaluations on the same scale, but some few of them either retained their existing dollar parities, as in the case of Switzerland, or devalued only to a lesser extent. As an instance, after the liberation of Belgium an exchange parity was fixed of B.fcs.176⅝ per £1, but in September, 1949, Belgium decided not to follow fully sterling devaluation, and the parity was raised to only B.fcs.140 per £1. This, however, is not really a case of revaluation, as the exchange value of the currency was made dearer only in respect of those currencies which had devalued and not as against world currencies in general.

The most recent example of revaluation occurred in 1969. For some time German production costs had been low in relation to the same costs in other manufacturing countries. The currency became undervalued at its existing parity and the monetary authorities revalued it by about 9 per cent. Prior to that occurrence the notable examples of revaluation took place in 1961 when both Germany and Holland revalued by about 5 per cent. However, revaluations are rare and must be regarded exceptionally.

CHAPTER II

THE MAIN CAUSES OF FLUCTUATIONS IN THE EXCHANGES

Visible and Invisible Trade; Seasonal Factors; Gold Exports of Gold Producing Countries

As long as any community is self-contained and self-sufficing it need have no relations with other communities involving the creation of debts, but as soon as it enters into any transactions with other communities which result in payments having to be made by one to the other, the problem of the exchange of currencies at once arises. Since a currency is, for the purpose of international exchange, no more than a commodity which facilitates the exchange of other commodities, its value in exchange for other currencies is entirely subject to the law of supply and demand. If the supply of a currency, i.e. the amount generally offered for sale, at any given moment exceeds the existing demand for that currency, its value in exchange must tend to fall since sellers must offer more units of that currency in exchange for others to induce further buyers to come forward when the existing demand has been satisfied. Conversely, if the general demand for a currency at any given moment exceeds the current supply, the exchange value of that currency in terms of others must appreciate, since buyers must offer to accept fewer units of the currency in exchange for others or to give more of other units for the same number of units of the wanted currency as before, in order to bring out fresh sellers when the existing supply has been absorbed. It follows, therefore, that the exchange value of a currency, which is the "rate of exchange," fluctuates continuously with every variation in the relationship between the current supply of and demand for the currency, and all the factors which go to make up and to affect current supply and demand are, consequently, of the first importance in considering movements in rates of exchange.

Existing Balance of Indebtedness

As will be seen from a study of the following paragraphs, the factors affecting the supply of and demand for a currency are numerous and varied, and some of them have only a psychological effect which can hardly be measured. It is quite impracticable for a line to be drawn under the accounts existing between any two

15

countries at any given moment, and for a resulting total or net balance of indebtedness between the two to be obtained. The commercial and financial relationships between nations are now so complicated and so extensive that payments for debts incurred between them on various accounts are being settled every minute of every working day, and future commitments are arranged for even years ahead. It is, therefore, those debts falling due for *immediate* settlement between nations that constitute the current supply of and demand for currencies, and which, consequently, have the greatest influence on immediate fluctuations in rates of exchange. These are known as "short-period factors," and they consist largely of tangible items, the effects of which can be seen and almost exactly calculated.

Economic and psychological factors are less easily seen and measured, and their effects on the exchanges may be apparent only after the lapse of a considerable period. They are, therefore, known as "long-term factors," and constitute the most complex problem of the exchanges.

Main Influences on the Exchanges

The principal factors affecting the exchange values of currencies may be summarized thus—

Short-term factors—(a) *Commercial.*

(b) *Financial.*

Long-term factors— (a) *Currency and Credit Conditions.*

(b) *Political and Industrial Conditions.*

These will now be considered seriatim.

COMMERCE

The exchange of commodities which we call "Trade" is the basis of all intercourse between nations, since the modern social system seems to demand that the world should live by buying and selling. If a London merchant buys coffee from a Brazilian grower, a debt is incurred by this country to Brazil. The creditor eventually requires payment in his own currency in order that he may discharge his own internal debts, and the debtor must therefore exchange his own currency by some means for that of his creditor, or the latter must find some means of exchanging for his own currency the right which he possesses to the currency of the debtor. Trade, however, is not one-sided, and there will be another Brazilian merchant who has bought, for example, hardware from a Sheffield merchant, and who has thereby incurred a debt due by Brazil to this country. If it is assumed that the two debts are each for £500, the situation will be that London merchant *A* owes £500 to Brazil merchant *B*, while Brazil merchant *Y* owes £500 to Sheffield merchant *Z*. The settlement of these two transactions might therefore be effected by *B* drawing a bill for £500 on *A* and selling it to *Y* in exchange for local currency at the prevailing rate of exchange between the pound and the cruzeiro (the Brazilian currency) and by *Y* sending the bill to his creditor *Z*, who would thereupon present it to *A* and obtain payment in pounds. *A* would then have discharged his debt in his own currency, while *Z* would have received the amount due to him in his own currency. Similarly, *B* would have received a sufficient amount of his own currency to discharge the debt due to him by *A* and, by paying over this amount in his own currency, *Y* would have discharged his debt to *Z*.

This principle of the off-setting of debts is, of course, vastly more complicated in practice. Each nation trades with many others, and debts due by one nation to another may be offset by debts due to the first nation by a third, while, particularly in the case of this country, debts may arise due both to and by us in respect of trade between two other nations which is financed through London. Thus, in the example given above, the purchase of coffee might have been made by a Danish merchant and financed through London, so that, by accepting the drafts on London of the Brazilian exporter, this country would incur a debt to Brazil while Denmark would incur a debt to this country in respect of the financial facilities granted. The movements of tangible goods between nations can be checked, and their quantities and values can be recorded by the various State officials appointed for this purpose in every country, and trade in all commodities of which the import and export can be so recorded is known as "Visible Trade" and is the basis of the "balance of trade."

There are, however, many other items which give rise to debts between countries which are of so intangible a nature that the recording of the values of all such items is impracticable. For example, a ship owned by a British company may carry a mixed cargo from Liverpool to Shanghai, and may then take a cargo of rice to San Francisco, a cargo of wheat from that port to a Greek port, a cargo of currants from there to Boston, and finally arrive back in this country with a mixed cargo of American goods. The local agents of the vessel at each port will have collected the respective freights and will have made certain disbursements on account of revictualling and refuelling the vessel. The shipowners in this country will receive in due course the net amounts due to them in respect of the ship's voyages, but the various items cannot be made the subject of official statistics in every port, and no official record of the incomings and outgoings can therefore be kept. There are many similar intangible items and they are commonly known as the "Invisible Trade" of a country. They constitute invisible imports and exports; an import being something for which a country has to pay and an export being something for which it has to receive payment.

The principal "invisible" items are—

Freights. Sums earned by our vessels,[1] whether carrying our own or foreign goods, are sums due to us for services exported. When British-owned goods are carried by foreign vessels,[1] we incur a debt to the owning country for our import of their services.

Disbursements of British ships in foreign ports are an import by us of the goods and services so obtained, while disbursements of foreign ships in British ports cause debts due to us by the foreign countries for such services and goods.

Insurance Premiums for risks insured with British companies by foreigners are debts due to us for services exported, while risks insured by our nationals with foreign companies are our imports of services for which we must pay.

Commissions and Brokerages. Where, for example, a German buyer uses the services of a London wool-broker to buy Argentine wool at the London sales, and the purchase is financed by means of a credit opened in London, the German buyer and the Argentine seller both import the services of a London broker, while the German, in addition, imports the services of the London bank or Accepting House through whom the credit for payment of the purchase is opened. All such charges, therefore, represent exports by the country rendering the service and imports by the country receiving it.

Tourists' Disbursements. When a national of one country visits another country, he spends a certain amount of money and presumably benefits in some way by his visit. His country may, therefore, be held to have imported, through him, a certain amount of health, enjoyment, and education, and the money spent abroad by the tourist represents the payment for these imports.

Profits sent home from branches or subsidiary concerns operating abroad represent, presumably, payment for facilities afforded to the foreign countries concerned and, therefore, of an import of services by them, as are *Royalties* on books, plays, films, etc.

Government Disbursements, such as reparations, maintenance of troops, police, and officials in foreign countries, pensions paid abroad, etc., represent payments for past or present imports of

[1] And, of course, aircraft and road transport.

services. Reparation payments can be considered as the re-import of loss previously caused to others; pensions, as a past import of services, etc.

Sales of ships are not registered as part of the visible trade of a country, and must therefore be included under the invisible items, although of a tangible nature. For example, a British ship may be sold to a Dutch buyer while lying in a Belgian port.

Loans and Interest Payments. These are really the most important of the invisible items, though some economists include them under the heading of Stock Exchange operations. A loan obviously creates the need for a payment by the lender to the borrower or his assigns. As between nations, a loan by one to another is in effect an import of the paper promises to pay of the borrower. If the proceeds of the loan are withdrawn in cash, in the form either of credit instruments or of bullion, it results in offerings of the currency of the lending country by the borrowing country, causing a tendency to depreciation in exchange value of the lender's currency.

If the proceeds of the loan are spent by the borrower within the lending country, the result is an increase in the exports, visible or invisible or both, of the lender, and the exchange value of the lender's currency is not affected. In any event, every foreign loan must eventually result in the export by the lender of goods, services, securities, or bullion to some other country, since those who purchase the lender's currency from the borrower will eventually use it in the purchase of one or other of these items from the lender. Where a country is over-lending abroad and the resulting offerings of its currency cause such a depreciation in the exchange value that gold is taken from it as being the cheapest method of discharging the temporary adverse balance of indebtedness, the orthodox theory of money holds that the consequent reduction in the basis of the internal credit structure, and the contraction of credit and raising of interest rates which this causes, will result in a fall in home prices until the relative cheapness externally of the currency, combined with the low internal prices, makes the country a cheap market for foreigners to buy in, and an increase in exports takes place until equilibrium between exchange values and internal prices with the world level is restored.

The payment of interest by borrowing countries to the lender is an invisible import of their paper promises to pay by the borrowers, and therefore constitutes a debt incurred by them to the lenders. Repayments of loans are again a re-import by the borrowing countries of their original paper promises to pay, and a debt is therefore due by them to the lenders.

SUMMARY BALANCE OF PAYMENTS

£ millions

	1966	1967	1968	1969
Seasonally adjusted Current account				
Exports and re-exports (f.o.b.) . .	5,122	5,042	6,143	7,013
Imports (f.o.b.)	5,214	5,576	6,807	7,153
Visible trade balance . . .	−92	−534	−664	−140
Net adjustment to recorded exports .	+60	+80	+130	+43
Payments to the United States for military aircraft and missiles . .	−41	−98	−109	−61
Visible balance	−73	−552	−643	−158
Invisibles (net)	+113	+230	+334	+524
Current balance	+40	−322	−309	+366
Long-term capital account[1]				
Official transactions:				
Loans from Export-Import Bank (net)	+51	+76	+74	+11
Other	−131	−133	−53	−106
Private investment:				
Abroad (net)	−304	−463	−732	−593
In the United Kingdom (net) . .	+277	+381	+622	+709
Balance of long-term capital .	−107	−139	−89	+21
Balance of current and long-term capital transactions . .	−67	−461	−398	+387
Net seasonal influences				
Not seasonally adjusted				
Balance of current and long-term capital transactions . . .	−67	−461	−398	+387
Balancing item	−37	+227	−145	+182
Monetary movements[1]				
Adjustment for maturing forwards .	—	−105	−251	—
Miscellaneous capital . . .	−110	−66	−17	+201
Net liabilities in:				
Sterling	+125	+167	+165	−603
Overseas sterling area currencies .	−45	+24	−46	+1
Foreign currencies	−146	+213	+53	−109
Account with I.M.F. . .	−2	−318	+525	−15
Transfer from dollar portfolio to reserves	+316	+204	—	—
Gold and convertible currency reserves	−34	+115	+114	−44
Balance of monetary movements .	+104	+234	+543	−569

1   Assets: increase−; decrease+. Liabilities: increase+; decrease−.

The table which is set out above shows the importance to this country of the net income derived from invisible items, which enables the U.K. to import far more goods, by value, than are exported.

A significant growth in recent years, which may enable us both to develop our own economy faster than would otherwise be possible, and also contribute to the rate of emergence of developing countries abroad, is associated with certain international activities of our manufacturers. They have set up branch factories and, jointly with local enterprisers, associate enterprises, in foreign countries, they have licenced foreign factories to make their products and have generally expanded sales of "know-how" overseas. Within the next decade or so there should be a growing return from these sources. However, it should not be thought that the investment of capital in foreign activities is always undertaken by transfers across the exchanges; U.K. manufacturers often send plant, machinery, tools and test gear to their foreign associates under agreements which provide that the value of the capital goods is used to pay for the U.K. manufacturers' shares in the new concern. This means that no transfer across the exchanges is required, and so the export of the capital goods is called an "unrequited export," a term also used to describe gifts and free samples for the same reason.

Industrial investments of the type explained in the last paragraph are not only from highly-developed countries to the emerging ones. In a world where specialization is the watch-word, there are often opportunities for know-how to be exchanged between industrialized nations, a process which has been referred to as "a useful process of cross-fertilization." U.K. manufacturers have played an important part here and their initiative stands to be rewarded by payments from abroad which by their nature cannot be shown in our balance of trade statistics.

To revert to the table, the item of "Invisibles (net)" includes the estimated income from banking and other commissions, brokerages earned by stockbrokers and members of the important commodity terminal markets on transactions conducted for foreign account. Such earnings can, of course, only be estimated since no exact returns are available.

At one period, these tables included a special item of "Defence Aid." This referred to the gifts made by America in cash and goods to Britain and other West European countries, under the Marshall Aid Plan and successive votes of credit thereafter, first commencing in April, 1948. These tided over the recipients during a time of great strain on their economies. Today, American aid takes more the form of military help to other recipients, especially in the Far East.

In connexion with visible trade one further point must be mentioned. The average price levels of imports and exports are registered by means of indices compiled by the Board of Trade from official statistics. If the average cost of imports rises, so does the import price index, and if the average value of exports falls, so does the export price index. Obviously, a low index figure for imports and a high one for exports is favourable to this country, and another index is compiled by a comparison of the import and export price indices, which is called the "Terms of Trade" index. If import prices rise while export prices remain steady or rise only to a lesser extent, the Terms of Trade index rises proportionately, but if export prices rise to a greater extent than do import prices, then the Terms of Trade index falls. Consequently, a low figure for this index indicates trade terms favourable to this country, while a high figure indicates an unfavourable position. The monthly statistics of visible trade published by the Board of Trade are not of real value in assessing the country's current balance of payments position. Imports shown as arriving during any one month may have been paid for previously, or payment for them may be delayed for some little time under credit facilities granted by the seller. The value of exports for any month certainly does not mean that the country will receive immediate payment from abroad for that amount. Almost invariably payment for exports is received from the foreign buyers some time after the export has actually taken place. At one time, the value of imports was quoted on a c.i.f. basis, while the value of exports and re-exports was given on an f.o.b. basis, but this no longer occurs. F.o.b. values are employed in the statistics published at intervals by H.M. Treasury giving the U.K. balance of payments on current account. Statistics must always lag behind current events and they are of use only in so far as they indicate trends which may either be developed further or which need counteracting.

FINANCIAL SHORT-TERM FACTORS

The various systems of State control over international trade and payments have reduced greatly the former importance of financial operations across the exchanges. When there were no restrictions on the free movement of capital between countries, or on speculative operations in foreign currencies, these factors frequently had a strong influence on exchange rates. Apart from long-term capital investments which, as explained above, are part of invisible trade, there used to be, and to a very limited extent there still is, a large volume of liquid balances in every country which would tend to move to other centres either for temporary investment at a more favourable rate of interest than could be obtained at home, or because of the greater safety which it was considered could be secured by depositing the funds abroad. For example, if credit conditions were easy in New York but rather stringent in London, so that the yield on first-class bills of exchange was only 6 per cent per annum in New York but was as high as 8 per cent per annum in London, the tendency would be for New York bankers to use some of their loanable funds for the purchase of sterling for investment in bills in London. The exchange risk involved in such an operation would be covered by means of a "forward" exchange deal, and the complete transaction was known as a "swap and investment" or a "swap and deposit" deal. Operations of this nature are described fully in a later chapter. On the other hand, if a foreign investor regarded the current exchange rate for sterling as being unduly low, he would buy sterling for short-term investment as a speculation and leave his exchange risk uncovered. Other purely speculative operations for or against any given currency were also conducted on a large scale and all too frequently a strong "bear" or "bull" attack on a currency would actually force the movement in the exchange rate which the speculators anticipated. Under existing restrictions on the purposes for which foreign currencies may be bought and sold, particularly in this country, movements of short-term capital have been minimized, while speculation in the exchanges has been almost eliminated for the general public. However, both in the U.K. and abroad to varying degrees, certain people (e.g. Foreign Exchange dealers) are permitted to "take a view." The result could exert considerable pressure upon exchange notes as was the case prior to the revaluation of the Deutschemark in 1969.

There are still, however, ample facilities afforded by the leading stock exchanges of the world for the genuine investment of funds. Subject to any restrictions on the export of capital which may exist in a foreign country, there is nothing to prevent a resident of that country from using his own currency to purchase sterling, which is then used to buy sterling securities on a stock exchange in this country. If foreign investors decide that the industrial and economic outlook of a certain country is favourable so that the exchange value of the currency of that country is likely to improve and the quoted prices of securities issued in that country are likely to rise, they will realize other investments or use surplus funds for the purchase of the currency concerned, which is then used for the purchase of securities. The effect on the exchange rate for the currency concerned is proportionate to the volume of investment, but there is always the prospect that the investments will be realized and the proceeds repatriated[1] when the foreign operator considers that the exchange rate and the security quotations have reached a

[1] If local Exchange Control regulations permit.

favourable height. The repatriation of the investment proceeds will, of course, affect the exchange rate adversely. On the other hand, a bad economic and industrial outlook for a country will cause foreign investors who already hold securities in that country to realize them and to repatriate the proceeds,[1] thus making still worse an already adverse position. Movements of invested money, therefore, while far less important than between the two wars, can still exercise a considerable influence on the exchanges.

Another financial factor is the practice of banks to hold what are known as "Working Balances" with banks in other countries. The need for such balances is discussed later and it is sufficient to say here that the size and permanency of such balances depends again on the view taken abroad of the economic and industrial state of the country. Banks must also take into account the level of world prices for the principal commodities. The steep increases in world prices for the base metals, wool, cotton and other primary products which have taken place since the last war has meant that international trade requires much larger funds for its finance. International banks, therefore, tend to vary the size of the working balances which they maintain in other countries with variations in the price level of the main products of those countries. A good outlook for a country induces foreign banks to hold maximum balances there, while a poor outlook causes an immediate drawing down of such balances. Although, in many cases, the exchange risk is covered by means of successive forward exchange operations, there is also a considerable volume of foreign money for which the exchange risk is not covered. In such cases the initial purchase of the currency concerned has a favourable influence on the exchange rate, but any drawing down of such balances affects the exchange rate adversely.

The course of an exchange rate can also be affected immediately by the action of foreign creditors and debtors in anticipating or delaying debt settlements. If the outlook for a country is good and its currency is showing signs of strength in terms of others, then foreign residents who either already owe, or who expect to incur in the near future, a debt to that country will hasten to acquire the currency necessary to effect settlement before this cost, in terms of their own currency, rises still higher. At the same time foreign residents who are already due or who expect shortly to receive money from the country in question will ask that settlement shall be delayed, in the hope that when it is eventually effected the value of the foreign currency in terms of their own will have risen so that the debt settlement yields them a larger sum in their own currency.

[1] If local Exchange Control regulations permit.

Conversely, if the outlook for a certain country is poor and the exchange value of its currency seems likely to weaken, then foreign creditors will at once press for the settlement of debts already due and will endeavour to obtain advance payment of debts accruing due in the near future, so as to obtain the benefit of the current rate of exchange before the debtor currency becomes still cheaper and so would yield them fewer units of their own currency. Foreign debtors, both present and future, however, will endeavour to delay settlement of their debts as long as possible in the hope that they will then be able to obtain the required amount of currency for a smaller number of their own currency units than would be required by the current rate of exchange. Such actions are known as "leads and lags," and are speculative in a way, but even recent experience has shown that their cumulative effect can cause marked pressure for or against a currency in world exchange markets.

In connexion with both securities and working balances, there is now a growing return to the former practice of what was known as "Stock Arbitrage" and "Money Arbitrage." Such operations also involve "Exchange Arbitrage." Arbitrage means the simultaneous buying and selling of any commodity in two or more centres. It involves the closest possible watch on prices and exchange rates so that immediate advantage may be taken of discrepancies shown by the quotations in different centres. Here again, the principle of the external price being the internal price combined with the current rate of exchange obtains. For example, an international operator in securities might find that, by combining local stock exchange quotations with current exchange rates, he could use dollars for the purchase of "Royal Dutch" shares in New York which he could sell simultaneously in London and Amsterdam at prices which, combined with the exchange rates between sterling and dollars and Dutch guilders and dollars, would show him a profit. The shares would, of course, be forwarded from New York to the buying markets, and those markets would be under the necessity of exchanging their local currency for dollars. The resulting adverse effect on the respective exchange rates, together with the satisfaction of the current demand for the security in question in the buying markets, would cause the purchasing power parity theory to operate: security prices, combined with exchange rates, would reach equilibrium.

LONG-TERM FACTORS

Any economic condition which eventually tends to affect the purchasing power of a currency must eventually affect the international exchange value of that currency. Such effects are frequently hastened by the speculative dealings in exchange of professional operators and, in some cases, such exchange operations actually curtail or diminish what would otherwise be the effects of the economic cause.

A revival of trade activity in a country, or the adoption of improved methods of production, may induce a burst of foreign buying of the products of that country. The resulting demand for the local currency will be increased by a speculative demand on the part of exchange operators, and the consequent rise in its international price may make the external selling price of its goods sufficiently high to discourage further buying. This effect will be added to by the probable rise in stock exchange values, helped by foreign buying, causing an expansion of credit and a rise in prices.

The principal economic causes that may be described as long-term factors affecting exchanges are *currency and credit conditions* and *political and industrial outlook and events*. Financial interests in every country are always watching the statistics of other countries, both financial and commercial, as these show the probable trend of the internal, as well as of the external, value of the country's currency. If, for instance, the published figures of the note circulation of a country show a steady increase which does not appear to be justified by the state of internal trade, the assumption is that over-issue is taking place and that the internal purchasing value of the currency will fall, i.e. internal prices will rise. This will have an adverse effect on the export trade of the country, and the foreign demand for its currency will tend to fall off eventually, causing a fall in its international exchange value. Exchange dealers abroad will, to some extent, anticipate this by "selling short" of the currency, thus immediately increasing the external supply relative to the demand. The fall in the international exchange value which results serves to offset the rise in internal prices and, if carried to the point at which gold is withdrawn from the country, the consequent reduction in the basis of the currency and credit must cause a contraction in the latter which, in turn, causes a fall in internal prices. As long as gold can enter or leave a country freely, movements in prices and exchange rates, due to the internal volume of currency and credit being too great or too small, are counteracted by the effects on that volume of an efflux or an influx of gold, but where the currency has no gold backing or where any gold backing is not allowed to perform its proper function, the exchange value of the currency can fluctuate unrestrictedly, unless it is under official control.

The national budget is another index to national finances which is closely scrutinized abroad. Evidence that a country is regulating its expenditure to its income is a "bull" point for the country since it tends towards a reduction in taxation, a lowering of overhead costs of production, and an increase in national savings. On the other hand, where it appears that a country is spending more than the state of its national prosperity justifies, adverse criticism is aroused since it is likely that an increase in taxation will have to be made, causing an increase of overhead costs and a reduction in the capacity for saving of the people. In the first case, speculators in exchange will "go long" of the currency, i.e. buy up currency in anticipation of a rise in its exchange value due to increased prosperity of the country, and in the second case, they will "sell short" of the currency in anticipation of a fall in its international value owing to the reduction of exports, due to high selling prices, and to the general falling-off in national prosperity.

The political outlook in a country is also a potent factor both in exchange speculation and in the international movement of capital. A stable government, the strict maintenance of law and order, the protection of property and of the rights of owners of wealth, will all induce an inflow of foreign capital, either for interest-gaining purposes or for safety, in spite of low interest rates. Political unrest, attempts to overthrow the government either by force or by constitutional methods, the growth of and possible accession to power of a body of political thought inimical to capital, will all induce the withdrawal of capital and prevent any further influx of funds from abroad. In the first case, speculators will be less active than in the second, since beneficial effects are slower to mature than are evil effects, but, on the one hand, a steady appreciation in the exchange value of the currency may be looked for over a long term, while, on the other hand, an immediate depreciation in exchange value will take place owing to speculators "selling short" in anticipation of the offerings of the currency which are almost bound to take place through the withdrawals of foreign-owned funds.

Current events and the future outlook in the internal industrial situation of a country will have similar effects. Settled and amicable conditions between capital and labour, a stable level of wages commensurate with selling prices on the level of world prices, evidence of enterprise and efficiency on the part of those responsible for the direction of industry, will all operate as long-term factors in causing an appreciation of the international exchange value of the currency. Foreign capital will be induced to flow into home industries, and a demand for the currency will be manifest on financial, as well as on trade, account. Conversely, labour troubles, strikes and lock-outs, antagonism between capital and labour, too high costs of production, delay in adapting methods of production to new ideas and conditions, etc., will all, particularly the first two, have immediate effects on the exchange value of the currency, as speculators will at once "sell short" in the expectation of a falling-off in the trade of the country owing to diminished production and/or increased production costs.

It can be seen, therefore, that speculation plays a large part in accelerating the effects of economic factors, which would normally be manifest only after the lapse of some time, and that such speculation may operate to prevent the full normal effects of the cause from taking place or may produce effects in excess of the normal. With an almost general return to some sort of gold basis of the currencies of the world, the field for speculation would become more limited, since fluctuations in exchange rates would be confined within the comparatively narrow margins represented by the rates at which gold could be moved profitably from one country to another, or by "control" operations on the part of the various national Authorities. In such circumstances it is probable that long-term factors would be allowed to work themselves out unassisted by speculation, except on the sudden appearance of adverse factors, which will always attract the "bear" speculator.

Seasonal Fluctuations in Exchanges

Where the imports and exports of a country vary with such factors as climate, harvesting of crops, tourist traffic, etc., the exchange value of the currency will necessarily vary with the resulting seasonal variations in its supply and demand. In the case of Australia, the grain and wool harvest is gathered from December to February, and sales of these products abroad cause a demand for Australian currency against other currencies. Similarly, South African wool, fruits, ostrich feathers, etc., are harvested in the late summer months, and at such times the value of the currency tends to rise owing to the demand for it in order to pay for these exports. The U.S.A., Canadian, Argentine, and other exchanges are subject to similar seasonal influences, while India is affected by the monsoon, Siberia by the long winter, etc. In most such cases, the banks of the country concerned endeavour to smooth out violent variations in the exchange value of the currency by offering supplies of other currencies which are in demand during the months other than the exporting season (which they can do either by building up balances in advance or by arranging finance credits in other centres), which places them in a position to cover their earlier sales by buying up the offerings of other currencies which come forward when the export season is in full swing.[1] Needless to say, the rates of exchange are allowed to move to a sufficient extent in either direction to afford a profit to the operating banks both on their sales of other currencies (which are made at rates adverse to the home buyers) and on their subsequent purchases (which are made at rates which show a profit on the original sale as well as covering all the expenses involved in maintaining balances abroad or in arranging credit facilities).

Gold Exports of Gold Producing Countries

There is no relation between the shipment of gold abroad to adjust a temporary adverse balance of indebtedness, and a shipment of gold abroad by a gold producing country for sale in another country. In the first case, the gold shipped represents savings, and is a payment of part of the accumulated wealth of a country in discharge of debts already incurred, for which full value has been received by the country exporting the gold. In the second case, the gold is shipped as an ordinary export of a commodity which has been produced internally in excess of the country's own needs. When a consignment of wool is shipped and sold abroad, the major part of the proceeds has already been paid out in the home country in the shape of wages, interest on capital, and other costs of production. The same is the case with the gold exported by a gold producing country. In order to produce it and to prepare it for export, heavy costs have been incurred in the shape of interest on the capital sunk in the mining company, machinery, wages, transport costs, etc., and only a small proportion of the market value of the gold represents a profit to the producers. It is only this profit which, when brought home, increases the wealth of the exporting country, but the total value goes to swell the favourable items in the trade balance. Thus, exports of gold from such countries as South Africa and Australia must be considered in a light totally different from that of exports out of the gold stock of a country which has to adopt this method of discharging an amount of debt equal to the full eventual "outturn" of the gold in the other centre.

---

[1] Such operations are at present left to the Central Bank or Exchange Fund to conduct if deemed necessary.

CHAPTER III

FACTORS LIMITING FLUCTUATIONS IN THE EXCHANGES

Control by Economic Forces; Control by Gold and Other Forms of Currency Standards; Planned Control

SINCE the main function of money is to act as a measure of value and a store of value, it is essential that it should retain the greatest possible stability of purchasing power. The growth, over the past century, of greatly diversified human wants and standards of living has rendered increasingly difficult the problem of maintaining stable money values. In the same way that prices measured in terms of money can vary internally through business booms or depressions, inflation or deflation of the money and credit system, and the forces of nature such as droughts, floods, earthquakes, etc., so the price of any unit of currency in terms of others can vary for these and other reasons. At the same time the farmer, the manufacturer and the trader alike require at least a reasonable stability in the purchasing power of the unit in terms of which their prices are expressed both for internal and external purposes. A widely fluctuating rate of exchange can make or mar an export market and can also seriously affect the internal standard of living. Britain, for instance, is largely dependent on supplies of foodstuffs and materials from abroad to sustain her people, and these she can obtain only if she can export and sell abroad sufficient quantities of her own products to provide the purchasing power needed to pay for her essential imports. If, therefore, the pound sterling cheapens for any reason in terms of other leading world currencies, it immediately increases the cost of Britain's essential imports, even though it temporarily makes her export prices favourable to foreign buyers. The enforced devaluation of sterling in November, 1967, certainly gave an immediate advantage to British exports to countries whose currencies had not been similarly devalued. Imports which had already arrived and had not been paid for, and all new imports, in currencies other than sterling, immediately increased in cost. This increased cost was very shortly reflected in a general rise in internal prices, which of course led to demands for wage increases. The sum total of these had to be added to manufacturing costs and within a comparatively short time export prices had risen to an extent which almost nullified the temporary advantage of devaluation. In the end, therefore, the country was little, if any, better off from the trading point of view, while the blow delivered to the prestige of sterling took some time to live down. Other measures, such as the establishing of the Prices and Incomes Board, were necessary to obviate a total lack of confidence in sterling. Sudden and violent movements in rates of exchange can, therefore, be nothing but detrimental to the economic and commercial life of a country, particularly if not accompanied by other controlling measures. There is still a striving for a means by which monetary stability, both internally and externally, can be attained. The possible alternatives can now be considered.

Economic Forces

Where a currency is not backed by, or linked to, any precious metal or other commodity or any other currency and is not subject to any artificial control, such as that exercised by the State, its exchange value in terms of other currency units is nominally free to fluctuate without limit. In fact, however, this has never proved to be the case, and it is this phenomenon which really forms the basis of the Purchasing Power Parity Theory. Assume that country A lives mainly by agriculture and supplies its wants, in the shape of capital and consumer goods, by buying them from countries B and C, to whom it sells its agricultural products. Its currency unit is free from State control and is not tied to any metal or commodity or to any other currency unit. Assume further that the currency unit of B is based on gold, while that of C is controlled by the State in relation to B's unit and that, in normal conditions, two of A's currency units equal one unit of either B or C. The maintenance of these exchange ratios depends upon A maintaining equilibrium between imports and exports. If, however, through drought or a scourge, the harvest in A is an almost total failure, the means of providing purchasing power in B and C will be lacking. Imports which have already arrived, but which have not yet been paid for, and payment for new imports, will set up a demand for the currencies of B and C greatly in excess of the available supply, and those who are forced to satisfy their needs for those currencies will offer more and more units of their own currency in exchange for each unit of B and C. Such a cheapening of A's unit, however, cannot continue indefinitely because a point is reached at which consumers are quite unwilling, or unable, to pay the much higher prices in their own currency resulting from the increased cost of imports due to the fall in the exchange value of the currency. A natural corrective of the position is therefore set in motion and the volume and value of imports will be quickly curtailed to match the decreased overseas purchasing power. This decrease will, to some extent, be offset by the inevitable rise in price of such of *A*'s crops as are available for export, but in the circumstances the main corrective would be in the restriction of trade between the three countries until such time as a new harvest once more gave *A* the necessary volume of external purchasing power. The example of Italian purchases of coal from either Poland or Germany can be used in reverse as an illustration of movements in exchange rates affecting the direction of exports and internal selling prices. The natural corrections of this nature, however, have now been superseded almost everywhere either by the adoption of a metallic monetary standard or by direct State control over currency exchange values.

Gold and Other Forms of Currency Standards

The curious attachment of mankind to the precious metals as a measure and store of value has already been mentioned, but it is now necessary to examine in detail how they are used for such a purpose. In earlier times currency systems consisted of actual metallic money in the form of coins, and these became progressively sounder both in design and in the exactness of their metallic content. As international trade developed, however, it was found that the amount of money work to be done, both internally and externally, would require a greater volume of metallic money than could be provided from the official stocks of the metal. A banking system had also been developing, in which the bankers accepted deposits of money against the issue of receipts and used these deposits to make loans to other customers. Experience showed that of the total of deposits only a comparatively small proportion was likely to be withdrawn within any given short period, and the bankers built up a credit system under which their liabilities became two or three times as great as their actual cash reserves. These paper promises to pay (or bank-notes) which were used as a means of giving credit became known as "faith money" because their general acceptance as money was entirely dependent on the faith or confidence which the community placed in the banker by whom the paper money was issued. This principle is now an integral part of every banking system, and banking or State reserves in the form of coin or metal in bulk cover only a small percentage of the nominal value of the paper money in circulation within the country. As was mentioned earlier, gold is now almost everywhere regarded as the orthodox backing for a paper currency, but the attachment of a currency to gold can take several forms. The basic requirement is that the standard unit of currency shall be given a fixed gold content by force of law which can be altered only by new legislation. Even though no standard coins are minted and the monetary needs of the country are served purely by paper currency and subsidiary coins, it is still possible for the country to maintain a gold standard for its currency if this basic requirement and the others mentioned below are present.

Monometallism

This monetary system, as its name denotes, consists in the employment of one metal as the basis of the standard coin and national unit of account. Under a pure monometallic standard only the one metal would be coined and used as legal tender. As has already been explained, gold has gradually come to be generally accepted as the most desirable measure of value, and the currency systems of the world are based on this metal. For motives of economy, various modifications of the true monometallic standard have taken place and the various types may be summarized thus—

Gold Specie Standard, under which full-weight gold coins of the required legal fineness circulate freely, gold in coin or bullion is allowed unhindered ingress and egress, the Central Authority is always prepared to buy or sell gold in unlimited quantities at legally fixed prices, and minting charges are negligible.

Gold Bullion Standard, under which no gold coins are in circulation, but the internal needs of the country are met by the use of paper money and subsidiary coins, the free import and export of gold in bulk is permitted, and the Central Authority is always prepared to buy or sell gold of a given fineness in unlimited quantities at legally fixed prices.

Gold Exchange Standard, under which the national unit of account is based on the standard unit of a Gold Specie or Bullion Standard country, paper money and subsidiary coins are used for internal purposes, but the external value of the national unit is maintained at about the fixed ratio with the gold unit through operations in the purchase or sale of the gold currency against the national unit by the Central Authority.

A Composite Legal Tender System is now usual under any monometallic standard. Under this system the standard money consists of coins of the standard metal (usually gold), or of official paper money which is freely convertible into gold or the right to gold, either of which are made legal tender to an unlimited amount. For the smaller domestic needs of the community subsidiary coins of a baser metal, such as silver, bronze or nickel, are minted, but these are made legal tender for a limited amount only.

As such subsidiary coins must have a lower intrinsic or metallic value than their legal or nominal value (in order to prevent them from being melted down or exported for profit), they are known as "Token" coins.

In all these cases fluctuations in the exchange value of the currency are limited to the rates of exchange which would be produced by movements of gold in bulk into and out of the country. A subsidiary kind of control of this nature is to be found in what is known as a *Currency Exchange Standard*, in which one currency is tied to another at a legal fixed parity of exchange, on either side of which only a small margin of fluctuation is allowed to provide for a profit in exchange operations. A currency so tied links its fortunes completely with those of the currency to which it has chosen to ally itself and which need not be, and in fact seldom is, on any form of gold standard. The outstanding example of the successful working of a Currency Exchange Standard is, of course, that given by members of the group of countries comprising what is popularly called the "Sterling Area" (see later). The New Zealand and Eire pounds are officially tied to the pound sterling at varying rates of exchange, while the Australian, South African, Indian, Pakistani and Ceylonese local currencies have a fixed legal sterling value. The exchange values of all these currencies, therefore, fluctuate with that of the pound sterling in terms of the currencies of all countries outside the group. Each country in the group is, however, master in its own house and is perfectly free to alter the exchange value of its currency in terms of sterling whenever it wishes. When sterling was devalued in 1967 some of the countries in the group did not retain their parity with sterling but preferred to retain their parity with the U.S. dollar. This decision reflects in some measure the changes that have gradually taken place both in world trading arrangements and commercial interdependence of countries. Australia, India and Pakistan were the principal countries concerned.

A Currency Exchange Standard is also in operation in other mutually associated groups of countries, as in the case of the Dutch and French Monetary Areas, although all the basic currencies, i.e. Dutch guilders and French metropolitan francs, are not on any form of gold standard. It is, however, a very convenient and cheap method of instituting some control over exchange fluctuations in respect of territories between which a considerable degree of interdependence already exists.

CHAPTER IV

MEANS AND METHODS OF DISCHARGING INTERNATIONAL INDEBTEDNESS

The International Banking System; Types of Credit Instruments

INTERNATIONAL indebtedness arises because nations trade with one another, exchanging goods and services, borrowing money from one another, paying interest on such borrowings and gradually repaying the capital and generally undertaking operations which result in the creation of a debt due from a resident of one country to a resident of another. Modern social and economic development has grown so complex that the diversified wants of mankind can be satisfied only by a highly-specialized international division of labour. As was shown in the first chapter, the primitive method of "barter" would be impossible today, and debts, whether internal or international, must be expressed in terms of money. There is no international money unit because practically every nation, in its desire to demonstrate its own individuality, has instituted its own national money or unit of account. Any creditor will normally require the eventual payment to him of his debt not in terms of some foreign currency but in terms of his own home currency, which is the only money he can use for his own internal purposes. It therefore follows that every international debt created means that sooner or later the money of the debtor country must be exchanged or translated into the money of the creditor country.

As long as the amounts owed by any country to any other are offset by the amounts owed to that country by the other, i.e. the bilateral balance of payments is in equilibrium, the question of exchanging the money of the one country for that of the other merely resolves itself into the establishment of some form of clearing house for the settlement of these mutual debts. The balance of indebtedness as between one country and another, however, continually fluctuates and these fluctuations are the immediate cause of fluctuations in exchange rates unless a rigid exchange control is in operation. International commerce and finance create debts, and the debts in the respective units of account create the need for the translation of one currency into another. The fact that the balance of indebtedness continually varies almost from hour to hour prevents any exact and permanent comparison of the two units being made. The actual value of one unit of currency in terms of the other is continually being thrashed out between the hammer of demand for that currency and the anvil of supply of it.

Many of the fluctuations in the day-to-day balance of payments between one country and others are due to temporary causes, such as seasonal purchases of grain, wool, tobacco, etc., which iron themselves out in due course. Others are more deep-seated and represent what the International Monetary Fund describes as a "fundamental disequilibrium" in a country's external balance of payments. Under any form of Gold Standard or under a planned control of fluctuations in exchange rates, a persistent adverse balance of payments is eventually corrected by the combined action of the following factors—

(a) Offerings of the currency by foreign holders who cannot use it, or wish urgently to dispose of it, cheapen its exchange value, which increases the cost of imports but decreases the external price of exports.

(b) Under any form of Gold Standard an efflux of gold reduces the credit base and causes a shortage of liquid loanable capital and a rise in interest rates, which in turn eventually cause liquidation of stocks of goods and a fall in internal prices, with, possibly, temporary unemployment.

(c) Under a planned control of the exchanges the Authorities would acquire unwanted home currency from foreign holders, which would be withdrawn from the domestic banking system and so would create almost the same conditions as those which follow an efflux of gold.

(d) In either case the cheapness of the exchange value of the currency, combined with the fall in internal prices, will make export prices attractive to foreign buyers, while imports will decrease owing to the rise in their cost through the low exchange value of the currency. At the same time, provided the internal economy of the country is basically sound, the shortage of liquid loanable capital and the rise in interest rates will induce an inflow of capital from abroad, which will give further support to the exchange value of the currency. These various adjustments will eventually restore rates and prices to approximately the purchasing power parity.

In the ordinary way, however, international indebtedness is settled by means of credit instruments of various kinds. In an example given in Chapter II it was shown how one credit instrument could be used to discharge two debts or more, and that creditors and debtors alike prefer to express their debts in terms of a currency of superior standing rather than in terms of currencies of lower prestige. If an individual receives a cheque in payment of a debt he does not, as a rule, walk about with it in his pocket until he can find someone who will exchange it for goods and services. He will normally keep a banking account into which he will pay the cheque for collection and credit, and when he, in turn, has a debt to pay, he will draw a cheque on his banking account in favour of his creditor. The bank, therefore, acts as a temporary reservoir for wealth. It collects debts which its account holders have to receive, and pays out for them the debts which they have to meet. The same process is applied to foreign debts since every foreign debt can be expressed by means of a credit instrument in the same way as an internal debt. It is only logical, therefore, that an international banking system has been developed to perform these services.

Banks Act as Clearing Houses for Debts

The difficulties in the way of every debtor who has to find a local creditor who has drawn on a debtor in a country to which the local debtor wishes to remit, and for the exact amount which is required to be remitted, are obvious. Consequently, while it is true that the status of the currencies of a debtor and a creditor decides largely whether the creditor shall draw or the debtor remit, there must be some central pool into which drawings on other centres can be sold and out of which remittances required can be purchased.

The banks and financial houses dealing in exchange are the natural channels through which debts can be bought and sold and, in the same way as debts due internally can be sold to a bank or money dealer by discounting a bill, rights to wealth in terms of other currencies can also be sold to such concerns at the prevailing rates for the class of credit instruments concerned. Similarly, debtors can purchase from exchange dealers credit instruments in terms of other currencies to suit their requirements, so that creditors and debtors alike are saved the trouble of selling and buying to and from each other after many difficulties. The small toll levied by the exchange dealer in the shape of a difference in the prices at which he buys and sells the same class of instrument is negligible in comparison with the cost of the trouble saved to the individual, and this business of the buying and selling of international debts constitutes one of the most valuable international services rendered by the banks of today.

In order to conduct such a business, banks must maintain relations and keep current accounts with other banks in all the principal centres of the world. These accounts are fed by the remittance abroad for collection and credit of all the various credit instruments payable in a given country which have been bought up by the bank from its local customers. Arrangements are also made for overdrafts to be created in case of need or for other credit facilities to be granted, such as acceptance credits. Out of the supply of funds in a foreign centre thus acquired, the bank is able to meet the requirements of those of its customers who wish to buy the right to an amount of the foreign currency in question, and it will draw on its account abroad in any form desired by the customer. It is not often, therefore, that trade credit instruments pass through more than two hands, the drawer and the bank who negotiates, or purchases, the instrument. Even if the owner of an instrument does not wish to sell it immediately to a bank, he will utilize the organization of the bank to have his debt collected in the foreign centre and the proceeds remitted home to him, less costs of collection. If the instrument is expressed in terms of the foreign currency, the collecting bank will have the proceeds credited to its account in the foreign centre and will exchange them into local currency, i.e. will buy the foreign currency in exchange for local currency at its ruling rate of exchange from its customer if he wishes.

The collection and the payment of debts and the exchanging of currencies, one for another, is, therefore, almost exclusively a banking function, so that it can truly be said that modern banks, with their international relations and ramifications, act as clearing houses for the world's debts.

FOREIGN ACCOUNTS

If a bank has to act in this manner, obviously it must be in a position to operate current and deposit accounts with banks abroad in its own name, in the same way that individuals operate on their domestic banking accounts. These accounts will be credited with all the items in the local currency remitted for credit of the account and will be debited with all payments which are instructed to be made from the account. It must be repeated that it is only possible to have useful possession of a currency in the country in which it passes current, and if a London bank buys, for instance, U.S. dollars from one customer and sells the same currency to another customer, the actual receipt and payment of the dollar amounts must take place in the U.S.A., while the purchase price is paid and the sales price received in sterling in London. Banks in this country, therefore, who act as international banking agents will maintain accounts with banks abroad in terms of the currencies of the respective countries, and these are known as "Correspondents' " accounts, or "Nostro" or "Our" accounts. In its own books of account it will show the foreign currency amounts side by side with the sterling equivalent. If a London bank purchases from a customer a sight draft in French francs at an agreed rate of exchange, it will debit the account in its books of the French bank to which it is remitting the instrument for collection, and will show in the currency column the face value of the draft and against it the sterling equivalent which has been paid or credited to the customer. When it receives advice from its correspondent that the item has been collected and credited to its foreign currency account it will also be advised of debits for stamps and collection charges. It will then credit these small items to the account in its books in name of the French bank and will show against them the sterling equivalent at the then current rate of exchange which it will debit to or claim from the customer. The eventual profit or loss on the working of these "Nostro" accounts is ascertained by valuing the established foreign currency balance at the end of an agreed period at the then current rate of exchange, and if this produces a larger amount than that shown as the difference between the debit and credit sterling columns, a profit has been made on the account. If, however, a transfer of sterling to the credit side of the account will be necessary to make the account balance, then a loss on the working of the account over the period will have been shown.

Conversely, foreign banks keep accounts with British banks in terms of sterling, which are run on the same lines as current accounts for home customers. These are known as "Vostro," or "Your," accounts. When referring to the account of any third party, whether it is an account in a foreign currency or in home currency, it is usually described as a "Loro," or "Their," account. To recapitulate—

"Nostro" accounts are accounts abroad kept in terms of the relative foreign currency and mean "Our account with you."

"Vostro" accounts are domestic accounts in the home currency and mean "Your account with us."

"Loro" accounts may be accounts either in a foreign or in the home currency and mean "Third party" accounts.

Principal Credit Instruments

There are many forms of instruments conveying rights to wealth, but, for the purposes of international finance and exchange, they can be classified under a few main heads. Each form varies from another chiefly in the speed with which the right to wealth which it expresses can be turned into cash, and its price, or "present value," varies with the loss of interest and risk of capital loss which must be borne by the purchaser or owner. The different rates of exchange which are consequently applied to different classes of credit instruments are discussed in a later chapter, but brief references are made to this point in the definitions which follow.

TELEGRAPHIC TRANSFERS (T.T.s.)

A T.T. is an order for the payment of money sent by telegraph, cable or telex, and it is by far the quickest method of transferring money from one centre to another. Telex is an exchange service similar to the telephone service whereby a printed message is recorded simultaneously at the point of origin and the point of destination by the use of teleprinters. Telex is now the most commonly used instrument for the transmission of T.T.s. The ability to execute such transfers must depend on the availability of funds in the other centre, and as only the banks and a few very large industrial concerns maintain current accounts abroad, their use is mainly confined to such institutions. Further, as no signature in writing, which could be compared with a specimen signature of the sender, can be included in the telegraphed instructions, a system of private codes by means of which the genuineness of the instructions can be tested and authenticated is essential, and such a system can only be worked between concerns having close relations with each other. As, by arrangement, funds are paid out in the foreign centre usually on the same day that payment is made in the home centre in local currency, there is no gain or loss of interest. Also, as the use of such instruments is almost exclusive to institutions of the highest class, the risk of non-payment is negligible. T.T.s, therefore, form the safest and quickest mode of transfer of funds, and the principal means by which bankers' funds are moved from place to place for short-term investment and of making transfers of large amounts, on either financial or trade account. As there is no loss of interest, no risk, no stamp duties, and the charge made in the rate at which they are sold by the selling bank is comparatively small, they constitute the best value for money in the eyes of a purchaser who requires funds in another centre immediately, but because of these advantages, their price, or the rate of exchange which they command, is the dearest of any form of credit remittance. Finally, as every other class of credit instrument only commands a lower price, i.e. a worse rate of exchange for the seller, owing to a certain loss of interest or greater risk to the buyer, cost of stamp duties or other expenses, etc., *the price of T.T.s may be considered the basic rate of exchange between the two countries concerned, as at any given moment.* Variations in rates of interest, or in local conditions affecting the safety of a remittance, may cause fluctuations in the price of other forms of remittance while leaving the price of T.T.s unchanged, but any variations in the price of T.T.s will usually be reflected at once by changes in the prices of other forms of instrument, unless other factors, such as interest rates, move in the opposite way at the same time. A later consideration of the Dominion rates of exchange will show clearly that the T.T. rate of exchange is the basic rate on which all other rates of exchange are built up.

MAIL TRANSFERS (M.T.s.)

A Mail Transfer is an order to pay sent by letter from principal to agent. It may be an order for an actual payment of cash to a third party, or for a credit to be passed to the account of the payee in the books of the agent. A current account between the signer and addressee is necessary, and such transfers perform all the functions of a cheque in effecting payment or transfer of funds but are not negotiable or transferable, need no stamp, and eliminate the risk of a cheque or draft coming into wrong hands. They also save the purchaser the trouble of endorsing and forwarding on a cheque or draft, as the instructions for the payment or credit of the funds are given in writing to the selling bank and passed on in its letter to the agent in the foreign centre. The purchaser pays cash for the instrument on ordering it, but the selling bank is not debited for the payment by its agent abroad until the letter arrives. This results in a loss of interest to the purchaser, since he or his creditor will not have the use of the funds transferred until the arrival of the instructions in the other centre, and a gain in interest to the selling bank, since it receives payment here before it is debited abroad. This difference in interest value is made up by an allowance in the price at which the instrument is sold, i.e. it is cheaper to buy than a T.T. to the extent of the interest due, and a correspondingly larger number of foreign units per pound are given, or fewer pence per foreign unit demanded, than for a T.T. These instruments, again, are almost exclusively used by banks and the international type of merchant firm, and in such cases, the risk which attaches to them is negligible.

Mail Transfers may be made by AIR MAIL or by SEA MAIL, but in ordinary circumstances, and now that all postal services to Europe at least are made by air lift, they are made by air unless a request to the contrary is made by a customer. For more distant countries, there is a variation between the quotations for air mail and sea mail transfers to allow for the additional loss of interest if the latter agent is used. It is always the period between the date on which an instrument is purchased and the date on which effective credit for the proceeds of the instrument is received that decides the interest allowance, usually by an adjustment of the exchange rate.

It will be obvious to bankers that the T.T. and M.T. have much in common with domestic "credit transfers" or "Bank Giro."

BILLS, DEMAND DRAFTS, CHEQUES AND BANKERS' DRAFTS

Though the volume of financial business may overshadow the balance of international indebtedness arising out of trade, and banking instruments of remittance be the most important from the point of view of the total amounts involved, yet the *number* of ordinary credit instruments used in the discharge of debts between nations is probably larger, though they may reach a smaller total amount. In the same way that the bill of exchange, sight draft, cheque or banker's payment is used for the settlement of internal debts, so such instruments may be used internationally, except that the liability of small firms or of individuals is less readily accepted by creditors.

Bills of exchange, as used internationally, may be divided into bank bills and trade bills and subdivided again into long and short bills. It can readily be understood that the greater security afforded by a bank bill causes it to command a better price (i.e. more advantageous to a seller) than that of a trade bill, and bank bills are much more used for the settlement of international debts than for internal purposes. Bank bills may arise out of financial operations or from bank credits opened in respect of commercial transactions. Trade bills are, of course, those drawn by one merchant firm or individual upon another, and do not usually appear in any discount market but are held and collected by the bank which purchases them from the owners in the first instance.

The tenor of a bill will depend upon the arrangement between the drawer and the drawee. Where new relations in trade are being opened up, it is usual for the seller to ask the buyer to arrange for payment by means of a bank credit, under which the seller will draw on a bank and will eventually obtain a bank acceptance which he can discount at the finest rate. This process involves the buyer in some expense and, as soon as relations between the two have become well established, he will ask the seller to draw on him direct and so save the cost of a bank credit. The seller will probably agree to draw sight drafts on the buyer, to which the shipping documents covering the relative goods will be attached and which will be handed over to the drawee by the collecting bank against payment of the draft.

The next stage may be that the seller allows a short term of credit to the buyer by sending him direct the documents covering the goods and trusting him to send an approved banker's draft in payment at once. This may be followed by the seller agreeing to accept the buyer's cheque in payment, to be forwarded by the buyer on the arrival of the documents. Eventually, the seller will have attained such confidence in the buyer that he will extend the period of credit allowed and draw at 30, 60, 90, 120, or more days after sight or date, and allow the buyer to obtain possession of the relative documents on his acceptance of such drafts.

Short bills are those drawn for periods not exceeding 30 days after date or sight, or which have not more than this period to run before maturity, while long bills are those which have a tenor or an unexpired period of currency of more than 30 days.

In practice, British banks are only asked to *buy*, i.e. negotiate, bills "at usance," whether short or long term. This is because the pound sterling is one of the largest units of account in the world and is widely used. Consequently, while British creditors draw bills on their foreign debtors in terms of the debtors' currency, it is nearly always the case that a foreign creditor of a British debtor will prefer to draw a bill in sterling on the debtor rather than for the latter to purchase from his bank and remit to him a bill "at usance" in the creditor's currency. Therefore, British banks do not sell usance bills in foreign currencies but only buy them.

The way in which the purchase price is adjusted to suit the tenor of any particular instrument is dealt with later, but it is important here to distinguish between bills drawn "after date" and "after sight." In the case of an "after date" bill, it begins to run towards maturity from the date stated on it and according to its tenor. If such a bill is not offered for negotiation until some days after it has been dated, it will have a correspondingly shorter time to run to maturity, and the loss of interest is reduced in proportion. On the other hand, an "after sight" bill cannot begin to run to its maturity until it is "sighted," which means that it must be presented to the drawee for acceptance before it commences to run to maturity. If such a bill is presented for negotiation, the period over which interest will be lost by the buyer is not only the actual tenor of the instrument but also the time which must elapse before it can be "sighted" and accepted by the drawee and any further period required for the homeward remittance of the proceeds of the bill on maturity. Transmission by air has shortened very materially these extra charges but, even so, they must be taken into account in the case of drafts drawn on very distant centres.

FOREIGN COUPONS AND DRAWN BONDS

Other instruments which banks are asked only to buy and not to sell are Foreign Coupons and Drawn Bonds. Many international security bonds have their interest coupons expressed as payable in one or other of the currencies of several centres, at the option of the holder, at a fixed rate of exchange. Apart from any Exchange Control regulations that may be in force, it therefore becomes a question for a British holder of such coupons as to the centre in which they shall be cashed as and when they fall due. If, for instance, a coupon representing interest on a security is expressed as being encashable for £1 in London or for 12½ Swiss francs in Zürich, and the current rate of exchange for Swiss francs is 12·25 per £, it will obviously be profitable for the British holder to arrange for the coupon to be encashed in Zürich as he will receive just over £1·02 instead of £1 for each coupon and the collecting charges will be only a small percentage of the difference. Many international security issues provide for capital redemption or repayment by periodical drawings of a certain number of bonds, as in a lottery. Drawn Bonds are those whose numbers are "drawn" in such a manner, and they then fall due for immediate repayment. They will be forwarded for encashment to the paying centre or, in the case of a choice of centres, to that centre which shows the highest return in home currency through the current rate of exchange.

In both these cases the buyer of the instruments loses interest until he receives credit after their encashment, and he must also bear the cost of packing, posting and insuring the parcels of coupons or bonds. An allowance for these items must, therefore, be made in the purchase price. The bond or coupon may, of course, be "collected" when the rate of exchange will be that current when proceeds are received. Loss of interest would not then be a factor in determining the rate of exchange to be applied.

STOCK DRAFT

Another form of sight instrument is the Stock Draft, which is simply a sight draft or cheque drawn by a stockbroker on some other stockbroking firm, or on a bank in another centre, in respect of the sale of stock by the home centre to the other centre, as securities are frequently bought and sold as between two centres. The purchasing centre will sometimes be content for the stock purchased to remain lodged in the safe custody of a first-class bank in the selling centre, but often there arises a private buyer who wants to have the stock locked up in his own safe, or an arbitrage operation in shares which calls for the physical delivery of the securities. In that case a seller of stock has to deliver to the other centre the actual stock or shares, and a stock draft is drawn against the collateral security which these represent, the actual stock or shares being attached to or enclosed with the stock draft. In addition to the names on the draft of the drawer and drawee, who are usually very good specializing firms of stockbrokers, the buyer of the draft has the security represented by the stock or shares which presumably could be sold should the draft be unpaid. But because the buyer incurs the expense and trouble of packing, posting and insuring a parcel of securities, as well as loss of interest until he receives credit for the proceeds, he must receive compensation in the price which he pays for the instrument.

REVERSE STOCK DRAFT

This operation involves a sale of foreign currency in contrast to the Stock Draft, which is the purchase of a draft in foreign currency. In certain cases a foreign seller of securities is not prepared to relinquish physical possession of them, except against payment on the spot. The home buyer must therefore arrange with his bank for the necessary amount in the foreign currency to be paid out in the foreign centre against delivery of a sight draft and the relative securities. The bank selling the foreign currency, and so acquiring ownership of the draft on the home buyer, will only receive reimbursement in sterling when the draft and the relative securities arrive from the foreign centre and can be presented to the home buyer. In this case, also, the buyer not only loses the interest on the capital sum involved, but must pay packing, posting and insuring costs, and any agent's charges.

COMMERCIAL AND PERSONAL CREDITS, TRAVELLERS' CHEQUES, ETC.

Credits established by British banks for account of a customer and for commercial purposes seldom, if ever, provide for the drawing of usance bills in a foreign currency. Any such credits would almost certainly involve payment at sight or on demand. If a foreign bank establishes a credit abroad in terms of its own currency and providing for usance bills to be drawn by a British beneficiary, such bills would be treated as short- or long-term bills according to their usance by any bank which was asked to negotiate them, and would be given the usual treatment accorded to such bills. Commercial credits in a foreign currency and all personal bank credits, travellers' cheques and circular notes are sight instruments, and are treated as such by any bank asked to issue such instruments or to make encashment against them. The issue by a British bank of such an instrument in a foreign currency is simply a sale of that currency against immediate payment in sterling and there is, therefore, a gain of interest until the foreign currency account abroad is debited with its encashment. When such instruments which have been issued abroad in terms of foreign currency are presented in this country for encashment, the bank is, in effect, purchasing a sight draft in the foreign currency against immediate payment in sterling and so must make the necessary allowance for loss of interest. After encashment the instrument itself, or the sight draft drawn against it, is forwarded by the buying bank to the foreign bank by whom the instrument was issued, for the face value to be credited to its foreign currency or "Nostro" account. It should be noted that such instruments cannot be purchased "with recourse" because the buying bank will not always be able to trace the presenter of the instrument. If, in fact, the encashment has been effected by fraud on the part of the presenter, the buying bank must stand the loss. Instruments of this nature issued in sterling by banks abroad do not involve an exchange operation, but are merely encashed by a correspondent bank in this country at their face value (less a small charge), and this amount is debited to the sterling account (the "Vostro" account) of the foreign bank with the correspondent bank.

Foreign Notes and Coin

Foreign "money" is usually handled by a special department in a big bank which confines itself to the purchase and sale of foreign currency in the form of notes and coin. A small balance is always held of the principal foreign moneys for the convenience of travellers and, in the ordinary way, sales within a little are offset by purchases. If, however, there is a seasonal demand for a Continental currency for tourist purposes, it may be necessary for the department to obtain direct, or through the foreign exchange department, a supply of notes in bulk. On the other hand, a similar seasonal supply may increase the stock of a particular currency to an unnecessary size, and a bulk sale will then be made to a correspondent bank abroad or to the foreign exchange department. In each case allowance must be made in the exchange rate for the costs of packing, posting and insuring the parcels of notes as these will have to be borne even where notes are imported from abroad.

Bullion

As long as the supply of credit instruments relative to the demand is sufficient to maintain the price, or rate of exchange, of the currency of one country in terms of others at about the Mint Par or Purchasing Power Par rates, the fluctuating balance of indebtedness is evidently not either heavily in favour of that country or against it. But should any undue disturbance of the equilibrium between supply and demand in that currency take place, the price of credit instruments will move to a point at which it would be cheaper to discharge debts in gold. As the whole of the world's credit structure has been built up on a gold basis, this metal will always be accepted by a creditor in discharge of his debt, and even with the few remaining silver-using countries, the import or export of the white metal will always suffice to adjust any temporary discrepancy between the supply of, and demand for, credit instruments.

The remittance of bullion, therefore, is the final method of settling any existing balance of indebtedness between any two countries, and such movements will take place whenever the rates of exchange justify the heavy expense involved, and provided that sufficient supplies of the metal can be respectively bought and sold in the debtor and creditor countries. This expense is so heavy that transfers of bullion are the most costly means of discharging international debts and, owing to the technical points involved and the saving of costs of transport by the remittance of large quantities at a time, these transfers are carried out mainly by banks or financial houses, as a final means of covering other exchange transactions, or, under special circumstances, by governments.

London as a Monetary Centre

For many years London was supreme amongst the monetary centres of the world, and her position as the world's chief financial centre was due partly to chance and partly to the national characteristics of her people, as the following summary of the main causes leading to this result shows—

1. From Elizabethan times, this country led the world in trade and industry, and our people possessed a genius for colonization. Wherever our ships and merchants traded, the pound sterling became in demand for the purpose of payment, and our colonists carried with them our monetary system as well as our laws.

2. This spread of our trade made the names of our leading merchants known all over the world, and our national temperament gave our traders and banks a reputation for honesty and fair dealing. This eventually resulted in banks and large merchant firms being asked to lend their names to bills on behalf of lesser-known firms

in this and in other countries, and the use of the sterling bill as a means of payment became international.

3. This use of sterling as an international currency was given a great stimulus by the chance which led this country to be the first country in the world to adopt gold as the basis of her currency, which meant that any debt expressed in sterling was thereby given a definite gold value. The gold basis also meant that the value of sterling in terms of other currencies could vary only within narrow limits, and the pound therefore became a stable currency and measure of value.

4. The establishment and maintenance of a free gold market in London gave the pound even greater prestige. The gold standard of currency meant that any person having the right to receive payment of a debt in sterling could demand payment of his debt in gold. The free gold market meant that, having obtained his gold, he could either sell it in exchange for some other currency or could withdraw the gold from the country if he wished. Similarly, a debtor whose debt was expressed in sterling could settle it, in case of need, by remitting gold to this country, and the quantity which he must remit was fixed by the gold basis of the pound, while the free gold market permitted the free import and disposal of such gold. Other countries adopted a gold standard of currency but did not permit free dealing in gold. They maintained a "one-way" gold market, which meant that while the responsible authority was usually ready to buy any gold offered to it at a price which might or might not be fixed, it would sell gold for export only when it felt inclined to do so, and usually possessed the legal right to encash notes in some other medium than gold if it so wished. For example, the Bank of France for many years possessed the right to encash its notes in either gold or silver at its option, so that a foreign creditor could never be sure of receiving a stable measure of value in exchange for his debt.

5. Our leading position in the world's trade, together with our lead in shipping and insurance, made us the world's creditor, on balance, for year after year for many years. This excess of trading income over expenditure gave us an ability to lend money to other countries, and such loans had the double effect of increasing our trade, as the proceeds of a loan were usually withdrawn ultimately in the shape of goods or services and rarely by gold, and of increasing our annual income from abroad by the amount of interest due to us and repayments of some of the capital lent.

6. The growth of the use of the sterling bill for trading purposes, and the necessity of setting up machinery for dealing with the issue and handling of foreign loans, led to the gradual building up of the

organization now known as the Money and Discount Market and to the development of the Stock Exchange as a capital market. Here, again, the level-headedness of our banks and merchants soon made these markets the most efficient in the world, and even today no other centre possesses such a highly-organized, sound, and active money and discount market as exists in London.

7. The geographical situation of this country between the Old World and the New, our freedom, both as individuals and as a nation, the absence of any serious political upheavals, the ability of our captains of industry and finance, the quality of the work of our artisans, and our well-balanced, placid, national temperament, have all aided in gaining for us the confidence of other nations and a reputation for soundness and fair play.

8. London's prestige has been enhanced in more recent years by our ability to evolve and develop more adequate means of financing trade, and media of international investment in line with the demanding conditions of a progressive world. Our industrialists, bankers, economists, merchants, civil servants and members of other professions have contributed an important part to the various discussions and negotiations which have taken place internationally. The activities of our factors, the development of Export Credit Guarantees to their present forms, the closer amity of our banks with their foreign counterparts, and the floating of substantial *dollar* loans on the London Stock Exchange are pointers indicating that, in a highly competitive world, London continues to hold her outstanding position as an international monetary centre.

CHAPTER V

THE THEORY AND WORKING OF GOLD POINTS

Limits to the Exchange Price of Credit Instruments; Specimen Calculations; Premium on Gold

THIS chapter has been reproduced almost in its original form because of its undoubted value in affording an understanding of the almost universal practice of relating currency values to gold. Nevertheless, it must be remembered that the object is to explain principles. In consequence, the rates of exchange used are out of date and there has been no decimalization. Admittedly, gold movements on private account are still greatly restricted and, in practice, are largely a matter of arrangement between governments and Central Banks. Also, any official declaration of a gold content for a national unit of currency is theoretical and has no practical value. The member countries of the International Monetary Fund declared exchange parities for their respective currencies with the U.S. dollar, and so indirectly with gold because of the American official gold price, but this is merely for accounting purposes. Very few countries allow the unhindered egress and ingress of gold, for residents as well as non-residents. Even in the United States gold coins are not in circulation, there is no free gold market and transactions in gold (except under special licences which are granted only sparingly) are conducted by the Federal Reserve Bank acting on behalf of the U.S. Treasury. None of the essentials for the effective linking of currencies to gold, either directly or indirectly, is therefore present, and in such circumstances gold movements in response to fluctuations in exchange rates are confined to official transactions between Central Authorities. If and when the principal world currencies are made fully "convertible," however, gold parities will have to be established and free gold markets opened and allowed to operate without hindrance sooner or later. When this stage is reached an understanding of the principles and practice of gold points will be essential to anyone concerned with practical foreign exchange.

It is not true to say, however, that no practical significance now attaches to the level of exchange rates at which it is more advantageous to use gold rather than credit instruments for the international movement of money. There are now active gold markets, in several Continental centres and in London, in which private operators can deal, and the "dollar parity price," i.e. the equivalent in U.S. dollars of the quotation in local currency calculated through the I.M.F. parity link, is of first importance. Illustrations of the possible limiting effects on exchange fluctuations of the "dollar parity" in the London Bullion Market are given later. The reader must remember that, although exchange rates and costs which are now obsolete have been used in other examples, the object is only to illustrate the underlying principles. The factors involved can be amended to accord with current conditions as, when and where they exist.

Within a country in which gold coins circulate freely, a debtor may effect payment by means of a credit instrument, bank notes or gold coins and, since either of the former methods of payment can be instantly converted into gold, the creditor is prepared to accept any of these forms of payment indiscriminately. Even where debtor and creditor reside in different parts of the country, the changing of a draft or note into gold is accomplished immediately on receipt, and credit instruments and gold become interchangeable as long as the debtor has a right to draw his draft.

The ability to effect payment in gold in another centre by means of a credit instrument, however, must depend upon whether the drawer has the right to funds which will enable the drawee to carry out his instructions. In a domestic banking system, the right to withdraw gold from a certain branch of one bank can be transferred immediately into a right to withdraw gold from another branch of the same bank, or even of another bank, and the adjustment of the gold holdings of the respective branches can be carried out by internal book-keeping or, in case of need, by remittances to and from the main stock at the head office, at the bank's expense.

Apart from the time factor, this principle is applied to international adjustments. In countries in which a legal gold value has been given to the standard unit of currency, and in which the Central Bank deals freely in gold, or a free gold market is allowed to operate and gold can enter or leave the country without hindrance, foreigners can draw on their balances to buy and withdraw gold, or can accumulate balances by remitting and selling gold. In such conditions a London bank which held a balance in French francs with a French correspondent could request that its balance should be used for the purchase of gold in Paris from the appropriate source (from the Central Authority or from the free gold market or from the correspondent's own reserves), and that the gold should then be shipped from Paris to London by air or sea, as desired. No system has yet been in force to provide, on an international scale, the facilities available in domestic banking for the withdrawal of specie in a centre other than that in which the drawer holds his credit balance, against an internal book-keeping entry between the two centres, direct or through some centre common to it, such as the head office of two branches of the same bank. At one time it was hoped that the Bank for International Settlements in Basle would act as the central repository for the gold reserves of its member banks, but in modern conditions gold and currency reserves are now held directly by the State Treasury or by a nationalized central bank, and the principle now seems to be that "a bar of gold in the vaults at home is worth two in vaults abroad, with the possible exception of Fort Knox!"

Limits to the Exchange Price of Credit Instruments

It has already been shown how the rate of exchange which the various forms of credit instruments will command varies with the speed at which they can be encashed after purchase, i.e. with the loss of interest to the purchaser, and with any necessary costs of collection and expenses of remittance, in addition to the varying status of the parties to the instrument. If in all countries full-weight gold coins circulated freely, and if the right to gold coins in one centre could be *immediately* transformed into the right to gold coins in another centre, the rates of exchange would never vary from the Mint Pars. In other words, if the supply of and demand for Telegraphic Transfers between two gold using countries were always evenly balanced, the exchange between those two centres would always be at the Mint Par. But it has been shown how many and varied are the influences affecting the relation between the demand for and supply of debts between nations, and the exchange dealers can sell rights to wealth in terms of other currencies only as long as they have at their disposal a balance in the other centre built up from the proceeds of debts due there which they have purchased, or credit facilities which enable them to draw even though their balances are exhausted. Similarly, they can only continue to buy up debts payable in other centres as long as there is a demand for remittances with which to pay debts due in those centres. The exchange price of other forms of credit instruments will always vary from the basic price of a T.T. to the extent of the loss of interest and expense involved, while the basic price of the T.T. itself will vary with the demand for and supply of remittances between any two centres.

As the basis of all credit instruments is gold, it follows that any serious discrepancy between the demand for and supply of such instruments can be adjusted by transferring gold to the centre whose currency is more in demand. But, as gold transfers must actually be made in fact and not by means of book entries, heavy expenses are incurred in making such transfers. These expenses are heavier than those involved by the use of any form of credit instrument, and the exchange price of credit remittances on one country can rise in a debtor country until the point is reached at which, for a given outlay in home currency, a debtor will obtain as much foreign currency by purchasing and paying all the expenses of shipping gold as he would by paying the market price for credit remittances, or when a creditor could obtain the same amount of home currency by the operation of withdrawing gold from the debtor country as he would by selling his draft on his debtor at the market price.

Definition of Gold Points

These points in rates of exchange between two gold using countries are known as *Gold Points* or *Specie Points*, and they represent *the exchange prices at which it is as cheap to use gold in discharge of international debts as to use any form of credit instrument.* To take a simple example, assume that the Australian sovereign and the English sovereign each contained the same amount of pure gold, and that the two coins were interchangeable for monetary purposes. In the ordinary way, debts between the two countries were settled by means of credit instruments, but if, for instance, there was a temporary adverse balance of payments against Australia, the demand for remittances on London would have steadily exceeded the supply, the available balances of exchange dealers would become exhausted, even should they have raised the prices at which they would have sold remittances on London (to discourage buyers), the cost of obtaining credit facilities in London out of which to sell further remittances would have made the price rise still higher, and, at last, the market price of a T.T. on London would have been so high in terms of Australian pounds that a debtor there would have found it as cheap to withdraw Australian sovereigns from his bank, paying all the expenses of transmission and incurring the loss of interest on his money while the gold was in transit, and eventually to have discharged his debt in London by paying over the gold coins, as to have met his debt by paying the market price in his own currency for a T.T. in sterling.

Gold Points Not Fixed

While the Mint Par of exchange remains the unalterable basis of comparison between two currencies on the same metallic standard as long as the Coinage Laws of the two countries remain unaltered, there are so many factors which determine the "outturn" (or product in terms of the other currency) of a gold shipment that the points in the rates of exchange at which such shipments would become possible and desirable could alter from day to day. Further, the primary essential for transfers of bullion would be that its exit from and entry to the two countries should be unhindered by legal or banking restrictions, and that the ability to obtain it in the one country and to sell it in the other should be untrammelled.

Causes of Variations in Gold Points

Any alteration in any of the factors which would determine the "outturn" of a bullion shipment would obviously alter the rate of exchange produced by transferring the metal, i.e. the Gold Point, and these various factors will now be considered in detail.

THE PRICE OF GOLD

Where full-weight gold coins could circulate freely in the two countries, the rate produced by transferring such coins from one centre to the other (without allowing for the costs of the operation) would be the Mint Par as long as the Central Authority in each centre was compelled to issue and receive any gold coins as representing in currency their value in pure gold *at a fixed price for gold*, or if the two coins could circulate in either country. As long as the Central Authority must both buy and sell gold, either pure or of a fixed fineness, at the same price, and dealings in the metal were unrestricted, a free gold market at the fixed price would exist, but dealers would automatically deal with the Central Authority, as no margin of profit would exist by dealing outside. This was the case in the U.S.A., prior to 1932, where the U.S. Treasury would both buy and sell fine gold at the price of $20·67183 per ounce, and no outside market in gold existed; under such conditions, dealers could calculate exactly the number of units of currency which they would pay or receive for gold bought from or sold to the Central Authority.

Should a Central Authority have legally fixed prices, one for buying and one for selling gold, or where it could vary its prices, or could even refuse to buy or sell should it wish to do so, a variable element is introduced into the calculation of the "outturn" of a shipment. In the case of this country, the Bank of England was at one time compelled to buy all gold offered to it at the price of 77s. 9d. per *standard* ounce, and was bound to sell gold for export in amounts of not less than 400 oz. at the price of 77s. 10½d. per standard ounce troy. These prices were equivalent to roughly 84s. 9$\frac{13}{16}$d., and 84s. 11½d.

per *fine* ounce, respectively, and there was therefore a margin between which bullionists could endeavour to deal in the outside market without recourse to the Bank of England. A buyer of gold in this country knew that he could always obtain it from the Bank at a price equivalent to 84s. 11½d. per ounce fine, but if he could buy it in the open market at, say, 84s. 10½d. per ounce, the cost of his remittance abroad was obviously less; in other words, to ship the amount of gold needed to produce a given amount of currency in another centre cost him less in his original outlay or, for the same outlay, he could obtain more foreign units eventually. Similarly, a seller of gold here could always sell it to the Bank at a price equivalent to 84s. 9$\frac{13}{16}$d. per fine ounce, but if he could obtain 84s. 10¾d. in the open market he would receive a larger amount of sterling for a given amount of gold which cost him a given sum in another currency. *The price at which gold can be bought and sold in the two centres* is therefore a factor of the first importance in arriving at a Gold Point, and the effects of variations in such prices are illustrated in the examples later in this chapter.

THE FINENESS OF GOLD AND REFINING CHARGES

The next point is the legal fineness of gold in the two countries and, where this differs, whether the Central Authority would accept gold of a different fineness or whether it would require all gold to be brought to its own measure of fineness before purchasing it, in which case, refining charges would be incurred by the prospective seller. This point was well shown in the case of gold shipments from this country to France during 1930. Owing to a very heavy drain of gold, the Bank of England announced that it could no longer oblige purchasers by selling gold in fine bars, but would fall back on its legal right to sell only bars $\frac{11}{12}$ths fine. The French standard of fineness was $\frac{9}{10}$ths, but the Bank of France had the right to refuse to buy anything but fine gold or gold $\frac{9}{10}$ths fine, and it informed the public that it was, at that time, prepared to buy only *fine* gold, so that all gold containing any proportion of base metal (as with bars bought from the Bank of England) would have to be refined before it could be sold to the Bank of France. This meant not only an additional expense to shippers of gold from this country to France on account of the costs of refining, but a further loss of interest during the time taken by the refining process and, as the facilities for refining both in London and in Paris were extremely limited, the refiners became so booked up that the process extended, at times, into as much as three weeks, so that the loss of interest was considerable. It should be noted that, when a gold shipment was being undertaken, no risk of fluctuations in the rate of exchange ruling in the market could be taken, but the currency which would be produced by the gold shipment had to be sold as soon as the shipment was arranged. Under normal circumstances, the shipper would pay for his gold in the exporting centre at once, but would receive credit in the other centre only when the gold arrived, and he therefore sold his "outturn" for delivery on the estimated date of arrival of the gold and lost interest on the money locked up at the rate ruling in the exporting centre. In the case of these shipments to France, however, the chief object of making them was to obtain francs in Paris as quickly as possible to cover sales of francs which had been made at very high prices, i.e. few francs to the pound, owing to very pressing demands for immediate funds in Paris. These immediate demands could be met only by creating temporary overdrafts in Paris and covering these by the eventual "outturn" of the gold shipments on arrival. Interest was therefore lost at the French overdraft rate which, owing to the unusual pressure for accommodation, was much higher than in London. As a result, fine gold in the open market commanded a premium equal to the loss of interest plus the refining charges, since by buying gold $\frac{11}{12}$ths fine from the Bank, even at a price equal to 84s. 11½d. per fine ounce, the buyer incurred costs which acted as an increase in price, and he would rather pay this increased price in the open market if, by doing so, he could save the trouble and delay of refining the standard gold. Consequently, when the charges and loss of interest equalled 1½d. per ounce, fine gold in the open market could be sold at 85s. 1d. per ounce, and when the refining charges were raised by the refiners (to take advantage of the opportunity of extra profit), and the delay in refining became still greater, the total extra cost equalled 2½d. per ounce, and fine gold in the open market was sold at 85s. 2d. per ounce. Gold shipments under these conditions became a matter of some hazard, and the exact Gold Point was almost impossible of calculation in advance. Normally, however, such hindrances either would not have existed or would have been such that their cost and effects would have been calculable and could have been allowed for.

In many instances, the receiving Central Authority required the gold offered to it for sale to be accompanied by an Assay Certificate or required to take assays of the consignment itself. In such cases, the *cost of assaying* had to be allowed for by the shipper, and a small additional loss of interest on the value of the bars reserved for assay and for which credit was not given until after the assay had been completed. Thus, the U.S. Mint gave immediate credit for about 97 per cent of a consignment of gold sold to it, but only gave credit for the remaining 3 per cent about three weeks or a month later, after the assay tests had been completed.

FREIGHT, OR COST OF CARRIAGE

This represents the actual cost of transporting the gold. Usually, a "through" rate of freight was obtained from the terminus in one centre to that in the other, to include carriage by rail, and/or air, and/or sea, with transhipment from one form of conveyance to another as required. The rate quoted was usually lower for large than for small shipments and was charged on the declared value, as the space occupied by a consignment of gold was quite out of proportion to its value. The market rates varied with the competition between the various forms of transport and between different companies engaged in the same form.

INSURANCE

This was the cost of the premiums which had to be paid to cover the risks attaching to the movement of gold. Every possible risk was usually included in the policy of insurance, and the rate of premium varied with the strength of competition between insurance companies, though a large consignment on one vessel or aeroplane usually resulted in a higher average rate of premium being charged as the leading underwriters would not accept more than a certain share of risk in such a shipment except under the payment of a higher rate of premium for the last part of the total cover. Thus, where a shipment of £500,000 had to be insured, the first £250,000 of the risk on one vessel would have been covered at the rate of, say, 1s. per cent, the next £100,000 at 1s. 6d. per cent, the next £100,000 at 2s. per cent, and the last £50,000 at 2s. 6d. per cent.

LOSS OF INTEREST

This item, as already explained, represented the cost to the shipper of the funds locked up during the time the gold was in transit, as cash had to be paid to obtain the gold, and the proceeds were available only after it had been moved to the other centre and accepted by the purchasing authority. This cost varied with the prevailing rates of interest (the financing being carried out either by using funds in the exporting centre or by overdrawing temporarily in the importing centre, whichever was the cheaper), and with the time taken in transit.

BROKERAGE

This item occurred as a recognized charge only in London, as no other open gold market existed in which specialized bullion brokers worked. Where gold was purchased in the open market, a bid could be entered only through a broker, and a commission of as high as ¼ per cent may have been levied on small amounts bought for private parties, but for amounts of, say, £100,000 dealt in on behalf of regular market operators the charge may have been as little as ¼ per mille. In cases where a shipper taking gold from the Central Authority had no facilities or labour available for the packing and handling of the gold, a firm of bullion merchants in any centre would have undertaken this service at a charge which would have been agreed upon beforehand.

PACKING AND HANDLING, BOXING, AND AGENCY CHARGES

As stated above, gold taken from a Central Authority in the form of coin or bars had to be carefully packed in stout wooden boxes or kegs, loaded into vans and carted to the terminus from which it was to be dispatched. On arrival at the other end, an agent of the shipper took charge of it, had it unloaded from the train, vessel or aeroplane, loaded into vans, and delivered to the purchasing authority. All these services had to be allowed for in the cost of the shipment (even the boxes cost several shillings each), but their cost could be exactly ascertained in advance and formed but a very small proportion of the total.

Calculation of Gold Points

For theoretical purposes, Gold Points were usually calculated by making allowance for the percentage of each form of expense on the rate of exchange produced by buying bar gold in one centre and selling it in the other, or, where no variation between buying and selling prices existed in each centre, the Mint Par rate could be used. For exact calculation, however, it was necessary to compile a *pro forma* invoice by working out the precise total cost and eventual "outturn" of a stated quantity of gold. The following examples illustrate both the approximate and the exact methods of calculation—

(*a*) Gold purchased from the Bank of England at 77s. 10½d. per standard ounce and sold to the U.S. Mint at \$20·67183 per fine ounce, would yield a gross "outturn" of \$4·8665 per £1 (or the then Mint Par).

From the equivalent rate thus obtained must be *deducted* the costs of the shipment, as the expenses reduce the eventual number of dollars obtained for each pound used by increasing the number of pounds required to produce a given number of dollars.

The net rate, or *Outgoing Gold Point* from London to New York was therefore obtained thus—

Gross "outturn" per £		$4·8665
Less Freight at 3s. %	$·0073	
Insurance at 1s. %	·00243	
Packing, cartage, and agency in New York at ¼⁰/₀₀	·001216	
Melting and assaying charges in New York at ¼⁰/₀₀	·001216	
[1]Interest on 97% of shipment for 8 days at 3% p.a.	·00315	
[1]Interest on balance of 3% for 30 days at 3% p.a.	·0002	
		·015512
(Interest taken on New York terms of 1 year of 360 days)		$4·850988

The eventual yield of such a shipment was therefore—

$$£1 = \$4 \cdot 850988 \text{ (or } \$4 \cdot 85\tfrac{3}{32} \text{ nearest),}$$

and if the market price of T.T.s were such that *fewer* dollars were offered per pound than this figure, dealers would have covered their requirements in New York by shipping gold from London rather than pay the price asked for credit remittances.

(*b*) To show the variable nature of Gold Points, if interest rates had risen until money was worth 6 per cent per annum, and the other factors remained unchanged, the Gold Point would be altered thus—

Gross "outturn" per £	$4·8665
Less Charges as above, but with interest calculated at 6% p.a.	·018862
	$4·847638

The Outgoing Gold Point from London to New York would then have become—

$$£1 = \$4 \cdot 847638 \text{ (or } \$4 \cdot 84\tfrac{49}{64} \text{ nearest),}$$

and the number of dollars offered per pound in the market in the shape of credit remittances would need to have fallen below this figure to have made gold shipments from London to New York profitable.

(*c*) But if gold could have been purchased in the open market more cheaply than from the Bank of England, the Gold Point would

---

[1] See p. 56

have undergone an alteration, if the costs of shipment remained unchanged. If gold could have been purchased in the open market at a price of 84s. 10½d. per fine ounce and sold to the U.S. Mint at $20·67183 per fine ounce, the gross "outturn" would have produced an equivalent rate of $4·87112 per £1. This means that the eventual net "outturn" would have yielded a greater number of dollars per £1, thus—

Gross "outturn" per £	.	$4·87112
Less Charges as above, worked on the new "outturn"	.	·015627
		$4·855493

and the Outgoing Gold Point from London to New York would then have been—

$$£1 = \$4\cdot855493 \text{ (or } \$4\cdot85\tfrac{35}{64} \text{ nearest).}$$

This should make clear the interdependence of the market price of gold and the rates of exchange between this country and others. The more nearly any gold rate of exchange approached the point at which gold could have been purchased from the Bank and shipped abroad with profit, the higher the price gold offered for sale in the open market will command, owing to competition between shippers. When exchange rates were well away from the Outgoing Gold Points, competition between buyers in the open market was correspondingly lacking, and the gold may eventually have been sold to the Bank at its statutory buying price through lack of outside buyers.

Conversely, if certain exchanges stood at such levels as to have induced an open market price for gold above the Bank's buying price, imports of gold may have been attracted from other centres on which the rate of exchange had nearly reached the point at which it would have been profitable to ship gold *to* London for sale to the Bank, rather than to give the number of foreign units demanded for each pound by the market price of credit remittances.

(*d*) The importance of this may be shown by the following examples of gold *imports* into this country—

Gold purchased from the U.S. Mint at $20·67183 per fine ounce and sold to the Bank of England at 77s. 9d. per standard ounce would yield a gross "outturn" of £1 for each $4·87438 expended.

The costs of shipment, however, would increase the number of dollars required to produce (or "lay down") a pound in London and so must be *added* to this figure.

The *Incoming Gold Point* from New York to London would be—

Initial cost in dollars per £	$4·87438
Add Usual charges, say, at 3°/₀₀, total	·014623
	$4·889003

If, therefore, the market price of credit remittances on London in terms of dollars should rise over $4·889003 (or $4·88$\frac{29}{32}$ nearest), gold would be the cheaper form of discharging debts due from America to this country.

(*e*) Should it be possible to sell gold in the open market at a better price per fine ounce than the equivalent of the Bank's statutory buying price per standard ounce, and the other factors remain unchanged, the Gold Point would be amended accordingly. If gold purchased from the U.S. Mint at $20·67183 per fine ounce could be sold in the open market in London at 84s. 10½d. per fine ounce, for example, the Incoming Gold Point from New York to London would then be—

Initial cost in dollars per £	$4·87112
Add Usual charges, say, at 3°/₀₀	·014613
	$4·885733

Gold would then be the cheapest method of discharging debts from America to this country should the market price of credit remittances on London in terms of dollars rise above $4·885733 (or $4·88$\frac{37}{64}$ nearest) per £1.

It can now be appreciated that there would be two points in every rate of exchange between two gold standard countries at which gold would tend to move from one to the other. As between this country and other gold standard countries, *the point in our rates of exchange at which gold would tend to flow into this country is known as the Incoming Gold Point, while the point at which it would tend to be exported by us is known as the Outgoing Gold Point* of the rate of exchange concerned. These points were by no means always operative in both directions, however, as there were many countries which were always ready to receive gold but which placed obstacles of all kinds in the way of gold exports. Owing to our constant endeavour to preserve a free gold market and to place no hindrances in the way of the entirely free movement of bullion, both into and out of this country, it may be said that our Outgoing Gold Points were always operative, i.e. we were always liable to lose gold should the value of the pound cheapen to the necessary extent, but that our Incoming Gold Points were only partially operative, dependent on the willingness of the other centre concerned to allow gold to leave the country, in terms of whose currency the pound had appreciated to the extent necessary to make gold shipments to us a profitable undertaking.

The exact working of the net "outturn" of a gold shipment is shown in the following *pro forma* invoices, as well as the precise equivalent rate of exchange produced by such shipments—

(f)   PRO FORMA INVOICE

FOR THE SHIPMENT OF 100,000 OZ. FINE GOLD FROM PARIS TO LONDON

Bank of France sells fine gold at 16,963·528 fcs. per kilo.
100,000 oz. equals 3,110·35 kilos.

3,110·35 kilos at 16,963·528 fcs. per kilo cost . .	Fcs.	52,762,509·30
Add Cost of Freight at 1s. % ($\frac{1}{10}$%)[1] . . .		26,350·00
Insurance at 6d. % ($\frac{1}{20}$%) . . .		13,175·00
Interest for 2 days at 3% p.a.[1] .		8,793·75
Packing, carting and agency charges .		2,081·95
Total cost	Fcs.	52,812,910·00

100,000 fine oz. sold to the Bank of England at 77s. 9d.
per standard oz. yields . . . . .   £424,090 18s. 2d.

Equivalent rate of exchange produced is

$$\frac{52812910}{424090 \cdot 909} = 124 \cdot 5324$$

Therefore the Incoming Gold Point from France to this country under the above conditions is 124·53¼ fcs. to £1.

If the gold could have been sold in the open market at 84s. 10½d. per fine ounce, the equivalent rate would have been found to be 124·47 fcs. per £1, and if it could have been sold as high as 84s. 11d. per fine ounce, the equivalent rate would have been only 124·40 fcs. per £1. Thus, the lower the price which could have been obtained for the gold by the shipper, the more francs must have depreciated in terms of pounds before gold shipments became profitable.

(g) The former German Reichsbank paid from Rms. 2,784 to Rms. 2,790 per kilo of fine gold, according to the strength of its desire to increase its gold holding. It is here assumed that the Reichsbank paid its highest price for the gold offered to it.

[1] Freight and insurance based on fcs. 52,700,000, and interest on a 360-day year.

PRO FORMA INVOICE

OF A SHIPMENT OF 100,000 OZ. FINE GOLD FROM LONDON TO BERLIN

		£	s.	d.
Cost of 100,000 fine oz. bought from the Bank of England at 77s. 10½d. per standard oz.		424,772	14	6
Add Cost of Freight by air at 1s. 6d. % . . £320				
Insurance at 6d. % 107				
Interest for 2 days at 3% p.a. . . 70				
Packing, cartage and agency . . 26				
		523	–	–
		£425,295	14	6

"Outturn" of 100,000 fine oz. in Berlin.
100,000 oz. equals 3,110·35 kilos.

	Rms.	
3,110·35 kilos sold to the Reichsbank at Rms. 2,790 per kilo yields	Rms.	8,677,876·50
Less Reichsbank assay charge of Rms. 6·00 per kilo		18,662·00
Net Return	Rms.	8,659,214·50

Equivalent rate produced by the above operation is

$$\frac{8659214\cdot50}{425295\cdot725} = 20\cdot36$$

Therefore the Outgoing Gold Point from London to Berlin under these conditions is £1 equals Rms. 20·36.

If gold could have been purchased in the open market at a lower price than the equivalent of the Bank's statutory selling price, the "outturn" (and the equivalent rate produced) would have been increased accordingly. Thus, if gold could have been purchased in the open market at 84s. 11d. per fine ounce, the equivalent rate would have been Rms. 20·37 per £1, and at 84s. 10½d. the equivalent rate would have been Rms. 20·38 per £1.

As will be noticed, the foregoing examples are based on pre-1931 figures and so are merely illustrative of principles.

The arithmetical processes used in arriving at these rates, or for calculating the rate produced by buying gold of a certain fineness in one country at a stated price and selling it in terms of the currency of another country at a stated price for gold of the same or of a different fineness, are set out in a later chapter.

Gold in the Open Market

In the absence of special factors, such as the fear of war or of the devaluation of a currency which would lead to a panic demand for gold for hoarding purposes, the price of gold offered for sale in any open market would be determined largely by the existence of legally fixed buying and selling prices for gold in any country or countries. As long as there remains one Central Authority, whether Government or Central Bank, which would be under a legal obligation to buy and sell gold at fixed prices in terms of its own currency, then the price of gold elsewhere would be governed by these fixed prices, combined with the current rates of exchange for the currency concerned. For example, from 1907 to 1933 the United States Mint was under a legal obligation to buy or sell gold in unlimited quantities at the fixed price of $20·67183 per fine ounce. After the end of the 1914–1918 war, and until the return of Britain to a Gold Standard in 1925, the U.S. Mint remained the only source in the world of an unlimited supply of, and demand for, gold at a fixed price. In consequence, gold prices in the London Bullion Market (which consistently remained the outstanding free gold market of the world) were based on the sterling-dollar rate of exchange.

Any seller of gold knew that he could sell his gold to the U.S. Mint at the statutory price and could then sell the dollars so obtained for any other currency. If, therefore, the dollar exchange stood at $4 per £, he could obtain a gross outturn of 20·67183 ÷ 4, which gives £5·168 nearly, or £5 3s. 4d. per fine ounce. Allowing, say, 1s. per ounce for transmission costs, no seller of gold would accept less than 102s. 4d. for his gold in the London market, while no buyer would pay more than about 104s. 6d., since he could buy dollars and use them to buy gold from the U.S. Mint for shipment to London at this price. If dollars had appreciated to $3 per pound, the price of gold would have risen correspondingly to 20·67183 ÷ 3, which would have given a basic price of about 137s. 10d. per fine ounce.

The return to the Gold Standard involved the re-establishment of fixed prices at which the Bank of England would buy and sell gold in unlimited quantities, but with a minimum quantity of 400 ounces, and this restored the exchange value of the £ as the basis of calculation of gold prices in the London Bullion Market. On the suspension of gold payments in Britain in 1931, which, of course, involved the suspension of the legal obligation of the Bank of England to buy and sell gold at fixed prices, only the U.S.A. and France were left with legally fixed gold prices, and these consequently became the basis for London prices.

With two potential gold dealers, the London buying price had to be based on whichever currency was the *dearer* in terms of pounds (since a sale of gold in the country with the dear currency would produce the greater sum in sterling), while the London selling price had to be based on whichever currency was the *cheaper* in terms of pounds (since a purchase of gold in the country with the cheap currency would cost a smaller sum in sterling). With the suspension of gold payments by the U.S.A. in April, 1933, France was left as the only country with legally fixed buying and selling prices for gold in unlimited quantities, and London gold prices had to be based on the French legal prices and on the French franc exchange rate. On 31st January, 1934, the U.S.A. fixed a new legal price for gold of $35 per fine ounce for both buying and selling and London once more had a dual basis for calculation.

Bullion Operations and Exchange Rates

It must be appreciated that a purchase of gold against local currency in one centre, and its subsequent sale in another centre for the currency of that centre, would necessarily involve a sale of the second currency against the first in one or other centre or elsewhere, so as to reimburse the operator for his original outlay. The size of any given bullion transaction would, therefore, be almost entirely dependent on the capacity of the foreign exchange markets of the world to absorb the currency which would be offered and to supply the currency which will be wanted, without causing any appreciable fluctuation in the exchange rate on which the operation was based. The process of conversion would not need to be confined to the exchange markets in the exporting and importing centres. Exchange arbitrage operations could be employed. However, in order to ensure that the foreign currency which would result from the gold transaction be sold at, or very close to, the rate of exchange which prompted the operation and give the required profit would demand a very high degree of technical skill. Competition between bullion operators would keep the margin of profit to a low level and a fluctuation of even one per mille in the exchange rate against the operator, e.g. a rise from $2 \cdot 81\frac{1}{2}$ to $2 \cdot 81\frac{3}{4}$ in the sterling-dollar rate when the operator proposed to ship gold from London to New York, would probably absorb all or most of the profit on the operation.

The following is an example of the relationship of exchange rates to gold prices, but it must be emphasized that the example is again purely theoretical as there is no free gold market in the U.S.A. and the Federal Reserve Bank, acting for the U.S. Mint, will deal in gold only with the Central Authorities in foreign countries and not with individual bullion operators. The fixed basic price in the U.S.A. of $35 per fine ounce for both buying and selling is subject to a charge of $\frac{1}{4}$ per cent in either case, which is equal to $00·0875 per fine ounce. The effective prices are therefore $34·9125 for buying and $35·0875 for selling per fine ounce. The costs of packing, handling, cartage, air freight and insurance, plus the profit margin, can be taken as amounting to another 4 per mille, so that if gold shipments between London and New York were practicable the outturn of exports from London would be \$34·77¼ per fine ounce, while the cost of imports into London would be \$35·22¾ per fine ounce. The official limits to fluctuations in the sterling-dollar exchange rate were \$2·78 to \$2·82 per £, and the price of gold in the London Bullion Market was about 250s. per fine ounce. As is shown by the following table, such a price would have made it unprofitable to import gold from New York even if the exchange stood at the upper limit of \$2·82 per £, while to have bought gold in London for sale in New York at such a price would have required an exchange rate of under \$2·80 per £ if such operations had been permissible.

APPROXIMATE INCOMING AND OUTGOING LONDON GOLD PRICES

T.T. London on New York	Equivalent London Gold Price for Gold Imports	Gold Exports
2·82	249s. 10d.	246s. 8d.
2·81½	250s. 3⅜d.	247s. 0⅝d.
2·81	250s. 9d.	247s. 6d.
2·80½	251s. 2d.	247s. 11d.
2·80	251s. 7½d.	248s. 4d.
2·79½	252s. 0¾d.	248s. 9⅞d.
2·79	252s. 6¼d.	249s. 3⅛d.
2·78½	252s. 11¾d.	249s. 8½d.
2·78	253s. 5¼d.	250s. 2d.

A cheap dollar means low gold prices; a dear dollar means high gold prices.

London "Dollar Parity"

This is the term used to describe the equivalent price in U.S. dollars per fine ounce of gold at any given level of the U.S. dollar/sterling exchange rate combined with the current sterling price for gold in the London Bullion Market. Thus, if the exchange rate were standing at \$2·81½ and the London price of gold were 250s. 1½d. per fine ounce, this gives a "dollar parity" of

$$\frac{250{\cdot}125 \times 2{\cdot}815}{20} = \$35{\cdot}20\tfrac{1}{2}.$$

If the exchange rate were \$2·79¾ and the London gold price were 250s. 9d., then the "dollar parity" would be—

$$\frac{250{\cdot}75 \times 2{\cdot}7975}{20} = \$35{\cdot}07\tfrac{3}{8} \text{ (nearest)}.$$

As stated above, the semi-practical limits to the fluctuations in the "dollar parity" are roughly $34·77¼ to $35·22¾, but in certain circumstances these limits could have been exceeded if neither the U.S. Treasury nor any other central authority were prepared to control the market.

Premium on Gold

The successive shocks to the confidence of owners of capital due to wars and rumours of wars, financial crises, stock exchange panics, and currency depreciation, have led in recent years to a tendency to hoard the only supposedly universal acceptable store of wealth— gold. When panic and distrust are at their height, the age-old instinct of self-preservation leads mankind to secrete wealth in some tangible form. The Frenchman sews up bank-notes in his mattress. The Scotsman keeps them in his tea caddy in the chimney corner. The African buries his ivory tusks in a secret place in the forest. The up-to-date method is to buy gold bars and lock them away in a safe deposit. The relative eagerness to hoard is nowadays shown by the premium, or excess of price over the normal, which buyers are prepared to pay over the normal. The difficulty over recent years, however, has been to establish a "normal"!

In the years immediately following the last war, when the U.S. was almost the only gold dealer in the world but would not deal with private interests, the price of gold on the so-called free markets in Alexandria, Bombay, Hong Kong and the countries of the Middle East rose to almost fantastic heights in comparison with the basic U.S. price. For some time, in fact, prices in these markets showed a premium of about 40 per cent over the basic dollar price, and large-scale smuggling of gold took place from countries where export restrictions were in force. This situation arose from three causes. First, there was the fear that the serious economic state of the war-shattered countries would lead (as, in fact, it did) to widespread and wholesale devaluation of currencies. Secondly, the "cold war" between the non-Communist and Communist worlds was always likely to break into a "hot war" without warning, with a consequent unprecedented destruction of life and property, so that a gold hoard appeared to many people to be the only possible method of preserving their wealth. Thirdly, the heavy upsurge in commodity prices in general which followed the war, and which reached its peak during the war in Korea, led to a widespread belief that the money price of gold would also have to be raised. South Africa, of course, was and still is strongly in favour of such a step, which would indeed appear to be only logical in view of the apparent anomaly of the 1934 price of a basic world commodity remaining unchanged in a world of greatly changed money prices for all other commodities and services. The American view is, however, strongly opposed to such a step. It is argued that to raise the money price of gold, on which the whole world system of credit is still based either directly or indirectly, would not only be directly inflationary in itself but would touch off a swift and steep inflationary spiral which in the end would once more show a gap between the money price of gold and the money price of other commodities and services. It is also argued that to raise the price of gold would induce the diversion of manpower and materials to the business of mining gold and that these forces would be far better employed in other forms of production that directly minister to the essential wants of mankind. There is still a strong body of opinion, however, which holds the view that sooner or later the money price of gold must be brought more into line with other money prices.

In the conditions outlined above the nominal "premium" on gold was, of course, artificial, and if and when convertible currencies and free gold markets are restored, a premium on the open market price will be rare. It could occur, for example, if it was generally believed that a currency was on the verge of devaluation and that the Central Authorities were likely to suspend sales of gold against that currency. In such a case owners of the currency would be ready to pay a price in the open market higher than the official price in order to make sure of obtaining at least a limited supply of the metal. This actually happened in 1960 when the stability of the U.S. dollar was generally distrusted and it was widely rumoured that the new President, who was taking office in the following January, intended to devalue the currency by raising the official gold price. Under these influences there was heavy buying of gold in every possible market and the London "dollar parity" rose to over $40. Emergency arrangements were, however, made between the American and British authorities and official sales of gold on the London market quickly steadied the price and gradually brought down the "parity" to under $35·20 again, but only at the expense of substantial losses to American reserves. It could also occur if there were general belief that war was imminent and that gold dealings would be controlled or suspended. Such conditions are, however, also largely artificial and the "premium" would represent panic rather than a planned operation.

Two-tier System

Since the foregoing was written there has been a significant development with regard to gold markets. Early in 1968 the demand for gold became extremely heavy because of a widespread belief that the official price of $35 per fine ounce could not be held. By mid-March the movement out of currency into gold had become so disturbing that the London Gold Market was closed initially for one day which was subsequently extended until the end of the month. This was to enable the active members of the gold pool (the central banks of Belgium, Italy, the Netherlands, Switzerland, the United Kingdom, the United States of America and Western Germany) to meet in Washington in order to decide what measures should be adopted to ease the position. The U.S.A. decided to continue to buy and sell gold at $35 per fine ounce with monetary authorities and expressed their resolve that all gold in their hands would be used for monetary purposes only. In consequence, no longer would they sell gold in the market nor did they consider it necessary to buy it. They further decided that they would not sell gold to monetary authorities to replace gold sold in the market. The co-operation of other monetary authorities was invited to make these policies effective, and the response was certainly adequate.

The effect of this was to bring into being a two-tier system under which there would be a basis for the operations of monetary authorities and also "free" gold markets in which a number of leading central banks have declared that they will not deal. These "free" markets would, therefore, be governed for price levels by supply and demand although the "free" market has experienced pressures which have forced the price to be as high as $43·825 in March, 1969, and as low as $34·75 in February, 1970. Up to the time of writing the two-tier system appears to be working efficiently.

CHAPTER VI

COMMONWEALTH EXCHANGES

Some Commonwealth Exchange Rates; The "Sterling Area"

THE exchanges between this country and those Commonwealth countries using a unit of currency fixed in relation to the U.K. £1 afford the simplest illustration of the principles on which are based rates of exchange for the different classes of remittances. While each Commonwealth country decides for itself its own internal and external monetary and fiscal policies, it is one of the fundamental ties of the Commonwealth that the currency of each member country is linked to sterling at rates of exchange that are fixed and controlled by the respective Governments acting through the central and commercial banks. The external reserves of most of these countries are largely kept in the form of sterling balances and investments in London, and the United Kingdom pound may be likened to the sun of the sterling system, with the Commonwealth currencies (and any others whose fortunes have been linked to those of the £) as surrounding groups of satellites, each attracted to the central sun but also having an independent existence of its own.

With the increasing economic and industrial development of the major Commonwealth countries, the problems attaching to the linking of their currencies with sterling have become more complex, but a remarkable degree of co-operation and stability has been achieved. It must be appreciated, however, that these countries are still in process of development and need outside capital to assist in their progress because their own margins of savings out of earnings cannot provide the volume of investment capital needed to promote their full development. Interest rates, therefore, tend to be appreciably higher than those in the more developed centres. Other factors contributing towards these comparatively high interest rates are the great distances and sparse populations which render banking services, such as the clearing of cheques, the movement of cash between bank head offices and branches, etc., very expensive, and the lack in most cases of an organized money and discount market.

The Commonwealth exchange rates are, of course, fixed by each country concerned. The London offices or correspondents of the local banks act only as agents and have to accept instructions from their principals as to the basic exchange rates that have to be used. The actual demand and usance rates quoted in London are fixed by agreement between the London offices and banks acting for the Commonwealth country concerned but, even so, they require the assent of the Authorities on the other side.

In every exchange the T.T. rate is the basic rate of exchange, since the funds are usually paid over in each centre on the same day so that no loss of interest is involved, while there are no stamp charges, very little, if any, risk of capital loss, and only very small expenses. All variations shown by other quoted rates from the basic T.T. rate are due either to a loss of interest, extra costs of collection or increased risk of capital loss. Extreme care is needed by the Authorities overseas in fixing a basic T.T. rate to remain in force until further notice. Every Commonwealth Government has external obligations, particularly in sterling, which require the retention for official purposes of a proportion of external earnings. It is, therefore, necessary to stimulate foreign demand for home products and services to an extent which will afford a surplus of external earnings over expenditure to meet Government requirements. On the other hand, the basic T.T. rate must not favour exports unduly at the expense of imports. All these countries are heavy importers of capital goods and, to a lesser extent, of consumer goods that are essential to their development and to the support of their economy. The basic T.T. rate must not make the currency so cheap as to handicap imports, even though it would stimulate artificially the export of goods and services. It does, therefore, involve some very important national considerations.

The rates for sight and tenor remittances are more the concen for the commercial banks and of the individual, and the margins by which such quotations vary from the basic T.T. rate are based on known factors. The commercial banker is a dealer in money, hiring it from his depositors as cheaply as he can, and re-hiring it to his borrowers at as large a margin of profit as force of competition will allow. Where a person sells an "undue" credit instrument to a banker, the latter regards such a purchase as a loan of funds, and bases his purchase price on what it would cost him, in turn, to convert the instrument into ready cash, i.e. the price at which he could resell it. In the case of an instrument payable in a centre abroad, the obvious place in which such instruments can be turned into ready cash is in the foreign centre itself, and it is the price of money ruling in that centre on which the home banker must base his buying price for such instruments. Further, an exchange banker must always cover his commitments so as to avoid an "open position," and he will normally cover a purchase of foreign currency in any form by an immediate sale of approximately the same amount of the foreign currency in the same or in some other form, and *vice versa*. The T.T. rate being the basic rate for exchange dealings in any currency, the banker will base his prices for other forms of remittance on the supposition that he will sell or buy a T.T. as cover for a purchase or sale, respectively, of another T.T. *or of any other kind of instrument*. Consequently, when buying a sight draft, for example, the banker will assume that he at once sells T.T. as cover. This means that he must order funds to be paid out at once in the foreign centre, whereas his account there will be credited with the proceeds of the draft purchased only after the lapse of a certain time. As a result his account in the foreign centre will, in theory, be overdrawn for such intervening period, and he therefore bases his purchase price for the draft on the cost to him of such an overdraft. On the other hand, where the banker *sells* a sight draft, or any other "undue" instrument, to a customer, he assumes that he will cover the sale by an immediate purchase of T.T. This operation would use up the home currency received from the sale and would leave the banker with foreign currency to his credit until the instrument sold was presented and paid to the debit of his account. Where money is plentiful in the foreign money market, it will be correspondingly cheap, and the credit rate of interest which he will receive on his account will be low. In such circumstances the banker finds that he is unable to pass on much to the buyer of the "undue" instrument by way of compensation for the loss of the use of the purchase money.

Some Commonwealth Exchange Rates

The following tables show the rates ruling in London in April, 1970, as agreed by the London offices and agents of the Central Authorities and commercial banks of the Commonwealth countries concerned—

COMMONWEALTH EXCHANGE RATES

LONDON ON AUSTRALIA
(BASIS £1 ENGLISH CURRENCY)

	Buying A.$	Selling A.$
T.T.	2·1514	2·1429

	Sea mail A.$	Air mail A.$	Air or Sea mail A.$
Sight or Demand . .	2·1773	2·1632	2·1429
30 days sight . .	2·1910	2·1769	—
60 days sight . .	2·2047	2·1906	—
90 days sight . .	2·2184	2·2043	—
120 days sight . .	2·2321	2·2180	—

LONDON ON NEW ZEALAND
(BASIS £1 ENGLISH CURRENCY)

	Buying N.Z.$		Selling N.Z.$
T.T.	2·1492		2·1367

	Sea mail N.Z.$	Air mail N.Z.$	Air or Sea mail N.Z.$
Sight or Demand . .	2·1749	2·1603	2·1367
30 days sight . .	2·1864	2·1718	—
60 days sight . .	2·1979	2·1833	—
90 days sight . .	2·2135	2·1948	—
120 days sight . .	2·2259	2·2102	—

Meaning of the Quotations

As stated in the tables, the amounts shown in the Commonwealth currencies are the equivalent of £1 sterling. Taking, first, the basic T.T. rates, the banks in London would require A$2·1514 from a customer for each £1 sterling paid to him for the purchase of a T.T., but would give only A$2·1429 for each £1 sterling paid to them in respect of a sale of a T.T. on Australia. The difference is, of course, the "Dealer's Turn" or exchange profit. In the case of New Zealand, the banks in London ask N.Z.$2·1492 for each £1 sterling paid to a customer in respect of a purchase from him of a T.T. on New Zealand, but they will give only N.Z.$2·1367 for each £1 sterling paid to them by a customer in respect of a sale of a T.T. on New Zealand by the bank.

The quotations for instruments described variously as sight or demand drafts, or mail transfers, and for drafts at usance, are based on exactly the same principles. For example, in the case of sight or demand drafts drawn on Australia, the banks in London would require A.$2·1773 per £1 sterling if they were asked to buy a draft on Australia which was to be dispatched by sea mail, but would require only A.$2·1632 if the draft were to be sent by airmail. The reasons for the various differences in rates are explained below. On the other hand, when selling a sight or demand draft on Australia to a customer, the banks in London would give only A.$2·1429 per £1 sterling whether the draft was to be dispatched by sea or air; it will be noted that this rate is the same as for remittances by T.T., which is also explained below. No rates are quoted by the London banks for selling bills at usance, since they do not re-sell the bills they have bought; to do so would be at variance with long-established banking tradition.

Calculation of Commonwealth Exchange Rates

In a later chapter the principles of dealing in foreign exchange are considered in detail, but it must be mentioned here that it is the business of an exchange dealer to make a profit by obtaining as many overseas units per £ as possible when buying from a customer, and to give as few overseas units per £ as possible when selling. His quotations will always be given on this basis where the quotation is expressed in terms of overseas units against a fixed unit of £1 or £100, and the margin between the buying and selling prices represents his profit. For example, in the case of the quotations for Australian pounds, the dealer's buying price for T.T.s is A.$2·1514, and his selling price is A.$2·1429 per £1 sterling. On every one hundred dollars worth of Australian currency, in the form of T.T.s, in which he deals, therefore, he makes a profit of only 85 cents, but it is usual to charge cable expenses, in addition, for transfers involving only comparatively small amounts. As stated above, the T.T. rate is fixed by agreement, both for buying and selling, and it is only altered by similar agreement, and then simultaneously by all the banks on both sides.

The calculation of the other rates is rather more complex. It has already been explained that when a bank buys an instrument which it cannot encash until after the lapse of a certain period of time, either because of the geographical factor or because the instrument is drawn at usance, or for both reasons, it must pay cash to the seller immediately and wait for reimbursement. It must, therefore, find some means of recouping itself for the resulting loss of interest, and this is usually done by an adjustment in the exchange rate. With a quotation of so many overseas units per £1 or £100, this is done by increasing the number of overseas units as the equivalent of the sterling unit. This adjustment will, of course, vary with the rate of interest on which the calculation must be based. In principle, if a bank buys an undue instrument, it will cover its exchange risk by an immediate sale of T.T. This will reduce its credit balance in the overseas centre and may even cause its account to become over-drawn. It must, therefore, presume that to replenish its resources overseas it would, in theory, resell (or discount) the undue instrument which it has purchased, and this it can only do at the rate of interest applicable to the instrument in question *in the overseas centre*. In other words, if a bank covers the exchange risk on the purchase of a

90d/s draft on Melbourne by a sale of T.T., it will assume that this sale would overdraw its account and that it would have to rediscount the 90d/s bill to provide immediate cash funds. *This it could only do at the rate of interest ruling in Melbourne for the type of bill concerned.* It is, therefore, the rate of interest ruling in the overseas centre which is used in the calculation of the loss of interest involved by the purchase of any undue instrument drawn on that centre. Bearing these principles in mind, the various quotations can now be explained as follows—

SIGHT OR DEMAND DRAFTS, OR M.T.s

Obviously the loss of interest will be less in the case of items of this nature remitted for payment by air mail than if they were remitted by sea mail. The buying rate for remittances by sea mail is therefore, always higher than that for remittances that are to be forwarded by air mail. In most cases the customer must give definite instructions that the remittance is to be sent by air and not by sea mail, and must pay the extra postage involved by that means of transmission.

In addition to an allowance for loss of interest, it is also banking practice to charge a commission for the collection of any credit instrument and this is included in the build-up of a sight rate from the basic T.T. rate. Taking, first, the Australian rates, the buying rate for sight drafts sent by air mail is A.$0·0115 higher than the T.T. rate, while the rate, if the instrument is sent by sea mail, is A.$0·0259 above the T.T. rate. Both these quotations include a collection commission of ¼ per cent, which is A.$0·0054 so that the interest allowance is A.$0·0061 by air mail and A.$0·0205 by sea mail. When buying any credit instrument a bank will naturally take the most pessimistic view of the time needed for the collection of the article, and it is the practice of the Australian banks to allow fourteen days for air mail and no less than forty-five days for sea mail. When selling sight drafts, whether they are to be dispatched by air or by sea, the bank will offer only A.$2·1429 per £1 sterling, which is the same as the T.T. rate. This is because the rate of interest obtainable on short-term funds, either in London or in Melbourne, is so low as to provide merely a small commission for the selling bank and the customer cannot, therefore, be given any interest allowance.

In the case of the New Zealand quotations, the buying rate for demand drafts to be forwarded by air mail is N.Z.$0·0111 above T.T. and N.Z.$0·0257 above T.T. for remittance by sea mail. These rates again include a commission charge of ¼ per cent, which is N.Z.$0·0054, and the interest allowance is therefore only N.Z.$0·0057 for air mail, but as much as N.Z.$0·0203 for sea mail. These allowances are based on interest for fifteen days in the case of air mail and for fifty-three days by sea mail. The selling price of demand drafts is again the same as the T.T. selling rate, for the reason given above.

DRAFTS AT USANCE

With one exception all the examples given in the table above the quotations for buying drafts at usance show a uniform increase over the sight quotations according to the tenor of the instrument. As the collection commission has been included in the sight quotations, the rates for drafts at tenor need only be adjusted for the loss of interest involved. For Australia, the rates rise by A.$0·0137 for each thirty days, which represents an allowance for loss of interest at $7\frac{3}{4}$ per cent per annum. The increase in the New Zealand quotations is N.Z.$0·0115 for each thirty days, which represents an interest rate of $6\frac{1}{2}$ per cent per annum. The exception is the difference between the 90 days and 120 days rates London on New Zealand where it increases to N.Z.$0·0154. This is because the rate of interest for the 120 days transactions is 7 per cent per annum. The reason being to discourage use of the longer term usance.

The method of calculation of rates for "undue" instruments is of great importance in foreign exchange work; the underlying principles should be clearly grasped, and the reasons for the various allowances thoroughly understood, at the outset. Remember that the basic rate and the true value of one currency in terms of another is the T.T. rate and that any instrument which involves a loss of interest to the purchaser or carries any risk of dishonour, requires a special rate of exchange in which allowance is made for such items on the basic T.T. rate. Instruments other than T.T.s are, as it were, ' discounted," so as to arrive at their "present value" by means of a percentage allowance on the T.T. rate and that the worse the instrument from the point of view of immediate cash, the lower will be its exchange rate, or price, as against the purchasing currency.

Fluctuations in Commonwealth Exchanges

The flow of payments across the Commonwealth exchanges is subject to fluctuations as are other exchanges and are affected by the usual exchange factors of trade, banking and financial operations, stock exchange operations, and currency and credit conditions. With all young and developing countries, large amounts of capital from abroad are needed for development purposes and, in consequence, it is usual for the trade figures for such countries to show heavy adverse balances during their early years, but the excess of imports thus shown represents the proceeds of foreign borrowings, and the apparent adverse balance is offset by invisible exports of paper promises to pay. As such countries establish themselves and their export trade expands, they should, by wise national financing, place themselves in the position of being able to supply steadily increasing amounts of capital for further development out of their own resources so as to decrease steadily further borrowings from abroad. At the same time, they should utilize a part of their favourable trade income in the redemption of part of their existing foreign debts so as to reduce steadily the annual burden of interest and capital repayments due to other countries.

The Sterling Area

This is a popular title given to the group of countries whose currencies are officially linked to the pound sterling but which, for the purposes of the Exchange Control Act, 1947, are entitled "the Scheduled Territories." The term "Sterling Area" was first used to describe the group of countries which attached themselves to sterling following the widespread suspension of gold payments in 1931. This group comprised what were then the British Dominions and Colonies (with the important exception of Canada, whose proximity to, and close trading and financial relationships with, the U.S.A. made it imperative for her to steer a middle course between the pound and the dollar), the Scandinavian countries, Portugal and, for some time, the Argentine Republic. All these countries linked their currencies to sterling at declared parities, and official action was taken to maintain the exchange rate with sterling at or about these parities. This association gradually broke up as the international payments system returned to more normal conditions.

With the outbreak of the 1939 war and the introduction of a complete system of Exchange Control in this country, the whole of the British Commonwealth of Nations, the Colonies, Dependencies and Mandated Territories, also assumed complete control over trade and foreign exchange on lines similar to those adopted by Britain. The need for the closest possible co-operation and co-ordination under the stress of war quickly led to the creation of a system under which Britain became the banker for a large group of countries, and responsible for the collection and allocation of foreign exchange on behalf of the whole group. Canada and Newfoundland, however, remained outside this Monetary Federation (again because of the ties with the U.S.A.), and Hong Kong also remained outside for a time owing to her exceptional position as an open market. This Colony was, however, subsequently brought into the system, which was also joined voluntarily by Eire and Egypt. With the dismemberment of Europe and the varying adherence of the Colonial possessions of allied countries to the allied cause, certain territories were from time to time added to or taken away from the Sterling Area, but the basic principle of linking the principal currency to sterling at a declared parity and using Britain as a banker and as the central pool of gold and currency reserves applied then as it does today. At the time of writing, the Sterling Area, or Scheduled Territories, includes the following—

The British Commonwealth (except Canada and Rhodesia), the Irish Republic, British Trust Territories, British Protectorates and Protected States, Iceland, the Hashemite Kingdom of Jordan, Kuwait, Libya, South Africa and South West Africa, the People's Republic of Southern Yemen, and Western Samoa.

CHAPTER VII

FOREIGN EXCHANGE TRANSACTIONS, TERMINOLOGY AND QUOTATIONS

Sanctions or "Limits"; Sales by the Dealer; Foreign Currency
Accounts; Exchange Maxims; The Foreign
Exchange Table and Article

THE buying and selling of foreign currencies, or dealing in foreign exchange, is a highly-specialized business for the professional, but the main principles involved can be quite easily understood by anyone. The professional dealers, who are the officials of the banks and financial houses entrusted with the buying and selling of foreign currencies on behalf of their institutions, have the responsibility of so adjusting their purchases and sales of any currencies that their balances in foreign centres are neither too large nor too heavily overdrawn. These dealers are in constant touch with the sources, both financial and commercial, from which the demand for, or supply of, any currency originates. If, for example, a sudden rise in interest rates should take place in New York above the level of interest prevailing elsewhere, there will be a general movement of funds to that centre for temporary investment, and exchange dealers all over the world will be met with a demand for dollars.[1] They will sell their available balances in dollars, and the proceeds of any dollar remittances which they may be able to purchase, at a steadily rising price for dollars in terms of their home currency as the strength of the demand makes itself felt. When the price of dollars has risen high enough, any credit facilities in America which the dealers may have will be utilized and, finally, should the price rise sufficiently high in any country with a free gold market, leading dealers there will arrange to ship gold to New York so as to use the "outturn" in dollars to meet the requirements of buyers.

Conversely, any exceptional offering of any currency, either on financial or commercial account, must be absorbed eventually by the exchange dealers. As the supply begins to overrun the normal demand, dealers will buy the currency only at successively lower prices, and it may eventually become so cheap that, in the case of a

---

[1] This assumes that reasonable conditions of world stability prevail, and that the chief countries permit the free exchange of their currencies for dollars.

country with a free gold market, dealers will use the proceeds of the remittances they have purchased to buy gold in that country and pay the expenses of bringing it home.

This again makes clear the control over the exchange value of a currency given by the existence of a free gold market within the country, and explains why, in the case of countries which will not or cannot either permit the free import and export of gold or exercise official control over the currency such as by means of a gold exchange standard, the exchange value of the currency can fluctuate very widely.

It has already been stated that exchange dealers act as clearing houses for international debts, buying rights to wealth in terms of other currencies from those who have them to sell and selling rights to wealth in terms of other currencies to those who wish to buy them. The usual forms of these rights to wealth, in the shape of credit remittances, have already been described, and the use of gold as a final means of discharging indebtedness, or of laying down funds in another centre, has also been dealt with. The operations of an exchange dealer are chiefly concerned with the buying and selling of such credit instruments and in arranging for the shipment of bullion in bulk when this is both possible and profitable. An exchange dealer will be asked to buy—

(a) TELEGRAPHIC TRANSFERS (T.T.s). These form the principal banking means of transferring funds in large amounts and are only offered in other cases by the largest commercial firms. As the buying dealer must pay out his home currency to the seller before he can be sure that the money has been paid over in the centre, and as he has no tangible security but must rely on the good faith of the seller, he will only take such instruments from a "good name" even if the seller is another bank or financial house.

(b) AIR AND SEA M.T.s. These credit transfers also are chiefly used only by banks, financial houses and the largest commercial firms, and as cash is paid at once to the seller while payment in the other centre takes place only some days later, the purchase is equivalent to a clean loan to the seller for the time being, and the question of "name," i.e. the standing of the seller, is of the utmost importance.

(c) CHEQUES AND SIGHT DRAFTS. These are usually tendered for purchase by commercial or private customers of the bank who have received them from debtors abroad, or who have drawn such instruments on their foreign debtors or on balances which they possess with banks abroad. The dealer will only purchase such articles "with recourse" to the seller and may refuse to purchase them if he has any reason to doubt the standing of the customer (see below).

(*d*) ENCASHMENTS UNDER CREDITS. Letters of credit issued by foreign connexions of the bank in terms of a foreign currency are frequently presented by foreigners travelling in this country, who wish to draw the sterling equivalent of all or part of the letter of credit to meet their expenses or disbursements in this country. The holder signs a form of receipt or a form of sight draft on the foreign issuer for the amount of foreign currency which he wishes to convert into sterling. The dealer purchases this as if it were a cheque in foreign currency and allows in his buying rate for the cost of the service rendered by his bank in making the encashment, as well as for the loss of interest through making the sterling payments at once, but only receiving credit in the foreign currency on the arrival of the instrument in the foreign centre, and for the cost of any necessary foreign stamp, etc.

(*e*) STOCK CHEQUE OR DRAFT. This is the term applied to a cheque or sight draft drawn on another centre in respect of a sale of stock and having the stock or share certificates attached to the cheque. International dealings in securities are mainly carrried out between stockbroking firms in the various centres between whom business relations have been firmly established for some time, and payment by the buying firm in one centre to the selling firm in the other centre is usually made by a Telegraphic Transfer on the appointed day, while the stock or share certificates are sent direct by the seller to the buyer. In some cases, however, the selling firm may not be prepared to part with the stock or shares except against payment in cash, while the buyer is not prepared to pay over his cash except against delivery of the security, or the seller may be unable to finance the operation himself and needs temporary accommodation. In such cases, the buyer may instruct his bank to honour the cheque drawn on it by the seller for a stated amount, if certain specified securities accompany the cheque and are found to be in order. A seller here, under such circumstances, will draw a cheque on a bank in the foreign centre designated by the buyer, or on the broker in the foreign centre through whom the sale was carried out, will attach to or deliver with this the parcel of stock or share certificates to which it refers, and will tender the whole for purchase to the exchange dealer at his own bank. The banker obtains a lien on the securities through his purchase, in addition to preserving recourse against the customer as drawer of the cheque, but he must allow in his buying rate for the instrument for the interest lost while the cheque is in transit as well as for the cost of packing, posting and insuring the parcel of securities, and should also take a margin to cover a possible drop in the market value of the securities.

(*f*) REVERSE STOCK CHEQUE. The home buyer of stock or shares in a foreign centre may be asked by the seller to arrange for cash to be paid out there against delivery of the securities. The buyer must then arrange with his home banker for such payment to be made in the foreign currency by the banker's local agent on presentation by the seller of the stated securities attached to a draft drawn by the seller on the buyer in terms of the *home* currency. The home banker will therefore be selling to his customer foreign currency for immediate payment abroad but for which he will receive reimbursement in the home currency only when the stock draft has arrived from the foreign centre and can be presented to and paid by his customer. The banker must therefore allow in the rate at which he sells the foreign currency for the loss of interest he will suffer, for any charges made by his agent, and for the cost of packing, posting and insuring the parcel.

(*g*) LONG BILLS. While it is still true that London draws few bills but accepts many, there is always a certain number of long bills which are drawn by firms and persons in this country on other centres on financial or trade account, and these are frequently offered for sale to exchange dealers.

Bills drawn in sterling on foreign centres usually bear special clauses which are dealt with in a later chapter, and such bills, except those claused "exchange as per endorsement," do not affect the foreign currency balances of the dealer, but are treated as an investment of sterling funds as in the case of an ordinary discount operation.

Bills drawn in or which may be converted into a foreign currency (as with the clause mentioned above) will be purchased by the dealer with recourse to the seller, and under the usual conditions as given below. The dealer will allow in his buying rate for loss of interest on the cash invested, cost of any foreign stamps, agents' charges, etc. The loss of interest in the case of an *after sight* draft will be for the time taken in transit plus the *full currency* of the bill, as it cannot be "sighted" until it arrives on the other side, while in the case of an *after date* draft, interest is lost only from the date of purchase until the date of maturity, since the bill commences to run from the date of drawing and no "sighting" is needed to fix the date of maturity.

(*h*) FOREIGN COUPONS AND DRAWN BONDS. It has already been explained how such articles as these now form part of the credit instruments used for expressing international debts, and a British holder of coupons or drawn bonds payable abroad in a foreign currency will offer them for sale to his bank in the same way as with any other credit instrument payable in another centre.

The exchange dealer must allow in his buying rate for interest lost during the time of mailing and for the estimated period which must elapse after arrival before the proceeds are eventually collected and credited to his account with his foreign agent, for the cost of packing, posting and insuring the parcel, and for the comparatively heavy charge which will be made by his agent for the service of collection of such items.

(i) FOREIGN COIN AND NOTES. In most of the big banks a special department exists, known as the "Foreign Money Department," for dealing in actual foreign money in the shape of the notes and coins of other countries. The amounts handled are usually small and arise through travellers from abroad wishing to convert what small change in their own currency they may have left after the journey, into small change in sterling, or through persons journeying from this country to places abroad wishing to purchase a certain amount in small change in the currency of the country to which they are going so as to be able to meet the usual expenses incurred on arrival.

In the ordinary way, the amounts involved are so small that the stocks maintained by the department represent only a trivial amount and overhead expenses are paid by taking a fairly wide margin between the buying and selling prices. Occasionally, however, stocks of the notes of a certain currency may mount up unduly (as in the case of U.S.A. notes during the American tourist season), or a specially large parcel may be offered for sale to the bank. In such cases the exchange dealer will have to buy the notes and remit them abroad for credit to his account, allowing in his buying rate for loss of interest during transit, packing, postage and insurance.

Sanctions or "Limits"

As mentioned above, the "name" of the seller of any exchange instrument is of the first importance to the buyer. Even as between the big banks themselves, each has a "limit" to the total of obligations of the others which may be allowed to remain outstanding at any one time and, as the grade of the other party descends, so the amount of the "limit" on that "name" decreases. The purchase of T.T.s involves the least risk, as any default in paying over the funds in the foreign centre is known in a few hours, and immediate steps are taken against the seller to obtain either payment of the foreign currency or a refund of the sterling paid to him.

In the case of cheques, demand drafts, longer-dated articles, coupons, drawn bonds, etc., the operation of purchase is similar to the discounting of a bill, and while attention is paid to the standing of the drawee or payer, even more is devoted to the standing of the customer from whom the articles are being purchased. With the exception of encashments under credits, for which the purchasing bank must assume responsibility, and so must take every precaution against fraud when effecting such payments, *banks will purchase exchange instruments only with recourse to the seller and only from regular customers.* In order to make the responsibility of the customer quite definite and relieve the bank from liability in respect of any acts of its agents or of any expenses incurred in connexion with instruments purchased, it is customary to take from the customer a General Form of Authority for Collection or Negotiation of Foreign Bills. By his signature to this form, the customer agrees that any such operations shall be at his entire risk and responsibility and that, in addition to any rights which the bank may acquire as holder of any such articles, the bank shall have the right to debit the customer's account immediately with the value of any such articles that may be unpaid, together with any charges which may have been incurred.

The granting of "Sanctions" or the fixing of "Limits" is carried out by the Managerial Department of the Head Office of the bank, and limits will be fixed by this department as to the total amount in respect of each of the classes of transaction that the customer may desire to carry out, which may be outstanding at any given time. The exchange dealer is responsible for seeing that the outstanding amount of foreign exchange transactions with any customer never exceeds the total of the sanction granted by the Head Office.

Sales by the Dealer

The exchange dealer will be asked to sell principally T.T.s to either banks at home and abroad, or large financial or commercial houses; Air and Sea M.T.s to other banks and to financial and commercial houses; bank drafts to commercial firms and private persons; letters of credit, either personal or commercial, for payments to be effected abroad in terms of a foreign currency by the bank's agents; and the Foreign Money Department will be asked to sell small amounts in actual foreign coin and notes to persons proceeding abroad.

In all of these cases the dealer will endeavour to sell at a better price for himself than that at which he has purchased similar instruments, the margin of difference constituting his profit. He will make no allowance to a buyer for any expenses, such as stamps, etc., which the latter must incur before he can obtain payment, and it may be accepted that a bank will always pass on to the customer any expenses that it must itself incur, such as cable and airmail costs, but will make no allowance for such expenses when incurred by the customer. Additionally, an exchange commission is charged to the customer on a fixed scale.

The exchange dealer endeavours to carry out his operations in such a manner as will show a reasonable profit for his bank by buying at one rate and selling at another. It is by no means essential that he should cover a purchase or sale of one class of instrument by a sale or purchase of another instrument of the same type, and, in fact, much of the dealer's profit is derived from covering one class of transaction by means of a different class of transaction, e.g. he may cover a purchase of "cheque" by a sale of T.T., or a purchase of long bills by a sale of forward T.T., depending upon the funds which he may have available at home and in the foreign centre and the relative rates of interest which he can obtain.

It is not the practice of London banks to permit their exchange dealers to "run a position." This means that the dealer is expected to set off within narrow limits the total of his purchases and sales of any currency each day, and is not allowed to leave any substantial amount of currency "uncovered," i.e. he must not show an unduly heavy over-bought or over-sold position at the end of the day.

In order to keep in exact touch with the state of his accounts in other centres, the exchange dealer keeps a "position" sheet or book which is started each morning with the approximate total credit balance or overdraft in each foreign centre (most banks maintain accounts with several banks in each principal foreign centre), as agreed at the close of the previous day by the book-keeping department.

As he transacts each operation of purchase or sale, the exchange dealer will either debit or credit the amount of currency to the balance in the relative centre, making a note at the side of the class of instrument dealt in. He can thus see at a glance whether he is becoming over-bought or over-sold and effect adjusting operations accordingly. Space does not permit of an examination of the entire book-keeping system of a foreign branch, but brief reference is made in the chapter on the London Foreign Exchange Market to the process of dealing with a T.T., and this may be taken as typical of the entries needed. It may be mentioned that in international banking, certain terms are employed to distinguish accounts kept by the banks with each other. The accounts which a bank keeps with other banks are termed by it "Nostro" accounts. The accounts kept with it by other banks are termed by it "Vostro" accounts. Entries passed to the account of a third party are said to be for "Loro" account, e.g. a remittance made by one bank to another for account of a third bank may be sent by the remitter "for credit of Loro a/c (— bank)," meaning "their account with you."

Foreign Currency Accounts for Account of Customers

Banks are sometimes asked by customers, such as international merchants, to accept deposits in foreign currency. Such deposits are held, with Exchange Control permission, on "Retained Currency Account" at the entire risk and responsibility of the customer; the bank assumes no liability for the solvency or acts of its agent in the foreign centre. The customer must sign a form admitting these points, and the deposit is then *held in the foreign centre* as part of the bank's own balance there. If at the time the bank is allowed interest by the foreign agent, it either allows the customer no interest at all, or only a lower rate so as to show a margin of profit. As and when the customer wants payment made out of such an account to his creditor abroad, he must ask the bank to effect such payment by credit transfer, or to issue a draft drawn on the foreign agent abroad; in other words, the customer has no facilities for drawing cheques on the foreign currency account, or of making any disbursement except by instructing the bank to make it.

The exchange dealer will be able to use such deposits in the same way as a bank uses the sterling deposits of its customers.

Most of such sums will be placed on deposit for a fixed period and the dealer will have a fairly accurate idea of the times at which the remainder is likely to be withdrawn. He can, therefore, use the funds so provided in the course of his operations in exchange, as long as he always retains a sufficient margin of available credit on his account in the foreign centre to meet any withdrawals made by the depositors. All such deposits are, of course, registered in separate accounts in the name of each customer in the books of the home bank. The foreign agent, however, cannot distinguish between funds paid in to the credit of the account of the home bank in its books, and so shows merely a total debit or credit balance in the home bank's "Vostro" account. It is, therefore, necessary to reconcile the balance abroad as shown by the statement of account received from the agent, by arriving at the aggregate of the bank's own balance and the balances in foreign currency of its depositors, and by allowing in the usual way for items in transit which will eventually be credited or debited to the account by the agent, as entries to a "Nostro" account abroad must be passed by the home bank as and when transactions take place, and adjusted as to any charges and as to the date for interest purposes (known as the "value date") on receipt of the advice from the agent.

Exchange Maxims and the Making of Prices

Exchange dealers throughout the world are the persons immediately responsible for making the prices at which they will buy and sell various classes of remittances in different currencies, and it is the competition between these dealers, based on the offerings and demands for currencies received from their customers or on their own account, which eventually hammers out the current rate of exchange. The method of building up from the basic T.T. rate prices for instruments involving a loss of interest or expenses has already been referred to and will be dealt with again in a later chapter.

The maxim to be applied to all remittances is—

"The better the bill, the better the rate."

This means that an instrument involving little expense in collection and small loss of interest to the buyer will be more valuable, i.e. will command a better price for the seller, than will an instrument costing more to collect and involving a greater loss of interest. It also means that an instrument issued by and/or on a first-class name will yield a better price to the seller than will an instrument of similar tenor or usance issued by and/or on a name of lesser standing. Thus a cheque on New York would have a greater "present value," i.e. would command a better rate of exchange for the seller, than could a 60 days draft on New York, both drawn on a bank by a bank, while a 60 days commercial draft on New York would not command such a good rate of exchange for the seller as would the 60 days bank draft.

Currency and Pence Rates

The method of quoting the prices or rates of exchange for different currencies takes one of two forms. In the case of the exchanges between this country and others, the rates are quoted either in terms of a variable number of foreign units to the fixed unit of £1, or in terms of a variable number of pence sterling per fixed foreign unit. Rates quoted in terms of foreign units per £1 are known as "currency" rates while those quoted in terms of pence per foreign unit are known as "pence" rates. "Currency" rates are also known as *indirect*, or *uncertain*, since the sterling cost of a single foreign unit can be obtained only by a division sum, i.e. indirectly, and the number of foreign units to the £ can vary, i.e. is uncertain and movable. "Pence" rates are also known as *direct*, or *certain*, for the opposite reasons to those given above.

Most of the rates quoted in London are currency rates owing to the early predominance of the £ in international finance, and to the fact that it is the largest standard unit in the world. Other centres necessarily quote "direct" rates on London, except those quoted in pence here when London is quoted as an "indirect" rate, and their quotations on each other are nearly always of the "direct" type, e.g. Paris quotes New York in terms of francs per fixed unit of $1, while New York quotes Paris in cents per unit of 100 fcs.

Occasionally the value of one currency is said to be at a "premium" or at a "discount" in terms of another. Remembering that "premium" is synonymous with "dearer" and "discount" with "cheaper," it can be seen that such expressions mean that the first currency is dearer or cheaper in terms of the second currency than the ratio established between them by the Mint Par, e.g. if the Mint Par between London and New York were $2·40 to £1, a rate in London on New York of $2·395 to £1 would mean that dollars were at a premium in London since the pound would purchase fewer dollars than the Mint Par ratio, while a rate of $2·405 would show that more dollars than the fixed ratio could be obtained per pound, and that dollars were at a discount in London.

Buying and Selling Prices, or the "Two-way Price"

An exchange dealer quotes what is known as a "two-way" price, which means that he quotes two rates always, at one of which he will buy and at the other of which he will sell the foreign currency. In all *currency* rates, the dealer will obviously endeavour to *sell as few foreign units per pound* as he can persuade the buyer to accept, and will endeavour to *buy as many foreign units for each pound* he parts with as he can force the seller to give him. The principle is the same as that by which a retail greengrocer endeavours to obtain oranges from a wholesaler at the rate of fifteen per 5 pence and to resell them to a confiding public at the rate of ten per 5 pence.

For currency rates then, the maxim is—

"Buy high, sell low"

and this basic principle can be summed up in a piece of doggerel (for those who like that sort of thing) thus—

When buying foreign units at so many to the pound,
You need a rate that's very high—the highest to be found.
But when engaged in selling, in voice sepulchral say,
"I can't give you many units, the rate is down today!"

It is, of course, much simpler to memorize the brief admonition to "Buy high, sell low," but there are many who like their educational pastry made with a very light hand!

When rates are quoted in pence per foreign unit, however, the maxim is reversed. *For pence rates* the dealer must—

"Buy low, sell high,"

in the same way as with buying and selling any commodity in terms of pounds and pence. No aid to memory should be needed in this connexion.

A distinction must be drawn between rates quoted by a dealer to his customers and the so-called *market* rates. If a dealer makes a price of 2·40½–¾ in U.S. dollars to a customer, it means that he is prepared to sell a T.T. on New York (or other principal centre) to the customer, giving $2·40½ for each pound paid by the latter, and that he will buy a T.T. from the customer, taking $2·40¾ for each pound he pays to the latter. The margin of ¼ cent per pound is the *Dealer's Turn* and constitutes his profit as long as he can sell at one rate and buy at the other. Similarly, if he quotes a rate for Indian rupees of £5·5105–£5·5605, it means that he will sell rupees to his customer at a charge of £5·5605 per 100 rupees or will buy rupees from the latter, paying over only £5·5105 per 100 rupees.

The "market" rates are those ruling between the dealers them-selves as members of the market, and consist of offerings by dealers who wish to sell at one price and bids by dealers who wish to buy at another price. Thus, a "market" rate on Frankfurt of 8·86¾–8·87 would mean that certain dealers were prepared to sell marks at the rate of 8·86¾ per pound, while others were prepared to buy if they could obtain 8·87 marks per pound. The actual rate at which a deal is effected in the market is a matter of negotiation and depends on the relative keenness of buyer and seller, and on their respective bargaining powers. Failing any giving way on the part of the other party, a dealer who was forced to cover in the market an operation carried out with a customer, would have to buy marks at the market's selling price of 8·86¾ or sell them at the market's buying price of 8·87. In the case of a pence rate, if the market quoted Bombay as £5·5105–£5·5605, a dealer might only be able eventually to sell to the market at £5·5105 per 100 rupees, or to buy from it by paying £5·5606 per 100 rupees.

It is usual to regard movements in exchange rates from a *national* point of view. The old Mercantile Theory held that the inflow of gold to a country showed that it was trading at a profit, while an outflow of gold showed that it was trading at a loss or was sending abroad more than its surplus income. Consequently it is customary to regard a movement in exchange rates towards the point at which gold is likely to flow into this country as being good from the national point of view, and to regard as adverse to the country as a whole, movements in rates towards the point at which gold is likely to be exported. From a national viewpoint, in the case of *currency* rates—

"High rates are for us"
"Low rates are against us,"

and in the case of *pence* rates—

"Low rates are for us"
"High rates are against us."

From the point of view of the individual, whether a rate is favourable or adverse will depend upon whether the individual is a buyer or a seller. A rate on New York of $2·40½ would be *favourable* from the national viewpoint with a Mint Par of $2·40, as the rate then would be moving *towards our Import Gold Point*. Such a rate is also favourable to an individual who has a debt to discharge in dollars and who is, therefore, a buyer of that currency and wishes to obtain as many dollars as possible for each pound he spends. But such a rate is unfavourable to an individual who has to receive dollars in payment of a debt, since he is, therefore, a seller of dollars and will wish to "sell low," i.e. give as few dollars as possible for each pound he receives. A high pence rate would be *adverse* to this country generally, as it would show that the cost of the foreign unit had grown so dear that *gold might shortly be exported*, and would be adverse to an individual who had to buy some of the currency in question, but would be favourable to a creditor who had the foreign currency for sale, since he would receive a larger number of pence per foreign unit than the ratio set up by the normal parity.

Other Exchange Expressions

The terms "Favourable" and "Unfavourable" are most often used to describe, from the *national* point of view, movements in exchange rates, but other more indefinite terms are occasionally to be found in articles on the foreign exchanges in the Press. Those who are not well versed in exchange terminology would do well to confine themselves to the use of the expressions "favourable" and "unfavourable" when describing movements in exchange from the point of view of this country, or to the use of "appreciate" and "depreciate" when describing a movement in the value of any particular currency. For example, if the rate of exchange in London on Brussels moves from fcs. 119·25 to fcs. 119·10 per pound, Belgian francs have "appreciated" in value, since fewer are obtainable per pound, while if the rate in London on Bombay moves from £5·5605 to £5·5105 per 100 rupees, the rupee has "depreciated" in value, since it will cost less in terms of sterling.

All other technical expressions are variations of the above terms. The depreciation or appreciation of a currency may be expressed in four ways—

(a) The currency has become "cheaper" or "dearer."

(b) There has been a "rise" or "fall" in the exchange rate, when this is quoted as a currency rate, though unfortunately financial writers often refer to a "rise" or "fall" in a currency when they mean that the *value*, and not the rate, has risen or fallen.

(c) The currency is "weaker" (or "easier") or "firmer" (or "harder"), though here again it is sometimes stated that the dollar rate was "weaker" when it is not intended to convey that dollars had depreciated in value but that the rate had "weakened" so that fewer dollars were obtainable per pound.

(d) The use of the terms "premium" and "discount" has already been explained, but it is sometimes said by financial writers that the premium or discount has "run off" (particularly with reference to the margins quoted for "forward" rates against "spot" rates), when it is meant to convey that a movement towards parity in either case has taken place.

The student should now be able to read with understanding both the Foreign Exchange Table and the letterpress accompanying it in the daily and weekly Press.

The Foreign Exchange Table

For the purposes of comparison, a table of foreign exchange rates as they would have appeared in leading daily newspapers on 31st March, 1938, is first given below and is followed by the much smaller (and in some ways, less informative) table of rates quoted in the London Foreign Exchange Market and published in *The Financial Times* of 12th May, 1970. At the time of writing, also, the daily report on business in the market is usually very brief and consists of not more than half a dozen lines. In order to introduce as many of the current technical expressions as possible, therefore, an imaginary extract from a financial daily has been composed and follows the tables so as to form a basis for the subsequent translation of market jargon!

Prior to the 1914 war and on the principle that "London draws few bills but accepts many," the exchange value of the pound was determined by conditions in the exchange markets in foreign centres. London, in fact, followed the quotations ruling abroad rather than deciding them here. London quotations were fixed at bi-weekly meetings of exchange dealers and brokers, and such lists of exchange rates as were published by the daily papers were the quotations received by telegram from foreign centres. By the early 1920s, however, the economic and financial disturbances which followed the war had caused great instability in exchange rates, and as sterling was still the leading world currency, even though gold payments remained suspended, it was London which took the lead in quoting exchange values for foreign currencies. As is described later, the bi-weekly meetings and leisurely procedure gave place to a market conducted by telephone at almost all hours of the day and night, and London exchange quotations became of the first importance to the whole world. Also, in view of the rapid and wide fluctuations in exchange rates, almost all the business was conducted on the basis of T.T.s, and quotations for cheques and usance bills became the exception rather than the rule as was previously the case.

For a long time there were considerable discrepancies in the manner of presentation of these lists of exchange rates by various newspapers. Some papers quoted a two-way price which was actually the market rate ruling at or towards the close of business; others quoted a two-way price which represented the highest and lowest dealing rates during the day; others, again, quoted a "middle" or "mean" rate which was half-way between the highest and lowest rates of the day. After the suspension of gold payments in 1931, however, the recognized representatives of the bankers and the foreign exchange brokers agreed that some uniform method of presentation was necessary, and arrangements were made to supply the Press with an agreed type of quotation to be used in compiling the full table of rates. Table 1 overleaf is a complete example of this method of presentation.

In September, 1939, H.M. Treasury assumed control of all foreign exchange operations and fixed official dealing rates for all the principal currencies. The Bank of England became the foreign exchange market and all banks authorized to deal in foreign exchange had at first to cover each deal with the Bank at the official buying or selling price, but were later allowed to cover only any surplus or deficit of a currency at the end of the day's dealings. In December, 1951, the London Foreign Exchange Market was reopened, although with certain limitations on its activities, and deals could be carried through at rates within the official limits at which the Bank controlled the market. The original official limits

TABLE 1

LONDON QUOTATIONS

Centre	Quoted	Par prior to 29/9/31	30th March, 1938, Close	29th March, 1938, Close
New York T.T. (1%)	Dol. to £	4·86⅔	4.96¾–96⅞	4·97⅜–4·97½
Montreal (T.T.)	Dol. to £	4·86⅔	4·99¼–4·99¾	4·99½–4·99⅞
Amsterdam (2%)	Fl. to £	12·107	8·96¾–8·97	8·96⅞–97⅛
Berlin (4%)	Mks. to £	20·43	12·37–·37½	12·37¼–·38¼
Berlin (4%)	Reg. Mks.	—	50¾%dis.	51½%dis.
Brussels (2%)	Belga to £	35	29·37–29·38	29·39½–·40½
Madrid (5%)	Ptas. to £	25·22½	80–140††	80–140††
Milan (4½%)	Lire to £	92·46	94⅜–94$\frac{7}{16}$	94$\frac{7}{16}$–94$\frac{9}{16}$
Paris (3%)	Fr. to £	124·21	163⅛–163¼	162$\frac{15}{16}$–163
Zürich (1½%)	Fr. to £	25·2215	21·66–·66½	21·66–21·67
Copenhagen (4%)	Kr. to £	18·159	22·38–22·42	22·38–22·42
Danzig (4%)	Gul. to £	25·00	26–26½	26–26½
Helsingfors (4%)	Mks. to £	193·23	225¾–226½	225¾–226½
Kovno (5½%)	Litas to £	48·66	29–30	29–30
Oslo (3½%)	Kr. to £	18·159	19·88–19·92	19·88–19·92
Riga (5%)	Lats to £	25·22½	24¾–25¾	24¾–25¾
Stockholm (2½%)	Kr. to £	18·159	19·38–19·42	19·38–19·42
Tallinn (4½%)	E. Kr. to £	18·159	17¾–18¾	17¾–18¾
Alexandria	Pstrs. to £	97½	97⅜–97⅝	97⅜–97⅝
Athens (6%)	Drch. to £	375	540–555	540–555
Belgrade (5%)	Din. to £	276·316	212–222	212–222
Bucharest (4½%)	Lei to £	813·6	665–690	665–690
Budapest (4%)	Pen. to £	27·8	24⅞–25⅜ *f*	24⅞–25⅜ *f*
*Constantinople	Pstrs. to £	110	621¶	621¶
Lisbon (4%)	Esc. to £	110	110–110⅜	110–110⅜
*b*Moscow	Rbls. to £	9·458	26·36–·36¾	26·32–26·32¾
Prague (3%)	Kr. to £	164·25	142–142⅜	142¼–142⅝
Sofia	Levas to £	673·659	390–420	390–420
Vienna (3½%)	Sch. to £	34·58	††	††
Warsaw (4½%)	Zloty to £	43·38	26⅛–26⅝	26⅛–26⅝
*Bangkok	d. to baht	21·82d.	22–22¼d.	22–22¼d.
*Batavia (3%)	Fl. to £	12·107	8·93–8·96	8·93–8·96
Bombay (3%)	d. to rupee	18d.	18$\frac{3}{32}$–18$\frac{5}{32}$d.	18$\frac{3}{32}$–18$\frac{5}{32}$d.
Calcutta (3%)	d. to rupee	18d.	18$\frac{3}{32}$–18$\frac{5}{32}$d.	18$\frac{3}{32}$–18$\frac{5}{32}$d.
*Hong Kong	d. to doll.	—	1/2¾–1/2⅞	1/2$\frac{11}{16}$–1/2$\frac{13}{16}$
Kobe (3·285%)	d. to yen	24·57d.	1/1$\frac{29}{32}$–1/2$\frac{1}{32}$	1/1$\frac{29}{32}$–1/2$\frac{1}{32}$
*Manila	d. to peso	24·66d.	1/11⅝–2/0⅛	1/11⅝–2/0⅛
*Saigon	d. to pstre.	—	1/2½–1/3	1/2½–1/3
*Shanghai	d. to doll.	—	1/0½–1/1	/11⅞–1/0¼
*Singapore	d. to doll.	—	2/3$\frac{15}{16}$–2/4$\frac{1}{32}$	2/3$\frac{15}{16}$–2/4$\frac{1}{32}$
Teheran	Rials to £	—	80½††	80½††
*a*B. Aires (3½%)		11·46	15·00†	15·00†
f B. Aires	paper	—	20·05–20·10	20·00–20·05
*g*B. Aires	peso to £	—	16·12‡	16·12‡
Bogota	peso to £	—	8½–9	8½–9
Rio de Janeiro	d. to mil.	5·89	2$\frac{13}{16}$*a*¶	2$\frac{13}{16}$*a*¶
†*Lima (6%)	Sols. to £	17·38	20††	20††
*e**Montevideo	d. to dol.	51d.	31⅝d.	31⅝d.
*i*Montevideo	—	—	27$\frac{31}{32}$d.	27$\frac{31}{32}$d.
f Montevideo	—	—	20¼–20¾d.	20½–21d.
Mexico	Peso to £	—	*n.q.*	*n.q.*
*k**Valparaiso	Dol. to £	—	124·37††	124·37††

* Rate quoted on London. ‡ Official rate. † 90 days. § Sight. †† Nominal ¶ Seller. *n.q.* No quotation.

a Official rate for export bills. *b* Approximate. *e* Exporters' rate. *f* Free market rate. *g* Central Bank selling rate, including commission of ¾ per cent. *i* Importers' rate. *k* Latest export rate.

N.B.—Following are the rates applicable for payment to the Bank of England for the Clearing Offices: Italy, 94·54 lire; Spain, 77 pesetas; Turkey, 625 piastres.

TABLE 2

FOREIGN EXCHANGES

May 11, 1970	Bank Rate %	Market Rates	
		Day's Spread	Close
New York . . .	6	2·40$\frac{3}{8}$–$\frac{3}{4}$	2·40$\frac{1}{2}$–$\frac{5}{8}$
Montreal . . .	8	2·57$\frac{7}{8}$–58$\frac{1}{8}$	2·58–$\frac{1}{8}$
Amsterdam . .	6	8·71$\frac{1}{2}$–73$\frac{1}{2}$	8·72–$\frac{1}{2}$
Brussels . . .	7$\frac{1}{2}$	119·35–50	119·40–50
Copenhagen . .	9	18·05$\frac{1}{2}$–07	18·06–$\frac{1}{2}$
Frankfurt . . .	7$\frac{1}{2}$	8·72$\frac{1}{2}$–74$\frac{1}{2}$	8·73$\frac{1}{8}$–$\frac{5}{8}$
Lisbon . . .	*3$\frac{1}{2}$	68·20–70	68·45–60
Madrid . . .	†6$\frac{1}{2}$	167·50–90	167·65–80
Milan . . .	5$\frac{1}{2}$	1,512–14	1,512$\frac{3}{4}$–13$\frac{1}{4}$
Oslo . . .	4$\frac{1}{2}$	17·18$\frac{1}{2}$–20$\frac{1}{2}$	17·19$\frac{1}{8}$–$\frac{5}{8}$
Paris . . .	8	13·27–29	13·27$\frac{5}{8}$–28$\frac{1}{8}$
Stockholm . .	7	12·50$\frac{1}{4}$–52$\frac{1}{2}$	12·51$\frac{1}{2}$–52
Tokyo . . .	6·25	860$\frac{1}{2}$–863	861$\frac{1}{2}$–862$\frac{1}{2}$
Vienna . . .	5	62·15–45	62·28–33
Zurich . . .	3$\frac{3}{4}$	10·32$\frac{3}{4}$–34$\frac{3}{4}$	10·33$\frac{5}{8}$–34$\frac{1}{8}$

N.B. Bank of England official limits for U.S. $2·38–42. * Bank of Portugal discount rate. † Basic discount rate under new system.

OTHER MARKET RATES

Australia . . .	2·1429–1514	Malaysia . .	7·3715–7·404
New Zealand . .	2·1367–1492	Argentine . .	‡8·37–8·45
South Africa . .	1·7121–7207		‡8·50–8·75
†India . . .	5·5280–5·5605	Brazil . . .	10·70–77
†Pakistan . . .	8·737–763		10–12$\frac{1}{2}$
Ceylon . . .	1/4$\frac{25}{32}$–$\frac{29}{32}$	France . . .	13·30–50
*Hong Kong . .	14·530–14·614	W. Germany . .	8·70–8·90
Luxembourg . .	119·40–50	Spain . . .	168–170
Belgium . . .	120$\frac{1}{2}$–122	Greece . . .	71$\frac{7}{8}$–72$\frac{1}{8}$
Italy . . .	§1·510–30	Switzerland . .	10·30–40

Note rate quoted by specialist dealers, other rates may be quoted elsewhere. † £'s 100 Rps. ‡ Rate for new pesos equal to 100 old. § Rate for denominations under Lr.10·000, rate for denominations of Lr.10·000 quoted at 1·520–40, and for higher denominations at 1·530–50. * Hong Kong dollars to the pound. U.S., Canada 93·22–24.

FORWARD RATES

—	One month	Three months
New York . . .	$\frac{1}{16}$ c. pm–$\frac{1}{16}$ c. dis	$\frac{1}{4}$–$\frac{1}{8}$ c. pm
Montreal . . .	$\frac{3}{16}$ $\frac{1}{16}$ c. pm	$\frac{7}{16}$–$\frac{5}{16}$ c. pm
Amsterdam . . .	$\frac{1}{4}$ c. pm–$\frac{1}{4}$ c. dis	1$\frac{1}{2}$–1 c. pm
Brussels . . .	Par–10 c. dis	8 c. pm–2 c. dis
Copenhagen . .	Par–5 ore dis	5–10 ore dis
Frankfurt . . .	$\frac{3}{4}$–1$\frac{1}{4}$ pf dis	1$\frac{3}{4}$–2$\frac{1}{4}$ pf dis
Lisbon . . .	20 c. pm–20 c. dis	15 c. pm–35 c. dis
Milan . . .	Par–2 lire dis	$\frac{1}{4}$–3$\frac{1}{4}$ lire dis
Oslo . . .	3 ore pm–2 ore dis	3 ore pm–2 ore dis
Paris . . .	2–2$\frac{1}{2}$ c. dis	3$\frac{1}{4}$–4$\frac{1}{4}$ c. dis
Stockholm . . .	Par–$\frac{1}{2}$ ore dis	Par–$\frac{1}{2}$ ore dis
Vienna . . .	25 gro pm 5 gro dis	40 gro pm–par
Zurich . . .	$\frac{5}{8}$–1$\frac{1}{8}$ c. dis	$\frac{3}{4}$–$\frac{1}{4}$ c. pm

(Taken from *The Financial Times* of 12th May, 1970)

were amended in December, 1958, when sterling was given a wide degree of external convertibility. Meanwhile, gradual relaxations of official restrictions had allowed a return to a limited scope for exchange arbitrage and, eventually, the list of spot and forward quotations reached the form of Table 2. There is still no official quotation in London for the currencies of Finland and Turkey, the Iron Curtain countries, Central and South America, and the Middle East and Far East outside the Sterling Area, but these currencies may be dealt in by London dealers for very limited purposes against cover obtained in the foreign country concerned. Pride of place in the exchange rate table is given to the American dollar, with the Canadian dollar next owing to its close connexion with its neighbour, but the other centres follow in alphabetical order. The omission of quotations for the previous business day is a disadvantage because it prevents a study of the immediate trend of quotations.

The Foreign Exchange Article

At one time the leading daily newspapers considered foreign exchange business to be of sufficient importance and general interest as to require an article of several hundred words to accompany the table of foreign exchange rates. Since the reopening of the London Foreign Exchange Market, however, its business has been dismissed in a few score words or less. The following extract has therefore had to be invented as an adjunct to Table 2 in order to introduce the reader to expressions in general use in foreign exchange circles.

Sterling firmed against the dollar until at one time the authorities intervened to re-purchase some of the currency it had sold yesterday at 2·40¾. After dealings at 2·40¾, and then slightly under this rate, the flurry subsided and the rate closed at 2·40½–⅝. Canadian dollars, previously bid on commercial account, no longer so firm against the pound, weakened to 2·58–⅛, though two points firmer on the cross at 0·9324. Both dollars were on offer on the forward positions for the closing of oversold sterling deals, reacting from previous levels to ⅜ c. premium for 3 months which reflects interest differentials.

Recent bidding for Dutch guilders died down, the trend being reversed for most of the day, but in later dealings there was evidence of profit-taking to bring the rate back to 8·72¼. The Belgian franc followed much the same course as its Benelux partner, but in both cases forwards were neglected at about previous levels.

D-Marks came on offer weakening to 8·74, but turned rather firmer towards the close of business. Lire followed the general trend and touched 1514 before reacting to 1513. Swiss francs were also on offer up to 10·34¼; it was reported that the offerings arose from repatriation of commercial profits meeting with an unwilling market so business was not in proportion to the movement in the rate.

On balance, Scandinavians displayed an easier tendency, as did escudos and schillings, so altogether sterling had a very good day.

Translated into ordinary language this would read—

The rate of exchange for the pound sterling against the U.S.A. dollar moved numerically upwards in favour of sterling reflecting buying of sterling which means dollars were offered in exchange: it is implied that experience in the market on previous days had been the opposite, with bidding for dollars by dealers offering sterling to such an extent that the Exchange Equalization Account, operating through the Bank of England, had found it necessary to sell some of their holdings of U.S. dollars in order to prevent the dollar price of the pound falling below 2·40⅝ which would have been an unjustifiably cheap price in current economic circumstances. Today, however, with dollars offered—that is, pounds in demand—the quick rise in the dollar rate was equally unjustified so when dollars were offered at 2·40¾ to £1, the Bank of England bought them from dealers; thus by their action on both days they prevented wide fluctuations in the international price of the pound. The reference to a rate "slightly under" a quotable fraction means that dealers bought and sold at the type of rate used in New York, where the pound is quoted to four decimal places; dealers were bidding $2·4074 or perhaps $2·4073 to £1 but not as low as the next quotable fraction which is 2·40 ¹¹⁄₁₆. In the late afternoon, there were other buyers of dollars besides, so less dollars and cents exchanged for the pound and when business closed down in London there were buyers in the market at 2·40⅝, and sellers offering at 2·40½.

Previously, importers from Canada seeking to pay for their purchases at a time when few sellers of Canadian dollars were in evidence, had caused that currency to appreciate so that less dollars and cents could be got for each pound paid; today, since they had bought all they wanted, there were more sellers than buyers causing Canadian dollars to cheapen.

So many banks in London deal in both Canadian as well as U.S. dollars that it is possible to arrange direct exchanges between these two currencies. The rate quoted is similar to that employed in New York, known as the "Cross Rate," where a price is given to four places of decimal of the U.S. dollar to $1 Canadian. Although Canadian dollars had lost value against the pound, this change was not so large as for the U.S. dollar, so instead of a cross rate of U.S. $0·9322 =£1 Canadian, it was quoted as U.S. $0·9324.

In the forward exchange market there had been in the preceding business days such a preponderance of buyers of U.S. and Canadian dollars that the premium on three months had risen to a high premium; on the day reported those who had been selling pounds for forward delivery (i.e. had bought dollars) were changing their minds and now selling dollars so the high premium ran off to a level where the margin reflected the higher rate of interest ruling in London as compared to that in New York.

Whereas yesterday buyers of Dutch guilders (otherwise known as "florins") had predominated, today sellers were stronger and their offerings caused guilders to become cheaper until late in the day when some buying made them dearer, though still cheaper than at the opening in the morning. The Belgian franc was the subject of the same sort of influences as the guilder, Belgium and Holland being very close economically through their partnership in the Benelux Union. In the forward exchange market for these currencies, there was so little business that there was no testing of the forward margins quoted by dealers which were therefore left without change.

In the case of the German, Italian and Swiss currencies, all of which were offered by sellers for most of the day, sterling appreciated (i.e. all these currencies became cheaper to us) until late dealings when some buying was in evidence. In the case of the Swiss exchange, one at least of the strong sellers was selling francs which arose from a profitable commercial operation in that country, or perhaps a series of operations, and since there were so few buyers this made the Swiss currency cheaper than if the normal condition of many buyers and sellers had existed.

Since the crowns of Norway, Sweden and Denmark, and Portugese and Austrian currencies had also come on offer, like the others referred to above, one can conclude that the pound sterling was in universal demand.

The following table, taken from *The Financial Times* of 2nd February 1971, shows the local units of currency in various countries and territories of the world, together with the approximate sterling value of those currencies on the date quoted—

WORLD VALUE OF THE POUND

The following list contains the latest market or official rates available on February 1, except where otherwise indicated. Market rates are the average of buying and selling rates except where they are shown to be selling rates only. In some cases market rates have been calculated from the market rates of foreign currencies to which they are tied.

Exchanges in the U.K. and most of the countries listed are officially controlled and the rates shown should not be taken as being applicable to any particular transactions without reference to an authorized dealer.

Abbreviations: (S) member of the sterling area; (O) official rate; (F) free rate; (T) tourist rate; (n/c) non-commercial rate; (n.a.) not available; (B) banker's rate; (Br.) broker's rate; (d) local unit expressed in terms of U.K. pence; (A) approximate rate; no direct quotation available; (sg) selling rate; (nom.) nominal.

Place and Local Unit(s)		Value of £ sterling	Place and Local Unit(s)		Value of £ sterling
Afghanistan	Afghani	200	Cape Verde Is.	Cape V. Escudo	68·37½
Albania	New Lek	{ 12 (O) / 30 (T)	Ceylon (S)	Ceylon Rupee	16·⅞ (d) [k
Algeria	Dinar	11·65 (sg.)	Chile	C. Escudo	{ 29·41 (B) / 34·29½ (Br.)
Andorra	{ French Franc / Spanish Peseta	13·20 / 166·32½	China	Renminbi	5·908
Angola	Ang. Escudo	68·37½	Colombia	C. Peso	45½ (F) [f
Antigua (S)	E. Caribbean $	4·80	Congo Ex. Bel	Zaire	1·185745 [g
Argentina	Ar. Peso	9·56 [h	Costa Rica	Colon(es)	15·924
Australia (S)	Aus. $	2·1471½	Cuba	Cuban Peso	2·39
Austria	Schilling	61·70½	Cyprus (S)	Cyprus £	1·0
Azores	Portug. Escudo	68·37½	Czechoslov'ka	Koruna	{ 17·28 (O) / 33·84 (n/c) / 38·74 (T)
Bahamas (S)	Ba. Dollar	2·4 [r	Dahomey	C.F.A. Franc	660
Bahrein (S)	Dinar	1·142	Denmark	Danish Krone(r)	17·90½
Balearic Is.	Spa. Peseta	166·32½	Djibuti	Djibuti Franc	502·79
Barbados (S)	E. Caribbean $	4·80	Dominica (S)	E. Caribbean $	4·80
Belgium	B. Franc	118·67	Domin. Rep.	Dominican Peso	2·39
Bermuda (S)	Bda. $ [s	2·4			
Bhutan	Indian Rupee	18·04	Ecuador	Sucre	{ (O) n.a. [w / (F) n.a.
Bolivia	Bolivian Peso	28·12½	Egypt	Egyptian £	1·046 (A)
Botswana (S)	S.A. Rand (–)	1·716	Eritrea	Ethiopian $	6
Brazil	Cruzeiro	11·56½ [b	Ethiopia	Ethiopian $	6
Br. Hond's (S)	Br. Hdrs. $	4·0	Eq't'l Guinea	Peseta	166·32½
Br. Solmn Is. (S)Aus. $		2·1471½			
Br. Virgin Is. (S)U.S. $		2·39	Falkland Is. (S)	Falkland Is. £	1·0
Brunei (S)	[dBrunei $	7·3725	Faroe Is.	Danish Krone(r)	17·90½
Bulgaria	Lev (Leva)	{ 2·81 (O) / 4·8 (T)	Fiji Is. (S)	Fiji $	2·09¾ [n
Burma	Kyat	21 (d)	Finland	Markka	9·97
Burundi	Burundi Franc	{ 207·61 / 245 (F)	Formosa	New Taiwan $	96·24
			France	French Franc	13·20
Cambodia	Riel	133 (sg)	Fr. C'ty in Af. [aC.F.A. Franc		660
Cameroun Rp.	C.F.A. Franc	660	Fr. Guiana	Local Franc	13·20
Canada	Canadian $	2·43⅜ [v	Fr. Pac. Is.	C.F.P. Franc	240·00
Canary Is.	Spanish Peseta	166·32½	Gambia (S)	Gambia £	1·0

Place	Local Unit(s)	Value of £ sterling
Germany (East)	Ostmark	10·01
Germany (West)	Deutschemark	8·617⅞
Ghana (S)	Cedi	2·45
Gibraltar (S)	Gibraltar £	1·0
Gilbert & Ellice Is. (S)	Aust. Dollar	2·1471½
Greece	Drachma (mae)	71$\frac{7}{16}$
Greenland	Danish Krone (r)	17·90⅛
Grenada (S)	E. Caribbean $	4·80
Guadaloupe	Local Franc	13·20
Guam	U.S. $	2·39
Guatemala	Quetzal(es)	2·39
Guinea	Guinea Franc	586
Guyana (S)	Guyanan $	4·80
Haiti	Gourde	11·95
Honduras Rp.	Lempira	4·78
Hong Kong (S)	H.K. $	14·572 [o
Hungary	Forint	28·18 (O) 72 (T)
Iceland (S)	I. Krona (Kronur)	209·15 (A)
India (S)	Ind. Rupee	18·04
Indonesia	Rupiah	907·2 [q
Iran	Rial	182
Iraq	Iraq Dinar	0·857
Irish Rep. (S)	Irish £	1·00
Israel	Israel £	8·40
Italy	Lira (Lire)	1,490⅛
Ivory Coast	C.F.A. Franc	660
Jamaica (S)	Jmca Dollar	2·00
Japan	Yen (–)	854¼
Jordan (S)	Jn. Dinar	0·862
Kenya	Ken Shilling	17·17⅜
Korea (Nth)	Won (–)	6·17
Korea (Sth)	Won (–)	730
Kuwait (S)	Kuwait Dinar	0·85715
Laos	Kip	576 (O) [i 1·200 (F)
Lebanon	Lebanese £	7·75 (F)
Lesotho (S)	S. Afn. Rand (–)	1·716
Liberia	Liberian $	2·39
Libya (S)	Libyan £	0·857
Liecht'nst'n	Swiss Franc	10·30½
Luxembourg	Lux. Franc	118·67
Macao	Pataca	14·41
Madeira	Portug'se escudo	68·37½
Malagasy Rp.	MG Franc	660
Malawi (S)	Pound	1·00
Malaysia (S)	[d Malaysian $	7·36625
Maldive Is. (S)	Mal. Rupee	11·40
Mali Rp.	Mali Franc	1,320
Malta (S)	Maltese £	1
Martinique	Local Franc	13·20
Mauritania	C.F.A. Franc	660
Mauritius (S)	Maur. Rupee	13·33
Mexico	Mexican Peso	29·83
Miquelon	C.F.A. Franc	660
Monaco	French Franc	13·20
Mongolia	Tugrit	9·60 (O) 14·40 (T)
Montserrat (S)	E. Caribbean	4·80
Morocco	Dirham	11·95 (sg)
Mozambique	Moz. Escudo	68·37½
Muscat & Oman (S)	Rial Saidi [u	1
Nauru Is.	Aust. Dollar	2·1471½
Nepal	Nepalese Rupee	24·3013
Netherlands	Guilder	8·61⅞

Place	Local Unit(s)	Value of £ sterling
Netherlands Guiana	Surinam Guilder	4·50
Neth. W. Ind.	Antillian Guild.	4·50
New Guinea (S)	Aust. Dollar	2·1471½
New Hebrides	Franc	213·33
N. Zealand (S)	N.Z. Dollar	2·1429½
Nicaragua	Cordoba	16·77½
Niger Rp.	C.F.A. Franc	660
Nigeria (S)	Nigeria £	0·85712
Norway	Nrwgn Kron(r)	17·04
Pakistan (S)	Pkst. Rupee	8·76 [l
Panama	Balboa	2·39
Panama Canal Zone	U.S. $	2·39
Papua (S)	Aust. Dollar	2·1471½
Paraguay	Guarani(es)	297½ (F)
Peru	Sol(es)	n.a.
Philippines	Ph Peso	15·40
Pitcairn Is. (S)	£ Sterling	—
	New Zealand $	2·1429½
Poland	Zloty	9·6 57·6 (T) [m
Portugal	Pgse Escudo	68·37½
Port Guinea	Guinea Escudo	68·37½
Port Timor	Timor Escudo	68·37½
Principe Is.	Guinea Escudo	68·37½
Puerto Rico	U.S. $	2·39
Qatar (S)	Q. Dubai Riyal	11·445
Reunion Ile de la	C.F.A. Franc	660
Rhodesia	Pound	n.a.
Rumania	Leu (Lei)	14·4 43·2 (n/c) 43·2 (T) 240 (O)
Rwanda	Rwanda Franc	305 (F)
St. Christopher (S)	E. Caribbean $	4·80
St. Helena (S)	£ Sterling	—
St. Lucia (S)	E. Caribbean $	4·80
St. Pierre	C.F.A. Franc	660
St. Vincent (S)	E. Caribbean $	4·80
Salvador El	Colon(es)	5·98
Samoa (Am)	U.S. $	2·39
San Marino	Italian Lira (lire)	1·490⅛
Sao Tome	Guinea Escudo	68·37½
Saudi Arabia	Ryal	10·765
Seychelles (S)	S. Rupee	13·33
Sierra Leone (S)	Leone	2·0
Singapore (S)	[d Singapore $	7·36625
Somali Rep	Som. Shilling	17·1415
Sth. Africa (S)	Rand (–)	1·716
S.W. Africa Territories (S)	S.A. Rand	1·716
Southern Yemen (S)	S. Arbn. Dinar	1·0
Spain	Peseta	166·32½
Span. Ports in North Africa	Peseta	166·32½
Sudan Rp.	Sudan £	0·8358
Swaziland (S)	S.A. Rand (–)	1·716
Sweden	S. Krona (Kronor)	12·36⅜
Switzerland	Swiss Franc	10·30½
Syria	Syria £	9⅛ (O) (A) 10·3 (F) (A)
Tanzania (S)	Tan Shilling	17·1093 (sg)
Thailand	Baht	50·03
Tibet	Renminbi	5·908
	Indian Rupee	18·04

Place and Local Unit(s)		Value of £ sterling	Place and Local Unit(s)		Value of £ sterling
Togo Rp.	C.F.A. Franc	660	Vietnam (Nth)	Dong	{ 8·83 (O)
Tonga Is. (S)	Pa'anga	2·143			{ 13·24 (T)
Trinidad (S)	Trin. & Tobago $	4·80	Vietnam	Piastre	{ 192 (O) (P)
Trucial Shk (S)	[c]	[c]	(Sth N.)		{ 283·2
Tunisia	Tunisian Dinar	1·24 (sg)	V'gin Is. U.S.	U.S. $	2·39
Turkey	Turkey £	35·9375 (sg)	Voltaic Rp.	C.F.A. Franc	660
			W. New Guinea	New Guinea Guilder	8·61¾
Uganda (S)	Ug. Shilling	17·17⅜			
Utd. States	U.S. Dollar	2·39	Western	Samoan Thaler	1·72
Uruguay	Uruguay Peso	593	Samoa (S)		
U.S.S.R.	Rouble	2·1530			
			Yemen	Ryal	n.a.
			Yugoslavia	New Y. Dinar	30
Vatican	Italian Lira (Lire)	1·490⅜			
Venezuela	Bolivar(es)	10·71 (F) [e]	Zambia (S)	Kwacha	1·71425 [j]

a That part of the French community in Africa formerly part of French West Africa or French Equatorial Africa.
b Government Tax of 0·2 per cent. London note rate 12–15.
c Of the Trucial Sheikdoms, Abu Dhabi has adopted the Bahrain dinar; Dubai, Ras al Khaimah and Sharjah have introduced the Qatar Dubai ryal as, it is reported, have the other Trucial States Ajman, Fujairah and Umm al Qawain.
d Malaysia and Singapore and Brunei on June 12, 1967, issued their own currencies, which for the time being will be freely interchangeable.
e Rate of oil and iron ore exports not available.
f Rate of most transactions including exports, imports and non-trade transactions previously covered by the certificate rate; exceptions are preferential rates for oil exports and crude oil imports which are not currently available.
g Free market rate in Brussels approximately 1·56 (cheques and transfers).
h A new peso, equal to 100 old, has been introduced. London note rate 10½–11½.
i London note rate 1,500–2,000.
The Kwacha (equal to 100 Ngwee) was introduced on January 16, 1968. The Zambian pound remains legal tender until further notice.
k Under a certificate scheme, details of which were given in the Financial Times on May 6, 1968, the Central Bank of Ceylon will buy sterling at Rs. 19·20 to the £, compared with the official rate of Rs.14·28.
l Pounds per 100 rupees. The quotation is given in this form in line with the new market practice. Tourists receive a 45 per cent bonus on foreign currency surrendered to banks in Pakistan.
m There is a special tourist rate of 40 zlotys to the dollar on exchange beyond a certain amount.
n Decimal currency was introduced in January, 1969—based on a Fijian dollar at a rate of 2F. dollars to the F. pound.
o Hong Kong dollar to £1 sterling.
p The Jamaican pound has been replaced by a decimalized currency based on the J. dollar equal to half the old J. pound.
q The exchange rate system has been revised, and a general official parity of 378 rupiahs to the U.S. dollar introduced. London note rate 1,100–1,400.
r The Bahamian dollar was up-valued on February 2.
s Bermuda has introduced a decimal currency, based on the Bda dollar, at a rate of 2·4 to the Bda pound, which remains legal tender for the time being.
t A decimal currency, the dollar, equal to 10 Rhodesian shillings was introduced by the independent regime on February 17. The RH pound has a parity of U.S. $2·80. The parity of the RH dollar is U.S. $1.40.
u A new currency, the Rial Saida, at gold parity with the pound has replaced the Gulf Rupee.
v It was announced on May 31 that the Canadian dollar was to be allowed to move freely in the exchange market.
w Dealings have been suspended since August 16 when the sucre was devalued from 18 to 25 to one U.S. dollar.

CHAPTER VIII

THE ARITHMETIC OF THE EXCHANGES

Calculation of Cheque, Sight, or Demand Rates; "Long" and "Tel Quel" Rates

(It should be noted that the exchange and interest rates used in this chapter are often not those ruling at time of publication, being merely incidental to the illustration of arithmetical methods.)

No advanced or abstruse arithmetical processes whatever are used in the performance of foreign exchange calculations. All that is necessary is ordinary ability to add, subtract, multiply and divide, but the author, in the course of marking many thousands of test and examination papers, has found a lamentable failure on the part of students generally in carrying out even these simple and elementary processes. The actual method used is not of prime importance. Educational methods vary, and what one learns at school in the way of arithmetic usually accompanies one in later life. The "standard" method of contracted multiplication and the "Italian" method of contracted division are admirable for those who are thoroughly accustomed to their use, but they are not indispensable aids to exchange calculations. The author must confess that he still uses, when unobserved, the "farmer's" methods both of multiplication and of division, that is, he sets down every figure of multiplier and multiplicand, or divisor and dividend (even when these run into eight, ten, or more digits), and does not juggle with decimal points but treats them with the respect they deserve.

The point that is of the utmost importance is that *all foreign exchange calculations must be worked with extreme accuracy.* Any result should always be obtained correct to five places of decimals at least for rates of exchange and three places at least for principal amounts, and methods of prediction and approximation should be used with great caution, if not entirely avoided. The constant use of a rough check is also strongly advised to minimize the risk of mistakes in the correct place for the decimal point.

As regards fractions, it must be noted that *all the fractions used in Foreign Exchange are multiples of* $\frac{1}{64}$, i.e. $\frac{1}{64}$, $\frac{1}{32}$, $\frac{1}{16}$, $\frac{1}{8}$, $\frac{13}{64}$, $\frac{11}{16}$, $\frac{29}{32}$, etc., and no other fractions, such as $\frac{3}{11}$, $\frac{2}{3}$, $\frac{5}{7}$, etc., are ever used. The student is advised to practise turning fractions into decimals mentally, to facilitate calculations, and this can be done by memorizing the "eighths" fractions in decimals, and then adding the decimals for $\frac{1}{16}$, $\frac{1}{32}$ or $\frac{1}{64}$ as required. Thus—

$$\frac{1}{8} = \cdot125 \qquad\qquad \frac{5}{8} = \cdot625$$
$$\frac{1}{4} = \cdot25 \qquad\qquad \frac{3}{4} = \cdot75$$
$$\frac{3}{8} = \cdot375 \qquad\qquad \frac{7}{8} = \cdot875$$
$$\frac{1}{2} = \cdot5$$

while $\frac{1}{16}$ is $\cdot0625$, $\frac{1}{32}$ is $\cdot03125$, and $\frac{1}{64}$ is $\cdot015625$, so that to decimalize, say $\frac{11}{16}$, take the "eighth" below it which is $\frac{5}{8}$, which is $\cdot625$, and add $\frac{1}{16}$, which is $\cdot0625$, making $\cdot6875$ as the decimal equivalent of $\frac{11}{16}$. Or to decimalize, say, $\frac{59}{64}$, divide the numerator by 8, which gives 7 as the nearest "eighth" below, so that $\frac{7}{8}$ is the basis; this leaves $\frac{3}{64}$, which is $\frac{1}{32}$ plus $\frac{1}{64}$, which is $\cdot03125$ plus $\cdot015625$; therefore add $\cdot875$, $\cdot03125$ and $\cdot015625$, which gives $\cdot921875$ as the decimal equivalent of $\frac{59}{64}$.

Interest Calculations

The rapid calculation of interest is also a matter of importance to the exchange dealer. In practice, all allowances in respect of interest lost on different types of remittance are made in the rate of exchange and not by adjusting the principal. Therefore, the rate of exchange is always regarded as the amount of principal on which interest is to be found. The interest formula of $I = \dfrac{P \times R \times N}{100}$ where P is the principal, R the rate per cent per annum, and N the number of years, is in constant use. When a number of days is in question, the formula becomes, $I = \dfrac{P \times N \times R}{100 \times 365}$ and a somewhat clumsy division sum is often involved.

The Third, Tenth and Tenth Rule

In order to minimize the arithmetical working in interest calculations with the above formula, the following short method is of considerable use. First multiply both numerator and denominator by 2, thus giving a divisor of 73,000. To effect the division without dividing, take the amount of the numerator and divide it by 100,000, i.e. move the decimal point *five* places to the left, then add to the resulting figure one-third of itself, then one-tenth of that figure, then one-tenth of that figure, and add the whole together. Finally, deduct from the total so obtained one ten-thousandth of itself, and the result is the required amount of interest.

For example, if it is required to find the interest margin between T.T. and "cheque" New York, the T.T. rate being $4·86 per £, the time of mailing being 8 days, and the rate of interest 3 per cent per annum, set out the problem thus—

$$I = \frac{4·86 \times 8 \times 3 \times 2}{100 \times 365 \times 2}$$

$$= \frac{233·28}{73000}$$

Therefore, take the numerator divided by 100,000 .	·0023328
Add $\frac{1}{3}$rd of this	·0007776
„ $\frac{1}{10}$th of this	·00007776
„ $\frac{1}{10}$th of this	·000007776
	·003195936
Deduct $\frac{1}{10000}$th of this	·000000319
Result	$·003195617

Therefore the interest margin would be ·003196 of a dollar, which is ·3196 of a cent, or $\frac{5}{16}$ nearest in the rate.

The use of this method is further exemplified in the working of Long rates later in this chapter.

Chain Rule[1]

This is another contracted method greatly used in foreign exchange calculations, and was once described in an examination paper by a cynical candidate as "a method of working Compound Proportion invented by Mr. — to make a simple problem more difficult!" It is generally considered, however, that this method is simplicity itself once the basic principle has been mastered. It is used in attaining a comparison or ratio between two quantities which are linked together through another or other quantities, and consists of a series of equations, commencing with a statement of the problem in the form of a query and continuing the equations in the form of a "chain" in that each equation must start in terms of the same quantity as that which concluded the previous equation. Mint Parities and Gold Points are invariably calculated by this method as is shown by the following examples—

(*a*) To find the Mint Par between this country and the U.S.A. if £1 contains 32·9144 grains of fine gold and 10 U.S. dollars are minted from 152·381 grains gold $\frac{9}{10}$ fine.

---

[1] See Clare's *A.B.C. of the Foreign Exchanges* (1892), Spalding's *Foreign Exchange and Foreign Bills*, p. 28, and others.

Chain Rule.   ?   \$ = £1.

If   £1 = 32·9144 grains fine

and if grs. fine   9 = 10 grains U.S. standard.

and if U.S. grs. st. 152·381 = 10 \$.

Note that the "chain" starts with the problem put in the form of a query, that each equation starts with the same kind of quantity as concluded the previous equation, and that the "chain" is completed by the concluding quantity in the final equation being the same as the commencing quantity in the first equation.

Now multiply the figures of each of the two sides and divide the total product of the right-hand side by the total product of the left-hand side, thus—

$$X = \frac{1 \times 32·9144 \times 10 \times 10}{1 \times 9 \times 152·381}$$

$$X = \frac{3291·44}{1371·429}$$

which, on being divided out, gives 2·40 dollars per pound. Therefore the Mint Par between the U.K. and the U.S.A. is—

$$\$2·40 = £1.$$

(b) To find the Mint Par between the U.S.A. and Belgium if the U.S. dollar contains 15 5/21 grains of gold nine-tenths fine and the franc contains 0·150632 gramme of fine gold.

            ? francs   = \$1

       if \$21   = 320 grains

   and if 10 grains std.   = 9 grains fine

   and if 480 grains   = 1 ounce

   and if   1 ounce   = 31·1035 grammes

   and if 0·150632 gramme = 1 franc

Then $X = \dfrac{1 \times 320 \times 9 \times 1 \times 31·1035 \times 1}{21 \times 10 \times 480 \times 1 \times ·150632}$

$$= \frac{89578·08}{15183·7056}$$

$$= 5·89962 \text{ (nearly).}$$

Therefore the Mint Par between the U.S.A. and Belgium is

$$\text{fcs } 5·89962 = \$1$$

Contracted Multiplication

While there is always a certain danger in too contracted methods, some labour-saving processes are quite permissible, though many of them afford scope for additional errors. In the "standard form" of contracted multiplication, the multiplier is set down so that the first significant figure becomes the units figure, the decimal point being moved to permit this, and the decimal point in the multiplicand being moved a similar number of places in the reverse direction. Multiplication is then carried out to one more decimal place than the number required correct by applying the units figure of the multiplier to that said figure in the multiplicand, which will give the necessary number of decimal places, the next figure in the multiplier being applied to the next figure in the multiplicand, and so on. The decimal point remains behind the units figure of the multiplier.

For example, to find the number of dollars produced in exchange for £142·25 at U.S.$2·40425 per £, as £142·25 forms the easier multiplier, set down thus—

$$
\begin{array}{r}
240\cdot4250 \\
1\cdot4225 \\
\hline
240\cdot4250 \\
96\cdot1700 \\
4\cdot8084 \\
\cdot4808 \\
\cdot1200 \\
\hline
342\cdot0042 \\
\hline
\end{array}
$$

The method is to multiply through by 1 from the last figure of the multiplicand, then by 4 from the figure 5 onwards, by 2 from the figure 2 onwards, and so on. (Should there be any figures to be carried from the figure before that on which multiplying is commenced allowance should be made but keeping the decimal point below that in the multiplier.)

Therefore the dollar equivalent of £142·25 at U.S. $2·40425 per £, is
U.S. $342·00

Other contracted methods may be used with advantage, but with care, and the student is advised to use the methods that come most easily to him, and in which he feels he is least likely to fall into error.

Italian Method of Division

This method merely consists in making the multiplication of the divisor by the series of figures in the quotient at the same time as the subtraction of the product from the dividend, the two operations being performed mentally, and only the result written down. When working correct to five places of decimals, it is not advisable to strike off any of the figures of the divisor until after the third place of decimals has been obtained in the quotient.

For example, to find the sterling equivalent of 4,853,808·60 fcs. at 124·25¾ fcs. per £, set out thus—

$$\text{Fcs. } 4,853,808\cdot 60 \text{ at } 124\cdot 2575 = \frac{48538086000}{1242575}$$

= 1242575)48538086000(39062·50001
　　　　　11260836
　　　　　　7766100
　　　　　　3106500
　　　　　　6213500
　　　　　　1125000

Therefore, the required sterling equivalent is £39,062·50001, which is £39062·50.

Percentages and Per Milleages

The meaning of these expressions should be clearly understood as they are greatly used in exchange operations. A percentage is a proportion per hundred, e.g. 1 per cent is one part in every hundred parts, such as £1 per £100, while per mille means per thousand, e.g. 1 per mille is one part in every thousand, such as £1 per £1,000. Care should also be taken to distinguish between a percentage and a fraction of a cent U.S. currency, e.g. ¼ per cent of a dollar rate of $2·80 per £ is ¼ of ·0280, or ·0070, which is nearly ¾ cent, whereas a proportion of ¼ c. in the rate is actually one quarter of a cent, which is ·25 of a cent or ·0025 of a dollar. Percentages or per milleages can also be used to advantage in checking roughly any calculations, such as interest when allowed for in a rate of exchange.

For example, 61 days at 3 per cent per annum is $\dfrac{61 \times 3}{100 \times 365}$

which is roughly $\dfrac{1}{100 \times 2}$ which is ½ per cent of the principal.

Consequently, 61 days interest at 3 per cent per annum on a rate for Belgian francs of 140·25 per £ must be about ½ per cent of 140·25, or $\dfrac{140\cdot 25}{100 \times 2}$ which gives $\dfrac{1\cdot 4025}{2}$ or ·70125 of a franc, which is 70⅛ centimes.[1] An answer to the exact calculation of this interest, therefore, which was not within a little of this figure would obviously

[1] Also, that 1 day at 9% p.a. is ¼°/₀₀ of the principal, taking a 360-day year can be used as a rough check.

be wrong, as where an answer of 21 centimes was obtained. Practice in the conversion of amounts into percentages or per milleages of a rate or of another amount is always useful, if only for the purpose of rough-checking exact calculations. For example, an exchange dealer may have made a profit of ¼ c. on $60,000, and wishes to give a rough estimate of the sterling profit immediately. He takes a round rate of $3 per £ which gives a sterling equivalent of the principal of £20,000. The profit of ¼ c. on each £ dealt in is equal to ·0025 on each $3, which is at the rate of $25 on $30,000, which is $1 on $1,200, which is a proportion of $\frac{1}{12}$ per cent. On £20,000, $\frac{1}{12}$ per cent is $\frac{1 \times 20000}{12 \times 100}$ or 16, so that the profit in sterling is approximately £16. These calculations are mental, but have been set out here in their entirety to show the methods by which the results are obtained.

Selection of Rates and Allowance for Profit

It has already been explained how a dealer endeavours to buy as many foreign units per pound as possible, and to sell as few per pound as possible (buy high and sell low in currency rates) or to give as few pence per foreign unit as possible when buying, and to take as many pence per foreign unit as possible when selling (buy low, sell high in pence rates). It has also been mentioned that when a dealer has to cover any of his operations in the market, he must buy at the market's selling price, or sell at the market's buying price, unless he can bargain successfully with other members of the market. The members of the general public who have occasion to deal in foreign exchange are mostly so well advised nowadays of the prevailing rates, and have, in many cases, acquired such an expert knowledge of exchange dealing, that they are able to put dealers into competition with each other so as to extort the best rate possible from one bank or another. As a result, the margins of profit left to dealers have been greatly reduced during recent years, and at the present time a dealer must allow his customer the actual market rate with only a very small proportion of profit, or may even have to quote between the market rate, in order to secure business, and trust to his powers of bargaining, or to a favourable movement in the rate, to show him a profit on the operation.

Where a dealer can allow himself a margin of profit, he takes it in the rate by—

(*a*) When buying, taking more foreign units per pound or giving fewer pence per foreign unit, or

(b) When selling, giving fewer foreign units per pound, or taking more pence per foreign unit.

For example, if the market price for T.T.s on New York is $2·40½ to $2·40⅝ per £, and a dealer can take a margin of profit of $\frac{1}{16}$ c. he would actually buy from a customer at 2·40⅝ plus $\frac{1}{16}$, making 2·40$\frac{11}{16}$, or would sell to the customer at 2·40½ less $\frac{1}{16}$, making 2·40$\frac{7}{16}$, so that his dealing prices with the customer would be 2·40$\frac{7}{16}$ to 2·40$\frac{11}{16}$. Similarly, if the T.T. rate on Calcutta was £5·5280 to £5·5605 in the market, and the dealer could take a margin of profit of £0·012, he would offer to buy from the customer at £5·5160 per 100 rupees, or to sell to him at £5·5725 per 100 rupees. Exchange profits are actually shown, for the time being, in the "Nostro" account with the foreign agent, either in the shape of a disproportionate sterling value of the currency balance held (where similar amounts of currency have been bought and sold at a profit in sterling) or in the shape of more currency bought with sterling received for a sale, in which case the profit is eventually turned into sterling by means of an excess of sales of the currency over purchases, to the extent of the accumulated profit.

Demand Rates

It has already been explained how the rate for Telegraphic Transfers between two centres must be regarded as the basic rate of exchange of the two currencies, since there is no loss of interest, practically no risk, no stamp duties, and only a very small proportionate charge for cable expenses. In the case of the Commonwealth Exchange rates, it was shown how the rate for sight or demand drafts varied from the basic T.T. rate to the extent of the interest lost by the buyer from the time he paid cash at home for the instrument until he eventually received credit in the books of his agent in the other centre, plus, on occasion, an extra margin for any assumed risk owing to the lesser standing of the drawer and for any exceptional stamp duties. The same principle applies to all instruments, the purchase of which involves loss of interest, extra risk, or appreciable stamp duties. Consequently, such allowances must always be made by the bank in the same way as it takes its exchange profit in the rate, and the following rules should be clearly understood—

(a) *In currency rates,* the buyer must receive an allowance for loss of interest, and this is done by giving him more foreign units per pound; therefore always ADD interest to currency rates, allowing the higher rate of interest when the bank is buying, and the lower rate of interest when the bank is selling;

(b) *In pence rates,* the buyer receives compensation for loss of interest by paying fewer pence per foreign unit; therefore, always DEDUCT interest from pence rates, at the higher rate when the bank is buying, and at the lower rate when it is selling;

(c) The allowance for profit is made in the usual way by adding to the currency rate or by deducting from the pence rate when buying, and by deducting from the currency rate or by adding to the pence rate when selling.

These rules are made clear by the following examples.[1] Where the T.T. rate on New York is $2·40$\frac{1}{8}$–$\frac{1}{4}$ per £, and the margin for cheque over cable is $\frac{3}{8}$ – $\frac{7}{16}$ c., the bank will—

> SELL *T.T.* at $2·40$\frac{1}{8}$ per £, *less* its profit of, say, $\frac{1}{32}$ c., making a net rate of $2·40$\frac{3}{32}$ per £;
>
> SELL *Cheque* at $2·40$\frac{1}{8}$ per £, *plus* its selling margin of interest of $\frac{3}{8}$c., making $2·40$\frac{1}{2}$, *less* its profit of $\frac{1}{32}$ c., making a net rate of $2·40$\frac{15}{32}$ per £;
>
> *BUY T.T.* at $2·40$\frac{1}{4}$ per £, *plus* its profit of $\frac{1}{32}$c., making a net rate of $2·40$\frac{9}{32}$ per £;
>
> *BUY Cheque* at $2·40$\frac{1}{4}$ per £, *plus* its buying margin for cheque of $\frac{7}{16}$ c., making $2·40$\frac{11}{16}$, *plus* its profit of $\frac{1}{32}$c., making a net rate of $2·40$\frac{23}{32}$ per £.

Where the T.T. rate on Calcutta is £5·5280 – £5·5605 and the margin for cheque against cable is £0·05 – £0·025, the bank will—

> SELL *T.T.* at £5·5605 per 100 rupees, *plus* its profit of, say, £0·0125, making a net rate of £5·5730.
>
> SELL *Cheque* at £5·5605 per 100 rupees, *less* its selling margin of interest of £0·025 making £5·5580, *plus* its profit of £0·0125, making a net rate of £5·5705 per 100 rupees.
>
> *BUY T.T.* at £5·5280 per 100 rupees, *less* its profit of £0·0125 making a net rate of £5·5155 per 100 rupees.
>
> *BUY Cheque* at £5·5280 per 100 rupees, *less* its buying margin of interest of £0·05 making £5·4780, *less* its profit of £0·0125, making a net rate of £5·4655 per 100 rupees.

It is highly important that the rules for making these allowances should be thoroughly understood, and the student is advised to study them at length, and perfect his knowledge by taking the published rates in the newspapers and working out buying and selling rates for himself, afterwards comparing his results with those that would have been obtained by following out the rules given above. All the above rates are assumed to be "market" rates, so that the eventual net rates obtained would be the dealer's actual dealing rates as quoted to customers in cases where he felt justified in taking such a margin of profit.

Basis of Interest for Demand Rates

The rates of interest commonly allowed for by a dealer in quoting Demand rates to customers are, for *buying,* the rate of interest at which he would be charged for an overdraft in the foreign centre,

---

[1] Allowances for expenses, such as brokerage, cables, etc., have been ignored in these simple examples.

since he is assumed to cover his purchase of cheque by a sale of T.T., and so overdraw his account abroad until the arrival and credit of the cheque; for *selling*, the rate of interest which he receives on current account in the foreign centre, since he is assumed to cover his sale of cheque by a purchase of T.T. on which he will be allowed interest by his agent abroad at the usual rate for current account balances until the cheque is presented and paid to his debit.

The "spread" between T.T. and cheque quoted in the market is based on the rate for Call Money ruling in the foreign centre, since holders of funds there will not sell T.T. and buy cheque unless they receive an allowance which represents at least the same rate of interest as could be earned by the foreign funds if loaned in the Money Market in the foreign centre, while sellers of cheque must be prepared to allow at least this rate of interest, and may be prepared to allow more if a sale of cheque against T.T. is necessary for them to avoid an expensive overdraft, or if they can employ the T.T. so obtained at a better rate of interest until the payment of the cheque, as by loaning the funds on the Stock Exchange in the foreign centre.

It must be remembered that in the case of a purchase and sale of cheque against T.T., the sterling payments for the cheque and for the T.T. are almost always "compensated," i.e. payment for the cheque is made by the buyer on the same day as he receives payment for the T.T. which he has sold, or, in other words, the purchase of the cheque and the sale of the T.T. are made "value same day." Thus, there is no gain or loss of interest on the sterling side of such transactions, and it is simply a case of the seller of the T.T. being deprived of the use of his foreign funds for a certain time, this use being enjoyed by the seller of the cheque, and the "cheque spread" (or margin between T.T. and cheque) merely gives compensation to the buyer of the cheque for the loss of the use of his immediately available funds, which he disposes of by his sale of T.T.

Another method by which any owner of immediately available funds can, as it were, loan them to another party for an exact period of time is by a sale of T.T. against the purchase of what is known as a Guaranteed Mail Transfer.[1] This is a Mail Transfer of which payment on a stated date is guaranteed by the seller. The lender sells foreign currency as spot against the guarantee of the borrower that the funds will be returned on an agreed date. The borrower must be prepared to pay a higher rate of interest than obtains in the home market, and the "cheque spread" is calculated as follows:

If the Call Money rate in New York is $1\frac{1}{2}$ per cent per annum, the

---

[1] Payment in home currency by the borrower for the T.T. and by the lender for the G.M.T. is made on the same day in the home centre.

overdraft rate there is 4 per cent per annum, one exchange operator has funds lying to his credit there as cover for drafts sold to customers on a low interest basis or against a forward sale of dollars, and another exchange operator is short of immediate funds owing to sale of T.T.s as cover for purchases of cheques on a high interest basis from customers, or against forward purchases, the former operator can only obtain 1½ per cent per annum if he uses his balance for a few days in the New York Money Market, while the latter would have to pay 4 per cent for an overdraft with his agent until the proceeds of his purchases were credited to his account there. There will probably be several operators in the market here in each of these positions, and force of competition between owners of funds and borrowers will eventually hammer out a dealing rate for cheque against T.T. based on a rate of interest somewhere between 1½ per cent and 4 per cent per annum, say 2¾ – 3 per cent. The actual margin or "spread" in any transaction will then depend on the length of time for which the funds are used, a "run" of 8 days needing an allowance of about ·19 of a cent, one of 10 days needing about ·23 of a cent, one of 12 days needing about ·28 of a cent, and so on. In each case the margin is for cheque *over* T.T., that is to say, the rate for cheque is always cheaper than that for T.T., and the margin will vary with the rate of interest agreed to by the parties, and the estimated time which will elapse between the date of purchase and the date of credit, in the case of cheques, demand drafts, or ordinary M.T.s, or the exact time allowed for in the case of a G.M.T. When these two factors have been decided, the working of the margin is merely a matter of a simple interest calculation as the following examples will show.

(a) At what rate would you sell T.T. and buy G.M.T. if the T.T. rate, London on New York, is $2·80 per £, if you wish to earn 3 per cent per annum on the dollars used, and if the G.M.T. is guaranteed for payment in 10 days time from the date of sale of the T.T., and purchase of the G.M.T.? (New York takes 360 days to the year.)

Answer —

$$\text{Interest} = \frac{2·80 \times 3 \times 10}{100 \times 360} = \frac{·028}{12} = \$·0023$$

∴ Margin for the G.M.T. will be 23 points over T.T., i.e. T.T. will be sold at $2·80, and G.M.T. purchased at $2·8023 per £.

(b) At what rate would you purchase a cheque on New York from a customer if the London market quotes $2·79⅞ – 2·80 per £ for

T.T.s, if you estimate that the cheque will not be credited to your account until 5 days after the date of purchase, if your agent in New York allows you $1\frac{1}{2}$ per cent per annum on credit balances and charges you 4 per cent per annum on overdrafts, and if you require a profit of $\frac{1}{2}$ per mille on the transaction? (New York allows 360 days to the year.)

Answer—

If the market quotes $2·79$\frac{7}{8}$ – 2·80 per £, the operator can only sell to the market at $2·80, and must therefore base his price on this rate. Also as he must assume that he will sell T.T. as cover for his purchase, and so will be overdrawn on his account in New York until the cheque is collected and credited to him, he must allow for interest at the overdraft rate of 4 per cent per annum.

Then, Interest $= \dfrac{2·80 \times 5 \times 4}{100 \times 360} = \dfrac{1·40}{90} = \$·00156.$

∴ Margin for cheque over T.T. is ·156 of a cent.
∴ Buying rate for cheque is $2·80 *plus* ·156 c. . . . $2·80156
Add profit at $\frac{1}{2}$ per mille (operator must take *more* dollars per £) . . . . ·00140
———————
$2·80296
———————

∴ Operator will buy cheque from customer at $2·8030, or $2·80$\frac{5}{16}$ nearest, per £.

(*c*) If cheque against T.T. New York is quoted at a margin of 16 points in the London market, with a T.T. rate of $2·40 per £, and the time of airmail is taken as 4 days, what rate of interest does this show to an operator who sells T.T. and buys cheque? (New York allows 360 days to the year.)

Answer. Using the usual formula—

(*I*) $\$·0016 = \dfrac{2·40 \times 4 \times R}{100 \times 360}$

∴ $24R = 144$

∴ $R = \dfrac{144}{24}.$

$= 6$

∴ Rate of interest represented by a margin of 16 points for a 4 days run on a T.T. rate of $2·40 per £ is 6 per cent per annum.

The same formula can be used to ascertain the number of days for which a G.M.T. must be fixed to allow of a certain margin over T.T. at a stated rate per cent per annum.

The operation of "swapping" T.T. against G.M.T., or cheque, was once such a usual method of using or obtaining temporary funds either in London or in New York, and so largely dealt in between the chief centres, that most operators had constructed tables showing the equivalent rate per cent per annum produced by any given margin, within practicable limits, for any given number of days up to 91 (for use in obtaining the equivalent rate per cent of a forward margin, which see later). Operations on cheque or G.M.T. can also be undertaken to provide funds on the home centre. If the margin for "short forwards," i.e. foreign currency for delivery a few days ahead, is at a discount over the T.T. or "spot" rate, the operator can sell cheque or G.M.T. for immediate cash in the home currency and cover himself by buying the foreign currency needed to meet the cheque "forward" for a date to coincide with the probable date of presentation of the cheque or maturity of the G.M.T. He will not have to pay for the "forward" purchase of the foreign currency until the date of delivery and so is left with the use of the home funds in the meantime. For such an operation to be profitable, the discount on the "short forward" must be great enough to reduce the rate of interest represented by the cheque margin to below the interest rate for short-term loans ruling on the home market.

"Long" Rates and "Tel Quel" Rates

Many countries have export trades in which it is so customary to allow a recognized period of credit to a buyer that such a lapse of time before payment has come to be accepted as a matter of course, or even of legal right, as in the case of the "three days grace" in this country. Consequently, bills drawn by or on that country have come to possess a "customary usance," or a certain tenor at which all such bills are drawn. Thus, in most of the South American countries, the "customary usance" is 90 days after sight, in the American cotton trade it is 60 days after sight, in certain French textile trades it is 30 days after date, and so on. Such bills came forward for purchase so regularly before the First World War that rates were quoted for them as a matter of course, and these rates were known as "Long" rates since they were for "long bills," or bills at tenor as distinct from demand drafts or cable transfers. The falling off in the use of trade bills and the almost universal use of the T.T., which was the result of the disturbance of commercial confidence and the wide fluctuations in rates of exchange following the war, led to the gradual dropping of the quotations for "long" rates in the London market, especially as the London banks had by then established their own Foreign Departments, and were prepared to purchase and hold against spot or forward sales any long bills in foreign currency which might be offered to them by their customers, instead of reselling them to the foreign banking houses as was their custom before the war. The use of the commercial bill, however, has been steadily reviving during the past few years, and it is essential that an exchange operator should be able to calculate quickly and accurately a "long" rate for any draft at usance which may be offered to him for purchase.

A "Tel Quel" rate (or a t.q. rate) is literally a rate for a bill "such as it is"; in other words, it is a rate of exchange calculated to apply to a bill having any period of time still to run. The original "long" rates were calculated on fixed usances, e.g. for the purchase of 90 d/d bills, to allow for the necessary loss of interest from the date of purchase until the estimated date of payment, plus expenses, but bills often came forward for purchase of which a certain portion of the usance had already expired. Thus, if a customer drew at 90 d/d on a buyer in Lisbon, sent the draft for acceptance and return, and offered it for sale here only after it had been returned to him duly accepted, the maturity date would be at least ten days nearer than the estimated maturity date allowed for in the quoted long rate for 90 d/d drafts just drawn, and the buyer would have to make an allowance to the seller in respect of the difference in interest lost. This could be done either by making an allowance in the long rate for the time already run or by calculating a new rate from the basic T.T. rate to allow for the loss of interest during the remaining period of the currency of the bill, plus expenses. In either case, the resulting rate was said to be a "tel quel" rate since it was exactly fitted to the particular bill.

In point of fact, most rates other than T.T. rates can be considered as "tel quel" rates. A rate for a demand draft is now calculated from the T.T. rate on the basis of interest lost and any incidental charges, and nearly every bill offered to a bank for purchase has either rather more or rather less than an exact 60 or 90 days to run, so that an exact allowance for interest must again be calculated. There is, then, no difference in the method of calculation from the basic T.T. rate of a demand, a long, or a "tel quel" rate. In all cases, allowance is made for interest lost (at the bank's rate for advances when buying or at its rate for deposits if selling), any stamps or collecting charges the cost of which must be borne by the buying bank, and an allowance for profit.

It may be repeated that a bank very rarely *sells* a tenor draft of its own drawing, and should it do so, it would make no allowance to the buyer for the cost of any stamps or collecting charges which would have to be borne by him but would, in fact, charge him with the cost of the English stamp on the draft and with an allowance for profit, and would only allow him interest at the lower rate for the exact period between the date of purchase and the estimated date of payment and debit to the bank's account in the foreign centre.

The following examples show the methods of calculating long and "tel quel" rates for buying drafts, in currency and pence rates, and a theoretical example of the sale of a tenor draft by a London bank to a customer. The principles are exactly the same as those set out for the calculation of demand rates, with the addition that costs of stamp and collection charges are allowed against the seller—

(*a*) At what rate would you purchase from a customer a 90 d/s documentary draft in dollars on San Francisco, if the T.T. rate London on New York is $2·79⅞ – 2·80 per £, if the time of mailing from London to New York is 4 days, from New York to San Francisco 3 days, and the return journey the same, if market discount rates for commercial paper are 3 per cent in London, and 4 per cent per annum in New York, if the stamp duty in the U.S.A. is ½ per mille *ad valorem*, if your agent makes a charge for collecting documentary drafts of ½ per mille *ad valorem*, and if you require a profit of $\frac{1}{32}$ c. in the rate? (U.S.A. takes 360 days to the year.)

N.B.—It is highly important to note that the rate of interest to be applied in the purchase of any tenor draft is the rate of discount at which the bank is prepared to buy such paper. In the case of inland bills, it is obviously the ruling rate in this country for the class of paper in question. In the case of foreign bills, it is the rate, at least, at which the buying bank could resell the draft so as to provide immediate foreign funds; in other words, the rate at which it could rediscount the draft should it so wish. Consequently, in all foreign exchange rates in which interest must be allowed for, *the rate of interest to be applied is the rate of interest ruling in the foreign centre*. In the case of cheque, or demand, or short rates, this rate of interest will be the rate for temporary overdrafts, when buying, or for short loans in the foreign Money Market, if selling. For drafts at longer tenor, the rate will be *the rate at which such drafts could be rediscounted in the foreign centre in case of need*, i.e. the foreign market discount rate for that class of paper, when buying, or for a fixed deposit of foreign funds for the period, if selling.

In this example, the rate of interest must, therefore, be the rate for such paper *ruling in New York*, which is given as 4 per cent per annum. The buying bank will be out of its money for 4 days mailing to New York, plus 3 days on to San Francisco, plus 90 days currency of the draft (since it cannot be "sighted" until it arrives in San Francisco, and so does not commence to run until then, while no days of grace obtain in the U.S.A.), plus 3 days for the return remittance from San Francisco to New York, making a total of 100 days from the date of purchase until the estimated date of credit of the proceeds in New York.

Working interest for this period at 4 per cent per annum on the rate at which the bank would buy T.T., viz. $4·86 per £, without allowing for profit, gives—

$$I = \frac{2\cdot80 \times 100 \times 4}{100 \times 360} = \frac{2\cdot80}{90} = \$\cdot031111$$

The bank must therefore take $·031111 *more* per £ than the T.T. rate to cover loss of interest.

It must also take *more* dollars per £, to cover the cost of U.S. stamp, agent's charges, and its own profit.

Therefore, the final buying rate will be—

		$
T.T. rate		2·80
Plus interest for 110 days at 4 per cent per annum .		·0311111
„ U.S. stamp at ½ per mille on $2·80 . . .		·0014
„ agent's charge of ½ per mille on $2·80 . . .		·0014
„ bank's profit		·0003125
		$2·8342236

∴ The required buying rate would be $2·8343, or $2·83 7/16 nearest, per £.

(*b*) At what rate would you purchase a 90 d/s draft on Calcutta if the London market rate for T.T.s is £5·5280–£5·5605, if the market rates of discount for such bills are 2½ per cent in London, and 6 per cent in Calcutta, if the time of mailing is 21 days, and there are no days of grace in India, if the foreign stamp duty is ½ per mille *ad valorem*, if your agent makes a collecting charge of ¼ per mille, and if you require a profit of £0·03125 in the rate for the bill in rupees?

The rate of interest applicable is that ruling in the foreign centre, which is 6 per cent per annum, and the total period between the date of purchase and probable date of credit is 21 plus 90 days, making 111 days in all. The bank can only sell T.T. Calcutta to the market, as cover, at £5·205 per 100 rupees, and so must base its buying rate on this price.

The interest at 6 per cent per annum for 11 days on £5·205 will be—

$$I = \frac{5\cdot5280 \times 111 \times 6 \times 2}{100 \times 365 \times 2}$$

$$= \frac{7363\cdot30}{73000}$$

$$= £0\cdot100867$$

(multiply numerator and denominator by 2 for $\frac{1}{3}$rd, $\frac{1}{10}$th and $\frac{1}{10}$th rule)

Take $\frac{1}{100000}$th of 7363·30 .	·073633
Add $\frac{1}{3}$rd of this . . .	·024544
,, $\frac{1}{10}$th of this . . .	·002454
,, $\frac{1}{10}$th of this . . .	·000245
	·100876
Deduct $\frac{1}{10000}$th of this .	·000010
	·100866

The bank must give fewer pounds per 100 rupees to cover this loss of interest and fewer pounds still to cover foreign stamp, agent's charge, and profit.

It will therefore calculate its buying rate thus—

	£	£
T.T. rate		5·5280
Deduct interest for 111 days at 6 per cent per annum on £5·5228 . . .	·100866	
,, foreign stamp at $\frac{1}{2}$ per mille . .	·002764	
,, agent's charge at $\frac{1}{4}$ per mille . .	·001382	
,, allowance for profit	·031250	
		·136262
	Net	£5·391738

∴ The required buying rate would be £5·391738 per 100 rupees.

(*c*) On 8th June, 1970, a customer presents to you for purchase, a bill on Copenhagen drawn fixed to mature on 30th September, 1970. If the London market quotes T.T.s on Copenhagen at 17·99½–18·00, if the market discount rates for such paper are 8 per cent in London and 9 per cent per annum in Copenhagen, if Danish stamp duty at $\frac{1}{2}$ per mille *ad valorem* must be paid, and if you require a profit of $\frac{1}{4}$ per mille, what buying rate would you quote to your customer?

The bill matures on 30th September, 1970. On 8th June, 1970, therefore, the bill has 114 days still to run (22 in June, 31 in July, 31 in August and 30 in September), and the bank will be out of its money for this period. T.T. could only be sold as cover in the London market at 18·00 per £, and the bill could be re-discounted in Copenhagen at 9 per cent per annum.

The interest to be allowed is—

$$I = \frac{18 \cdot 00 \times 114 \times 9 \times 2}{100 \times 365 \times 2}$$

$$= \frac{36936}{73000}$$

$$= \cdot 5059726$$

Take $\frac{1}{100000}$th of 36936	.	·36936
$\frac{1}{3}$rd . . .	.	·12312
$\frac{1}{10}$th . . .	.	·012312
$\frac{1}{10}$th . . .	.	·0012312
		·5060232
Less $\frac{1}{10000}$th . .	.	·0000506
		·5059726

The bank will require more foreign currency per £ to cover loss of interest and expenses, so the final buying rate will be calculated thus—

T.T. rate	18·00
Add interest for 114 days at 9 per cent per annum on 18·00	·5059726
,, Danish stamp duty at $\frac{1}{2}$ per mille on 18·00	·009
,, bank's profit at $\frac{1}{4}$ per mille on 18·00	·0045
	18·5194726

∴ The required quotation is Kr. 18·52 (nearest) per £.

(*d*) A New York banker has offered to him for purchase a 60 d/s draft on London for £2,389·77. The market rates in New York for T.T.s on London are $2·80\frac{1}{8} - \frac{1}{4}$ per £, discount rates are 3 per cent in London and 2 per cent per annum in New York, time of mailing is 5 days, English bill stamp may be ignored as it is only twopence, and the banker requires a profit of $\frac{1}{32}$ c. in the rate. At what rate will he purchase the bill from his customer?

The New York banker will have to pay out dollars on the spot and receive sterling in about 2 months time. He must therefore pay out as few dollars per £ as possible, and so must *deduct* from his buying rate for T.T.s all the necessary allowances. He can only sell sterling T.T. to the New York market as cover at the *lower* quoted rate, as a buyer of sterling would give as few dollars per £ as possible. He must therefore base his rate on $2·80\frac{1}{8}$ per £, and must take the London discount rate as he could only rediscount the bill there at that rate. He will be out of his money for 5 days mailing, plus 60 days currency of the bill after it has been "sighted," plus 3 days grace, making 68 days in all.

The interest will therefore be (taking London terms of 365 days to the year)—

$$I = \frac{2 \cdot 80125 \times 68 \times 3 \times 2}{100 \times 365 \times 2}$$

$$= \frac{1142 \cdot 91}{73000}$$

$$= \cdot 0156562$$

$\frac{1}{100000}$th of 1142·91	.	.	·0114291
Add $\frac{1}{3}$rd of this	.	.	·0038097
„ $\frac{1}{10}$th of this	.	.	·0003809
„ $\frac{1}{10}$th of this	.	.	·0000381
			·0156578
Less $\frac{1}{10000}$th of this	.		·0000016
			·0156562

He will now build up his 60 days rate by deducting from the T.T. rate the allowances for interest and expenses thus—

	$	$
T.T. rate		2·80125
Deduct—		
Interest for 68 days at 3% per annum on this rate	·0156562	
Banker's profit of $\frac{1}{32}$ c.	·0003125	
		·0159687
		$2·7852813

∴ The required rate is $2·7852 or $2·78½ nearest, per £.

Note again that the New York banker pays fewer dollars per £ in the same way that an English banker would pay fewer pence per foreign unit.

CHAPTER IX

FOREIGN EXCHANGE DEALINGS

"Arbitrage" and "Cross Rates"; Organization and Working
of the London Foreign Exchange Market

It is true that an exchange dealer is born and not made, but the men appointed by British banks to carry out the very responsible duties of dealing for the bank in foreign currencies are chosen not only because they appear to have a natural aptitude for the business but because they seem likely to respond well to the long and arduous period of training which they must undergo. The technical language of the business alone has to be acquired and, although the trainee studies under men who are already expert cambists, there is in the long run no teacher like experience. Also, the foreign exchange dealer who never made a mistake has yet to be born, and we must all learn from our mistakes. A bad mistake in dealing in foreign exchange, however, can cost the employer a lot of money and the employee his job, so that constant care and vigilance are needed to ensure that such mistakes as will inevitably be made are only little ones.

The phraseology of the exchange dealer has not been developed and adopted without reason. It is usual for the neophite in his early conversations with exchange brokers to use such double-edged expressions as "Sell me 50,000," when he means that the broker is to sell 50,000 units of currency for his account, and not that he wishes the broker to sell the currency to him, or "Take 50,000," when he wishes the broker to take from him, i.e. to sell for his account, 50,000 currency units, and not that he intends to take, i.e. buy, 50,000 units from the broker. The older hand will always use the accepted and unequivocal phrases of "I sell (or give) you 50,000," or "I buy (or take) 50,000." As is explained later, practically every transaction in foreign exchange between a bank and customer, or between a bank and broker, is conducted by word of mouth, and it is, therefore, impossible to be too precise when giving or confirming instructions and orders.

The exchange dealer of a bank is operating in the name, and for account of, his bank, and with the bank's money. A misunderstanding of the requirements of a customer, such as may result in a sale instead of a purchase of currency in the market, can prove very expensive when it has to be undone and the operation performed correctly. This risk is enhanced when instructions are given through the foreign clerk at a local branch. For example, a wine merchant who is importing some wine from Italy for resale to wholesalers in this country may explain the transaction rather badly over the telephone to the local branch of his bank, with the result that the foreign clerk telephones the foreign exchange dealer at the chief foreign branch or overseas department and says: "I have a customer who is selling goods costing lire 2m. What rate can you give me, please?" On such a statement the exchange dealer can only conclude that the customer is selling goods to Italy and will be *receiving* lire2m. in payment. He accordingly quotes the rate at which he will *buy* Italian lire from the customer. Actually, of course, the customer is buying goods from Italy and selling them over here and wishes to *buy* lire2m. in order to pay for the goods. If the exchange dealer has based his quotation on a market rate ruling at that time of 1516½ to 1517 lire per £, and by the time the misunderstanding is discovered (which will certainly be one day, if not two days, later when the customer receives confirmation of the contract from the bank) the Italian lire has appreciated and the rate stands at 1515–1515½, the bank will be involved in a loss of 2 lire per £ on the 2m. lire which the dealer understood he had bought and which he would have covered immediately by a sale to the market. As he will not receive cover from the customer, he must buy back lire in the market at the dearer rate then current, and he may even have to lose 1½ lire per £ on another 2m. lire, if the customer insists that he is entitled to receive the rate ruling at the time when he gave his order, as he ought not to be made to suffer through an internal misunderstanding in the bank. All requirements should, therefore, be stated as clearly and simply as possible and they should be repeated back equally clearly so that both parties can be certain that there is no misunderstanding.

Sources of Business

Business comes to the bank exchange dealer from many sources. On arriving at his desk he will find a summary of buying and selling orders received by post from the various branches of the bank on behalf of local customers. These summaries are prepared by various sections dealing specially with orders for the purchase or sale of foreign currencies in the shape of T.T.s or in the form of M.T.s or sight drafts, or with the advices received from foreign correspondents of credits to the "Nostro" account of the proceeds of drafts sent abroad for collection which have either been negotiated for the customer, i.e. discounted, or been sent for simple collection for his account. New drafts in foreign currencies will have come forward for negotiation for which special exchange rates may have to be calculated, while the coupon, dividend and stock departments will have foreign currency proceeds to sell for account of the customers to whom the items belonged. There will also be a mass of cables from abroad giving the closing exchange rates in the foreign markets concerned on the previous business day and probably containing, also, "limit" orders for the purchase or sale of foreign currencies against sterling, provided they can be carried out at the rate specified in the order. These form the basis of the day's dealings, and as soon as market rates have been established these orders will be "rated" by the dealer, i.e. he will fix an exchange rate for them, and the foreign currencies are bought and sold by the bank at these prices. He must then watch carefully to see if at any time a "limit" order can be executed, with, of course, a profit to the bank, bearing in mind all the time the maxim, *buy high, sell low*, for quotations in foreign units per pound. Then comes the ceaseless business of the day. Telephones are constantly ringing with inquiries from branches and big customers for quotations for this, that, or the other transaction. Other telephone calls will be from correspondents abroad inquiring as to the fate of their overnight orders, confirming the receipt and execution of orders from the home bank, giving new orders, making inquiries of all kinds and generally keeping the dealer on his toes. At the same time movements in the London market must be followed closely so that the quotations given in reply to all these inquiries shall be competitive and yet profitable for the bank. The whole business demands the most intense concentration and expenditure of nervous energy, but, once the bug is in the blood, few exchange dealers would prefer any other form of activity!

All the time, the head dealer is having questions called to him by his assistants such as—

"How will you deal in three months Paris for (so-and-so) Zürich?"

"X branch want a price for cashing fifty dollars under a letter of credit."

"How will you take a couple of hundred dollars in Can. Pac. coupons from so-and-so?"

"Y branch want to sell a bill on Hamburg for five thousand marks due 22nd September."

"How will you take Basle against Paris?"

"How will you sell dollars for tomorrow and buy next Wednesday?"

"Z branch want to buy six thousand rupees Bombay their option August," and many more.

Also, cables are continually coming in which must be decoded and any orders or proposals of business considered and replied to, and this goes on from about 9.45 a.m. to nearly 6.0 p.m. on any ordinary business day.

In many cases, branches are allowed to deal in the main currencies at rates which are either sent out overnight or telephoned in the morning from the foreign branch, but the amounts which may be so dealt in are limited to comparatively small sums, and any demands from customers for larger amounts to be either bought or sold by the branch must be referred to the foreign branch before a quotation is made to the customer. The daily totals of the small amounts dealt in are sent off in the evening to the foreign branch to be included in the dealer's "position" there the next morning. Also, the assistant dealers are given a certain amount of discretion as to the rates which they may quote without reference to the head dealer, and the latter is content to leave as much as possible to his subordinates while remaining responsible for the policy and general conduct of the department.

Value Date

This is the term used to define *the date on which a payment over of funds or an entry to an account becomes actually effective and/or subject to interest.*

In the case of payments by T.T., the value date is usually the same in both centres, i.e. payment over of the respective currency in each centre takes place on the same day, so that no gain or loss of interest accrues to either party. Such payments are said to be *Valeur Compensée*, or "value compensated," or "money here and there the same day," or, simply, "here and there."

As regards entries to an account, the value date is shown in a special column distinct from that containing the date of entry, and such a column is included in the ruling of the ledgers used by banks here for recording entries to their "Nostro" accounts. Whenever advice of a credit or debit entry is received from a foreign agent, the value date will be distinctly stated, and this is the date from which the entry became effective, and is frequently not the date on which the entry was passed. For example, an agent in a principal town may have received for collection items payable in a secondary centre which will take a day or two to collect. The sub-agent will collect these items in due course, and will credit the account of his principal, the first agent, value as on the date of collection. The agent himself will only receive advice of this credit from his sub-agent in course of mail, but will then proceed to credit his principal, the remitter, value as on the date on which he himself received credit from the sub-agent. Thus, items sent from New York to Denver on 22nd June might be received by the sub-agent on 24th June, and collected and credited by him to the chief agent value 25th June. His advice of credit might not reach the chief agent until 29th June, but the latter would pass an entry *under this date* crediting his principal *value 25th June*.

On the other hand, the chief agent might know exactly how long it would take for items on Denver to be collected and credited to his account, and might be prepared to give his principal immediate credit, "with recourse," should the items eventually be returned unpaid. In such a case he would pass an entry on 22nd June crediting his principal value 25th June. The first example is known as an entry with a "back value," and the second is known as an entry with a "forward value."

In order to arrive at the true balance for interest purposes of such accounts, the entries must be analysed by means of a "ladder" system so that all debits and credits bearing the same value date are summarized under that date, and the net difference is extended and added to or subtracted from the true balance as on the previous value date. Interest is then calculated on each true balance for the number of days between each value date.

Arbitrage in Exchange and Cross Rates

As has already been stated, arbitrage consists in the simultaneous buying and selling of a commodity in two or more markets to take advantage of temporary discrepancies in prices. As applied to dealings in foreign exchange, arbitrage consists of the purchase of one currency for another in one centre accompanied by an almost immediate resale against the same currency in another centre, or in operations conducted through three or more centres and involving several currencies. A transaction conducted between two centres only is known as *simple* or *direct* arbitrage. Where additional centres are involved, the operation is known as *compound* or *three (or more) point* arbitrage. Such operations must be carried out with the minimum of delay if advantage is to be taken of temporary price differences, and they require a high degree of technical skill.

If a London bank dealer has sold French francs to a customer that he requires to cover, he may find that, as against a quotation of $13 \cdot 30\frac{1}{4}$–$\frac{1}{2}$ in the London market, sterling is quoted in Paris at $13 \cdot 30\frac{1}{2}$–$\frac{3}{4}$. It is thus obviously more profitable for him to sell sterling in Paris against francs and so obtain 13·30½ fcs. per £ instead of 13·30¼ offered in the London market. This is an instance of *direct* arbitrage because francs were first exchanged for sterling in London through the sale by the dealer to his customer and the sterling was then reconverted into francs by being sold to a bank in Paris. If a French dealer buys Swiss francs against French francs from a correspondent in Switzerland, that is also a case of *direct* arbitrage.

In *compound* arbitrage a series of currency exchanges take place, with the object either of securing cheaper cover for a deal which has already been done or of making a profit out of the differences in quotations in the various centres. The following table shows the possibility of a successful *compound* arbitrage operation—

London on Paris	. .	13·30¼–13·30½
London on Amsterdam	.	8·71 –8·71¼
London on Frankfurt	.	8·84½–8·84¾
Paris on Frankfurt	. .	150·285–150·335 (francs per 100 D-marks)
Paris on Amsterdam	.	101·38 –101·40 (D-marks per 100 guilders)

A London operator could buy French francs in London against sterling at 13·30¼. He could then use the francs to buy D-marks in Paris at 150·335, and with his D-marks he could buy Dutch guilders in Frankfurt at 101·40. The guilders he could then sell in London at 8·71¼. This operation introduces what are known as *arbitrated rates* and sometimes (less correctly) "cross rates." These are the rates of exchange produced by a comparison of the quotations for any two currencies in terms of a third. In the table given above, the cross rate for Paris on Frankfurt for a purchase of French francs and a sale of D-marks would be obtained by Chain Rule thus—

$$? \text{ francs} = 100 \text{ D-mark}$$
$$\text{If } 8 \cdot 84\tfrac{3}{4} \text{ D-mks} = £1$$
$$\text{and } £1 = 13 \cdot 30\tfrac{1}{4} \text{ francs}$$

which gives an answer of 150·353. The selling price of 150·335 in Paris is therefore favourable. The *cross rate* for the Paris selling quotation for D-marks and the London selling price for French francs works out at just over the *direct* rate of 8·84¾. The eventual purchase of Dutch guilders in Frankfurt gives a *cross rate* with sterling of 8·726, showing a profit of 1·35 in Dutch cents per £1. Out of this profit the operator must, of course, pay the cost of his telephone calls to the various centres and all his confirmatory cables and London brokerages.

It must again be emphasized, however, that this is a purely imaginary illustration and no such wide margins of profit are likely to exist in practice. Exchange dealers everywhere are constantly on the alert for price differences so that whenever they exist they quickly disappear through immediate arbitrage operations. It is the principle which must be studied in order that it may be put into practice should opportunity offer.

The London Foreign Exchange Market; its Constitution

The next paragraph, and several of those which follow, are taken from a talk on the London Foreign Exchange Market given by the author [H. E. Evitt] to members of The Institute of Bankers in London in 1953. They appear here by courtesy of the Institute.

In this London of ours it is possible physically to observe (and to hear) such markets as the Billingsgate fish market, the Smithfield meat market and the Covent Garden fruit, vegetable and flower market in actual operation. Other markets, such as the Stock Exchange, the Baltic Exchange and the London Metal Exchange, operate by the physical presence and personal contact of their members, though it is not usually possible for the general public to watch their proceedings. The London Foreign Exchange Market, however, consists only of a cobweb of telephone wires and is peopled only by disembodied voices. It has no meeting place or physical existence and the only personal contacts enjoyed by its members take place on golf courses, sports grounds or places of refreshment, but it is none the less a very real and active entity which transacts a volume and value of business at least as large as that of any other recognized market in this country. Even with the limitations imposed on its activities by the present exchange control regulations, it works at lightning speed, and although all its business is conducted by word of mouth over the telephone, with nothing in writing exchanged until possibly some hours later, the number of errors and misunderstandings is amazingly small and must average less than one in a thousand.

The two sides of the London Foreign Exchange Market consist of the exchange dealers of the banks and financial houses handling foreign exchange business on the one hand, and the recognized firms of foreign exchange brokers on the other. The bank dealers act as principals and are the actual buyers and sellers of foreign currencies against sterling. The brokers are purely intermediaries and work on a fixed scale of commission or brokerage. They must not act as principals and deal for their own account, but they may be held responsible by a bank dealer for an exchange loss resulting from error or negligence on their part. They may only act as brokers between those banks and financial houses that are recognized as members of the market and may not operate for the general public or for any banks or other concerns outside the United Kingdom.

This is still the case, and in return the banks at one time undertook not to deal between themselves but to put all their business through the market by using the services of brokers, though this undertaking has been modified since the market was reopened in December, 1951, and in case of need the banks may now deal direct with each other. Very little advantage is taken of this facility, however, and practically all bank dealings are effected through the medium of the brokers.

This has always been the composition of the market, but the numbers on both sides have varied considerably. Prior to the 1914 war comparatively little use was made of the telephone for foreign exchange business, and as the quotations for foreign currencies in London were largely ruled by those obtaining in foreign centres, the bank dealers relied more on advices from abroad than on those from the brokers in London. An actual meeting of dealers and brokers took place each Tuesday and Thursday afternoon at the Royal Exchange, at which "cheque" and "long" rates were fixed for the principal currencies and which remained more or less unchanged until the next meeting, unless something exceptional, such as a change in a bank rate or a minor financial crisis, occurred in the meantime. The few exchange brokers regarded themselves as members of the Money Market and, dressed in morning coat and topper and bearing a shiny black note-book, they paid dignified calls on their banking friends. Life for the foreign exchange merchant was indeed very leisurely in those days! By 1919, however, the volume of business had increased enormously as the world-wide loss of confidence and lack of free facilities led to commercial business being conducted almost entirely on a cash basis, while, owing to the steep rise in prices, the amounts involved had also become much larger. More and more banks opened foreign exchange departments, and more and more newcomers entered the ranks of the brokers. During the 1920s speculation in currencies assumed almost fantastic proportions, and several fortunes were made and lost, while the exchange brokers reaped a harvest.

During the height of the boom there were about 120 banks and over 60 brokers recognized as members of the London Foreign Exchange Market. For a time there were no formal representatives to control and to speak for either side of the market, but when the bank managements realized the profitable nature of the business and the responsibilities placed on their exchange dealers, they formed a committee to regulate and standardize dealing practice and invited the brokers to form a similar committee. Much was done by these two committees to introduce uniformity and discipline into the market, but the bank managements refused to delegate executive powers to their committee, while certain of the brokers refused to be bound by the decisions of their own committee. In consequence, the two committees ceased to function, and the market was left to its own devices. Following the suspension of gold payments in September, 1931, however, and the assumption by the Bank of England of responsibility for the control of exchange rates, an official request was made that these two committees should be reconstituted. The banks formed the *London Foreign Exchange Bankers' Committee*, while the brokers formed themselves into an association called the *London Foreign Exchange Brokers' Association* and appointed a committee to sit jointly with the bankers for the management of market affairs.

Although the London Foreign Exchange Market was closed down on the outbreak of war in September, 1939, the Bankers' Committee continued to function in regard to the administration of the Exchange Control regulations. The Brokers' Association went into cold storage, and most of the staffs of the firms of brokers found employment with the Bank of England Exchange Control. When a market, limited to dealings in the Canadian dollar, was opened in December, 1950, the three or four firms of brokers who had kept themselves alive by dealing in the few Sterling Area currencies during the war were quick to take advantage of the opportunity to return to a wider market. They were soon followed by three or four more of the older firms who furbished up their rusty machinery, in the form of both office equipment and technical skill. When the much broader market was reopened in December, 1951, the Bank of England requested that the Brokers' Association should be revived but that membership of the Association should be strictly limited. At the present time, therefore, the market is controlled by agreement between the bankers' and brokers' committees who are empowered to regulate the working conditions of the market, such as fixing "value dates" for dealings in every currency, the rates of brokerage to be paid, the method of handling outstanding payments in a centre in which, for instance, a moratorium has been declared or restrictions placed suddenly on payments to foreign account, and similar practical matters.

Discipline is imposed by the treatment of any member by the others. If a bank dealer persistently infringes the accepted code of conduct, other dealers will refuse to "take the name" of the offending bank or finance house as the counterpart to a deal. If a broker is negligent, or inefficient, or impertinent, the bank dealer or dealers whom he has offended will punish him by "plugging up his line" for a certain period or, in extreme cases, the broker may be told to remove his private line altogether. Such instances are, however, extremely rare and although under pressure of business tempers may sometimes get a little frayed, the high feeling soon passes, and the usual friendly atmosphere is restored.

The Working of the Market

Market business is now conducted entirely by telephone and by means of private telephone lines between the brokers' offices and the exchange-dealing rooms of the banks. These private lines are installed by the brokers at their own expense and by permission of the bank concerned. In the early days of private lines each line terminated on a separate receiving instrument of the "coffee-grinder" type, and leading dealers would have thirty or more of these instruments on a long table or shelf. With a dozen bells all ringing together the clamour was unbearable, and in the early 1920s a French device of an "electric" dealing table was adapted and brought into use almost generally. These electric tables are quite expensive to purchase and install but cost very little to maintain. From the "frame," on which the private telephone line installed by the Post Office terminates, extra leads are taken and connected to terminals on the table, according to the number of positions that are required in the particular dealing room.

It is difficult for those who have not seen this most efficient piece of mechanism in operation to appreciate the speed at which it can be used. With proper co-operation from the other end, it is possible for a broker to advise a change of rate to ten bank dealers in not more than thirty seconds, probably less.

The brokers, working solely in the London market, have none of the facilities available to the dealers for following the quotations in other markets. Apart from what they may have read in the morning newspapers, therefore, they must rely on the help of their friends, the dealers, in deciding on the quotations which they shall use for "opening the market" at about 9.30 a.m.

It is, of course, physically impossible for any one broking firm to handle efficiently all the currencies quoted in the London market, and although all brokers handle American and Canadian dollars, the other currencies are split between them, so that two firms are recognized as dealers in French francs, two others as dealers in Dutch florins, and so on. Taking the generally quoted currency, the U.S. dollar, the broker will jot down on his pad what he thinks should be the opening rates for spot and forward deals up to six months, and will then chat to one of his dealer friends on something of the following lines—

BROKER: "Good morning, Sir. What do you suggest for this morning? I was going to call spot three-quarters seven-eighths, the one month one-quarter one-eighth, two months seven- to five-sixteenths, three months five-eighths in the middle and about one-quarter a month over that for the four, five and six."

DEALER: "Yes, you should be O.K. on the spot. I will support you for fifty at three-quarters and you can let me know if you see any three months at nine-sixteenths. I think you're a bit out in your four, five and six. On a spot close of three-quarters thirteen-sixteenths, New York sends me six months outright at nine and five-eighths seven-eighths, which would make the spread either side of one."

Let us now explain this jargon in ordinary language. The U.S. dollar rate is, of course, quoted in so many dollars and cents and fractions of a cent per pound. Everyone concerned is well aware of the first two figures, such as the two and four of a quotation of $2 \cdot 40\frac{1}{4}$–$2 \cdot 40\frac{7}{8}$; the third figure is known as the "big figure" and is only called into question on a rapidly moving market where the rate is fluctuating between, say, $2 \cdot 40\frac{1}{4}$–$2 \cdot 41\frac{1}{2}$. Usually only the fractions of a cent are quoted, so that our broker in his opening suggestion means that he proposes a rate of $2 \cdot 40\frac{3}{4}$–$2 \cdot 40\frac{7}{8}$ as the opening quotation for the spot. This is confirmed by the subsequent remark of the dealer that the six months outright forward rate from New York was $9\frac{5}{8}$–$\frac{7}{8}$, meaning that the full rate was $2 \cdot 39\frac{5}{8}$–$2 \cdot 39\frac{7}{8}$ or either side of one per cent under spot. The forward quotations are evidently at a premium because the selling price (which is always quoted first) is higher than the buying price, namely one-quarter of a cent against one-eighth of a cent. This premium for one month, of course, becomes larger for the longer periods and our broker is evidently groping in regard to the long forward dates because he can only suggest that the three-months quotation should be increased by one-quarter of a cent for each additional month up to six months. This would give a middle rate of $1\frac{3}{8}$ cents for the six months period, whereas the indication from New York is that the margin is more in the neighbourhood of one cent only. The brokers quote in the ordinary way only for the exact one to six months forward dates and a transaction for any intervening forward date, known as a "broken date," needs the calculation of a special quotation and even this may not prove workable on an exact proportionate basis. The regular forward dates are, of course, based on the "value date" for spot transactions, which is the date on which the exchange of the foreign currency for sterling actually takes place in the foreign centre and in London, and which is usually two business days after the date on which the deal is entered into. This applies not only to dealings in the London market but also to dealings between banks here and banks abroad. It is important to remember that there must be two clear business days in both centres. For example, now that Saturday is a holiday in the London Foreign Exchange Market, as in so many foreign centres, the value date for Friday deals is the following Tuesday; but if that day happens to be an official holiday in the foreign centre (e.g. Shrove Tuesday or a National "Independence Day") then the value date would be Wednesday.

In effect, therefore, the broker is suggesting to the bank dealer that there might be sellers of spot dollars at 2·40¾ and buyers at 2·40⅞ per pound, with which the dealer agrees and offers support "for 50 at ¾," meaning that he is a seller of $50,000 at 2·40¾. Note that, as with the initial figures of the exchange quotation, the "thousands" in a bid or offer of a dealer are understood, and the market talks of 20, 50 or 100 without the addition of the word "thousand" and will also speak of giving or taking a quarter or a half without the addition of the word "million." Our broker then has one firm side to his market, in that he has a definite seller of $50,000 at 2·40¾. His forward quotations mean that he thinks there should be sellers for delivery one month ahead at a quarter of a cent under spot and buyers at one-eighth of a cent under spot, sellers for two months ahead at seven-sixteenths and buyers at five-sixteenths cents under spot, with the three months position rather more vague, with possible sellers at something higher than five-eighths and buyers at something lower than five-eighths cents under spot. His dealer friend again puts him almost firm in the three months position by intimating that he is a possible buyer of three months dollars against spot at nine-sixteenths of a cent against him.

Thanking him politely, the broker then goes in turn to other dealers to check up on their ideas and eventually will have on his pad a set of rates at which he is reasonably confident of being able to work. His whole object in life is to find firm sellers and buyers at close prices so that he can attract business by being able to quote reliable rates, and his success as a broker depends entirely on the confidence which he induces in the dealers as a result of consistently reliable prices.

By perseverance and possibly a certain amount of cajolery he will eventually find buyers of spot at his upper price of 2·40⅞ and may be lucky enough to obtain offers of, and bids for, the forward positions at his suggested prices. He and his colleagues can then resume their round of the bank dealers with much more confidence and can make their approach as follows—

BROKER: "Three-quarters seven-eighths I deal in spot. One month I offer at a quarter—might bid an eighth. Two months I might get on at seven- to five-sixteenths. Three months I am a probable dealer at eleven- to nine-sixteenths."

DEALER: "Oh, three-quarters seven-eighths for spot. What happens at thirteen?"

BROKER (taking a chance): "I'd like to try and get you fifty there."

DEALER: "Well, don't bid it, but if it comes I will take it."

The broker at once rings up the first dealer who offered to support him for fifty at three-quarters and talks to him on something of the following lines—

BROKER: "Well, Sir, the market seems to have settled down at three-quarters seven-eighths, fairly well supported on both sides, but at the moment I might be able to place your fifty at thirteen-sixteenths."

DEALER: "How strong are you at three-quarters apart from myself?"

BROKER (either truthfully or guessing): "Oh, I should think another hundred or so would come at the price."

DEALER: "O.K., shoot my fifty at thirteen."

BROKER: "Very good Sir." (Feverishly rings the other dealer who asked to be informed of sellers at thirteen-sixteenths.) "If you're still interested, Sir, there is a chance of getting fifty at thirteen."

SECOND DEALER: "How do you find the market apart from myself?"

BROKER: "Very steady, with a hundred or more either side at three-quarters seven eighths."

SECOND DEALER: "Oh, very well, I'll take fifty at thirteen."

BROKER (Ringing first dealer and using sledge-hammer methods): Thank you, Mr. So-and-So, I've sold your fifty dollars at thirteen-sixteenths to the X Bank."

FIRST DEALER: "O.K., that's done."

BROKER (Ringing second dealer): "Thank you very much, Mr. So-and-So, I've bought you fifty dollars at thirteen-sixteenths from the Y Bank."

SECOND DEALER: "Fifty dollars from the Y Bank at thirteen, O.K."

This is all that happens to effect a sale and purchase of $50,000, or about £20,000, between two London banks. You will note that the two principals have no direct contact with each other but rely implicitly on the word of the broker. The need for the highest standard of integrity and reliability on the part of all concerned is very evident.

Each bank dealer then records his sale and purchase respectively on his "dealing sheet" and makes out a dealing slip which is passed to another section of his department. The broker will record the deal in his "dealing book," from which a clerk will make out written contracts advising the selling bank that U.S. $50,000 have been sold for its account to the Y Bank, in the form of T.T. New York, at $2·40 13/16, value current "value date", on which a brokerage of 1‰ has been charged. The buying bank receives a similar contract stating that U.S. $50,000 have been bought for its account from the X Bank, in the form of T.T. New York at 2·40 13/16, value the current "value date," with a brokerage of 1‰. These contracts are delivered by hand from the broker's office to the banks concerned, possibly two or three hours later, and are the first written record of the transaction.

Then comes the question of the payment and receipt of the dollars in New York on the agreed value date. The selling bank must instruct one of its New York correspondents to effect the payment and the buying bank must instruct one of its New York correspondents to receive the dollars. All London banks maintain several accounts with New York banks and work them alternately. The leading banks in the market give standing instructions to each other as to the names of the New York correspondents whom they will request to make or to receive dollar payments on stated days of the week. In other cases the instructions sections of the foreign exchange dealing departments will telephone one another, on receiving either the "dealing slip" or the broker's contract relative to any particular deal, to arrange which banks in New York will pay and receive the currency respectively. When these details have been arranged, written confirmations of the deal are sent by each bank to the other, and the necessary instructions to the New York correspondents are sent off by cable.[1] Arrangements are also made by the buying bank to ensure that the sterling equivalent is paid over to the selling bank on the agreed "value date," and it is seldom, if ever, that any hitch occurs in the paying-over either of the dollars in New York or the sterling in London. Should it happen that by accident some delay occurs in the paying-over of either the dollars in New York or the

---

[1] Physically, Telex is used whenever possible.

sterling in London, the party deprived of the receipt of the funds will claim interest for the period of the delay from the other party at the current overdraft rate of interest in the centre concerned. The same mechanism is used for dealings in all other quoted currencies and also in the case of forward contracts at the date of their maturity, except that instructions for the payment and receipt of the foreign currency in the foreign centre are usually sent by air mail a few days before the contract date so as to save cable charges.

In the case of transactions with domestic customers, the confirmation is sent off by post the same night or delivered by hand on the next business day if the customer resides in the vicinity. If the deal has been done through a branch, the written confirmation is sent to that branch, which is then charged with the duty of obtaining a similar confirmation from the customer which must agree in all respects with the confirmation from the foreign branch. Dealings with correspondent banks abroad may be confirmed verbally at the end of a telephone conversation in the course of which the deal was done, and written confirmation is then sent by air mail. The execution of an order received by cable is usually advised also by cable, with written confirmation subsequently. Great care must be taken that an accurate record of each and every deal in regard to the amount of foreign currency involved and the rate of exchange applied is kept on the *position sheet* or in the *position book*. It is essential that the dealer should be able to learn from the clerk keeping the "position," without an instant's delay, exactly how he stands in regard to surpluses or shortages of any particular currency. A dealer who is already "long" of a currency will be less disposed to buy more than if he had a "short" position in that currency. He must, therefore, vary his quotations not only in regard to the amount of currency involved and the standing of the customer or correspondent, but also in regard to his "position" in that currency. He will usually endeavour to keep his "book" as balanced as possible, particularly under the restrictions on the purposes for which foreign currency may be bought and sold and the limitations on the complete freedom of action of the dealer which are still in force at the time of writing. Once again it must be said, however, that an ounce of experience is worth a ton of theory, and there can be no substitute for the training which must be gained within the London Foreign Exchange Market itself.

In conclusion to this chapter, it should be noted that the brokers and dealers in the dollar market sometimes lapse into quotations of the American type, where the pound is quoted to four places of decimal of the dollar. Thus, if the broker is quoting $2·40\frac{3}{4}$ to $2·40\frac{7}{8}$ for spot, and he meets with a bid for, say, fifty thousand dollars "between," the deal could be negotiated by his going back to his seller at three-quarters and finding him not willing to give way as far as thirteen-sixteenths but nevertheless inclined to give way to a small extent over the three-quarters mark at which he put the broker firm. In such a case, the deal could be finalized at 2·4078 or 2·4079 dollars to the £; the concession is not so great as if he gave way to thirteen-sixteenths which, expressed as a decimal, is 2·408125.

CHAPTER X

ELIMINATION OF EXCHANGE RISKS

Forward Exchange; Calculation of "Outright" and "Option"
Forward Rates; Factors affecting Forward Margins; "Swap
and Investment" Operations

THERE is nothing abstruse or difficult in either the principles or the methods of dealing in forward exchange. The object of a "forward" deal in any commodity is to fix at once a price for a contract to be carried through on the future date agreed upon, and is intended to free both buyer and seller from any risk of loss which might accrue through fluctuations in the price of the commodity by the time both parties are ready actually to complete the transaction.

Forward Exchange may therefore be defined as *an operation in exchange whereby a rate is fixed at once for a purchase and sale of one currency for another which is to be completed at some future date.*

Under such an operation the exchange of one currency for another is arranged for a stipulated date at a rate of exchange fixed immediately, and, no matter what the current rate of exchange may be at the date of the actual exchange of currencies, the exchange is carried through at the rate fixed when the contract was entered into. It thus enables a creditor who has to receive payment of his debt in terms of a foreign currency at a future date, to fix at once the value of his debt in terms of his own currency, or enables a debtor who has to discharge a debt at some future date in terms of a foreign currency to fix at once the cost to him in terms of his own currency of discharging the debt when due. Each party can thus be rendered free from any risk of subsequent loss through fluctuations in exchange rates before the debt matures but, obviously, only one party to a debt need operate, and either the creditor can sell forward his right to the currency of the debtor or the debtor can buy forward the right to the currency of the creditor which he will eventually need to discharge his debt.

Uses of Forward Exchange

By such operations an importer of goods who has bought in terms of a foreign currency can fix at once the eventual cost to him of the goods by purchasing forward the amount of foreign currency he will require at a rate of exchange fixed at once. Similarly, an exporter who has sold goods abroad in terms of the foreign currency can determine his "outturn" in terms of his own currency by a forward sale of the foreign currency at a rate of exchange fixed immediately. Also a person who wishes to invest funds abroad for a short period can eliminate any risks of loss through fluctuations in rates of exchange by effecting a forward sale of the foreign currency which he is buying as "spot" for the purpose of the investment, so that when his investment matures, he has already fixed the rate of reconversion into his own currency.

Method of Dealing in Forward Exchange

As with all other exchange operations, the banks are the natural clearing houses for dealings in forward exchange. A bank will buy and sell "forward" currencies in the same way that it will buy and sell "spot" currencies. A customer or another bank, or any member of the exchange markets of the world, can offer to buy from or sell to that bank "forward" currency, i.e. currency for future delivery, and within limits will be quoted a rate as easily as for a "spot" transaction.

For example, an importer of goods from Germany may have received a quotation for a consignment from a likely seller there on terms which grant him three months credit, so that he will have to pay for the goods in marks in three months time if he accepts the offer. He can request his bank to quote him a rate at which it will sell to him German marks for delivery three months ahead and, on the basis of this rate, he can work out the eventual cost of the goods to him in sterling. If this is satisfactory, he will close with the bank's offer of the forward currency, and with the offer of the seller of the goods, and he will then know that, no matter what the current market rate for German marks may be on the date when he will have to discharge his debt, he has already fixed the rate of exchange at which he will have to pay for his marks.

Again, a bank in New York may wish to invest funds in three months London bills for the sake of a higher rate of interest to be obtained in London than in New York. To buy such bills it must first buy sterling and, if it does not "cover its exchange," it may lose all the profit from the higher interest rate, and even more, if the rate of exchange has moved adversely to it by the time the bills mature, and it wishes to reconvert the sterling into dollars. Thus, if it makes a purchase of sterling at the rate of $2·40 to the £ in order to invest in London when interest rates are 1 per cent per annum higher there than in New York, and uses the funds at this margin in London for three months, it will have made a profit for one quarter of a year at the rate of 1 per cent per annum, i.e. $\frac{1}{4}$ per cent on its investment, provided that it can buy back its dollars at not worse than $2·40 per £. If, however, the rate has moved to $2·38¼ per £, it will lose 1¾ cents on each pound it has purchased, which, over the period, is more than the gain in interest, since ¼ per cent of 2·40 is only ·006 cents per £. In order to eliminate this risk of loss, therefore, an investing bank or even a private short-term investor will combine the purchase of the "spot" currency in which it is proposed to invest, with a forward sale of the same currency for the date on which the investment will mature, thus fixing at once the eventual rate of reconversion of the foreign funds into the home currency.

A forward exchange deal is a definite contract, and a letter or form of contract is taken by the bank concerned from the party with whom the contract is made. As between banks or members of the market, a simple letter of confirmation of the deal is considered sufficient, but in the case of private customers, including commercial firms and all others than banks and market members, a definite form of contract undertaking due performance must be signed and handed to the bank. In many cases a certain "margin" is demanded by the contracting bank as security for the eventual performance of the contract, and this takes the form of a cash margin, held on a special account and bearing interest at an agreed rate, which must be maintained at anything from 10 per cent to 25 per cent of the *current* sterling value of the operation, according to the view taken by the bank of the standing of the customer. Once a forward contract is accepted by both parties, it must eventually be carried through, and a contracting bank therefore accepts a certain risk of loss should the other party fail to carry out his side of the bargain. For example, if a customer buys from a bank German marks for delivery in three months time at a rate of 8·74 per £, but fails to take delivery on the maturity date and leaves the marks on the bank's hands, the bank must sell them at the market price then current, which may be 8·76 per £, in which case the bank would stand to lose 2 pfennige on each pound's worth of marks sold to the customer. It is for this reason that a "margin" is often required so that it could be applied against any such loss, and in any case forward contracts with any other party are all subject to "limits" or "sanctions" from the managerial department. Where a "margin" is taken it is, of course, released when the forward contract has been finally discharged.

The details of a forward transaction with a bank are simply that a rate is fixed at once at which the foreign currency will be bought from or sold to the other party; the date on which the contract is to be completed must be stated and agreed upon before the rate is quoted and is an integral part of the contract; no money passes between the parties until the date of maturity arrives (except for any cash margin which may be demanded by the bank), but on that date the funds are paid over in the foreign centre, against payment of funds in the home centre on the same day, at the rate of exchange fixed under the contract. The bank will, of course, keep records of all such transactions, both in an account under the name of each customer dealt with, and in a "forward" account for each currency in its "Nostro" ledgers, so that its exchange position in "spot" and "forward" currency can be easily ascertained. No entries will be passed by the agent in the foreign centre until the date of maturity arrives, as he will not be advised to pay or receive the foreign funds until that date.

Forward dealings are carried out in the various exchange markets in the same way as "spot" deals, rates being arranged and contracts passed between brokers and banks, and between the banks themselves as for "spot" deals. The question of "name" is of greater importance for forward deals than for spot owing to the greater risk of loss through the position of one contracting party changing for the worse during the currency of the contract, and so rendering him unable to carry out his side of the bargain.

Forward Exchange Quotations

Forward rates of exchange are quoted as a "margin" or "difference" against the "spot" rate of the currency concerned, or as a "premium" or "discount" on the "spot" rate, or they may be quoted "outright," i.e. an actual forward rate of exchange in the currency, obtained by allowing for the forward "margin" over or under the current "spot" rate.

The following table, representative of those which appear in the daily Press, gives the market quotations for the forward "margins" in the principal world currencies.

It will be noted that the quotations are in terms of "pm," i.e. "premium," which means that the forward margin is *dearer* than, or *under*, the spot rate, or of "par," which means that the forward rate is on the same level, i.e. at par with the spot rate, or of "dis," i.e. "discount" meaning that the forward margin is *cheaper* than, or *over*, the spot rate. Remembering that "premium" is synonymous with "dearer" and "discount" with "cheaper," it can be seen that when the forward margin is *over* the spot rate (at a discount), the outright forward rate will be cheaper from a general point of view than the spot rate, and that when the forward margin is *under* the spot rate (at a premium), the outright forward rate will be dearer than the spot rate, speaking generally. This applies, however, only to

FORWARD RATES

	One month	Three Months
New York	$\frac{3}{16} - \frac{1}{16}$ c. pm	$\frac{3}{8} - \frac{1}{4}$ c. pm
Montreal	$\frac{1}{8}$ c. pm–par	$\frac{1}{8} - \frac{3}{16}$ c. pm
Amsterdam	$1\frac{3}{4}$–$1\frac{1}{4}$ c. pm	$4\frac{1}{4}$–$3\frac{3}{4}$ c. pm
Brussels	15 c. pm–par	25 05 c. pm
Copenhagen	2 ore pm–3 ore dis	3–8 ore dis
Frankfurt	1–$\frac{1}{2}$ pt. pm	$2\frac{1}{2}$–2 pf. pm
Lisbon	35 pm–35 c. dis	25 pm–40 c. dis
Milan	$5\frac{1}{2}$–$2\frac{1}{2}$ lire pm	8–5 lire pm
Oslo	5 ore pm–par	5 ore pm–par
Paris	$\frac{1}{2}$ c. pm–par	$\frac{1}{2}$ c. pm–par
Stockholm	$\frac{1}{2}$ ore pm–$\frac{1}{2}$ ore dis	1 ore pm–par
Vienna	30 gro pm–par	40 gro pm–par
Zurich	$\frac{1}{2}$ c. pm–par	$2\frac{1}{4}$–$1\frac{3}{4}$ c. pm

rates quoted in terms of foreign units to the pound, i.e. "currency" rates, and the maxims must be reversed when dealing with "pence" rates, but the number of forward deals in these latter rates is comparatively small, so that forward margins in "pence" rates are not usually quoted in the market or in the Press. The banks specializing in currencies for which the quotations are in pence are always ready to quote forward rates on request, and such rates are compiled in the same manner as for "currency" rates, which is set out below.

To show how the quotations given above should be used, the following examples may be taken.

The margins shown are in terms of the subsidiary unit of the currency concerned or in fractions thereof. Where the margin is at a discount, as in the case of Copenhagen, the rates quoted mean that for Danish kroner for delivery three months from date the margin is "sellers at 3 oere over spot" and "buyers at 8 oere over spot".

The market quotations are for the standard periods of one or three months from spot date, but it is possible to obtain quotations for up to six months from spot date or for any "broken" period in between, e.g. if the spot date is 6th July, the usual quotations would be for delivery on 6th August, 6th September and 6th October, but rates could be obtained for, say 6th November, or 6th January, or 22nd August, or 31st December, etc. The rates for periods other than those normally quoted are not always in strict proportion to the normal rates, and an outside buyer should expect to pay rather worse and a seller to obtain rather worse than the strictly proportionate rate for a "broken" period.

Returning to the example above, if the market quotes the spot (or T.T.) rate on Copenhagen as 18·00–01 per £, the market "outright" forward rates for the recognized periods would be—

	Sellers	Buyers
T.T.	18·00	18·01
3 months forward . . .	18·03	18·09

These rates are obtained by adding to the rate at which dealers are willing to sell T.T. the margin which they are prepared to give away to sell forward, and by adding to the rate at which they are prepared to buy T.T. the margin which they require over spot if they are asked to buy forward. It is always possible for a dealer to negotiate in the market in order to arrange a deal at a price midway between the extremes of prices in each case, in the same way as with spot, and his success or otherwise will depend on the tendency of the market and on the desire of another dealer to operate in the reverse way. For example, the three months "outright" forward rate in Danish kroner would probably be quoted as $18·04\frac{1}{2}$–08, instead of 18·03–09, as dealers on both sides would normally give way to the extent of 1 or $1\frac{1}{2}$ oere. In quoting "outright" forward rates to customers, a bank dealer, therefore, can usually be certain of obtaining a small margin of profit by undoing his deal in the market at a slightly better price, if he quotes the customer the extremes of the spot rate and the forward margin, but he may on occasion have to allow an additional margin of profit one way if the market appears to have a decided tendency in that direction.

In the case of, say, the Zürich rate for which the quoted margin is at a premium for the most part, the "outright" rates would be quoted *under* or *dearer* than spot and with a spot rate of $10·34\frac{1}{2}$ Swiss francs per £ would be—

	Sellers	Buyers
T.T.	10·34	$10·34\frac{1}{2}$
1 month forward . . .	$10·33\frac{1}{2}$	$10·34\frac{1}{2}$
3 months forward . . .	$10·31\frac{3}{4}$	$10·32\frac{3}{4}$

Note that the "outright" forward rates are obtained by a seller deducting from the spot rate at which he is willing to sell, the premium he requires for a sale for future delivery, and by a buyer deducting from the spot rate at which he is willing to buy the amount of premium which he is prepared to pay for the privilege of taking delivery at some future date. In the case of the one month position, buyers are not willing to pay any premium at all, and the forward rate is therefore at par with, i.e. the same as, the spot rate. Here again, dealings in the market could probably be effected at rates between the two extremes so that a bank dealer could undo an operation carried out with a customer and show a profit by selling to or buying from the customer at these extremes of prices and covering himself in the market at some intermediate rate.

Option Forwards

In many commodity markets and on some Stock Exchanges, it is possible to deal in an "option to deal," that is, by the payment of a sum of money, the giver purchases the right to deal in a certain quantity of the commodity or in a certain number of shares at a stated price, on or up to a stated future date. He is not bound to exercise his option to deal, but can get clear of his bargain merely by sacrificing the "option money."

In the Foreign Exchange market in this country, however, none of the banks will grant an "option to deal" in any foreign currency. They will only grant an *option as to the date of the eventual completion of the contract*, so that the dealings known as "option forwards" are "optional" only as to the date of completion by the other contracting party, and are never "options" as to the eventual completion of the contract, *which must be carried through* at the latest by the last day of the option to complete.

An "option forward" is therefore a contract under which one contracting party cannot state definitely at the time of entering into the contract on what exact date he will be able to complete the contract, and he therefore obtains the consent of the other party that *the contract may be completed on any date between two specified dates, or during a stated period*, at the option of the party to whom such option is granted. The giver of the option must obviously protect himself under such circumstances by taking the view that the contract may be completed on the worst possible day from his point of view, and must quote a price accordingly. Where an option is granted for completion of the contract on any day within one month from spot, for instance, and the spot rate is 20·50 per £ while the forward margin is 1–2 points discount, in the case of an option *sale* forward, the seller must take the view that the purchaser may demand delivery on the first day of the option, which would be the normal spot date, and so no discount at all can be allowed, but the spot selling price of 20·50 alone can be quoted; but in the case of a forward *purchase*, the buyer must take the view that the seller may not deliver until the last day of the option, in which case the full one month would have expired, and the full discount of 2 points would accrue to the buyer, and he must therefore quote a rate of 20·52 for buying a one month forward option.

In order to show clearly the difference between "outright" or "fixed" forwards and "option" forwards, the following table gives the rates which would be quoted by a bank to a customer for each class of operation, based on 1 month 1–3 oere discount, 2 months 2–4 oere discount, and 3 months 3–6 oere discount for Copenhagen—

	Sellers	Buyers
T.T.	18·00	18·00½
1 month forward fixed . . .	18·01	18·03½
1 month forward option . . .	18·00	18·03½
2 months forward fixed . . .	18·02	18·04½
2 months forward option for period.	18·00	18·04½
Option over second month only .	18·01	18·04½
3 months forward fixed . . .	18·03	18·06½
3 months forward option for period .	18·00	18·06½
Option over second and third months	18·01	18·06½
Option over third month only . .	18·02	18·06½

Note how the dealer gives away the smallest possible discount for selling any "option" forward but takes the fullest discount possible and for the full period when buying, whether the purchase is of a "fixed" or an "option" forward.

Where the forward margins are at a premium, based on 1 month 1c. pm–par, 2 months $1\frac{1}{4}$–$\frac{1}{4}$c. pm, and 3 months $1\frac{1}{2}$–$\frac{1}{2}$c. pm for Zurich —the table would read as follows

	Sellers	Buyers
T.T.	10·34	10·34½
1 month forward fixed . . .	10·33	10·34½
1 month forward option . . .	10·33	10·34½
2 months forward fixed . . .	10·32¾	10·34¼
2 months forward option for period.	10·32¾	10·34½
Option over second month only .	10·32¾	10·34½
3 months forward fixed . . .	10·32½	10·34
3 months forward option for period.	10·32½	10·34½
Option over second and third months	10·32½	10·34½
Option over third month only . .	10·32½	10·34¼

Calculation of Forward Rates

The relation of any forward rate to the spot rate for the same currency, i.e. the forward "margin" or "spread," depends, first, on the relative rates of interest obtainable on similar classes of securities in the two centres, and, secondly, on the relation between the demand for and the supply of forward currency in the world's markets.

The interest factor is the basic factor in arriving at a forward margin. If the rate of discount in Paris for three-months prime bank bills is 8 per cent per annum, while similar paper in London can be purchased at a rate of discount of 7 per cent per annum, there will be a flow of funds from London to Paris of such floating balances as are normally used in this type of investment, to take advantage of the higher yield shown by French bills. As long as movements in the exchange value of sterling in terms of the French franc are confined to within comparatively narrow limits, a certain proportion of transfers of such funds will be carried out "uncovered" as regards the exchange; that is, the London investor will run the risk of being able to buy back as many pounds per franc, when he wishes to repatriate his funds, as it cost him when he originally purchased the French francs in order to buy franc bills. This leads to a certain demand for spot francs, as has already been explained, with a consequent rise in the value of the French franc in terms of the pound.

In other cases and under less stable conditions, London investors will make a transfer of funds only if they can secure their exchange for eventual reconversion into sterling of the French francs they purchase; that is, they insist on covering their spot purchase of French francs by a forward sale of francs for a date approximating to the estimated maturity of the French investment. This means that there will be a general tendency in the world's exchange markets for operators to be asked to buy sterling on the spot against a resale of the sterling for a future date, both against francs. As a result spot pounds will be offered and forward pounds wanted, giving a tendency for the forward pound to be dearer than the spot, i.e. forward pounds will tend to go to a premium over spot as against francs, and a dealer wishing to carry out a "swap" in sterling against francs will have to give more sterling to buy his spot francs than he will receive for his forward resale of the francs against sterling.

Consequently, a certain loss is incurred in selling spot and buying forward pounds, and this loss must be set against the interest profit which will accrue by moving funds from London to Paris; but operators will give away only a part of their gross interest profit, in the form of a premium on the forward currency, and *the premium thus set up will never therefore, under normal conditions, represent a percentage cost equal to the percentage gain in interest, but will remain at a somewhat lower level.* The extent to which the premium on the forward currency will, under such conditions, approach a percentage equal to the percentage margin of interest, depends on the volume of funds in the low-interest centre available for transfer to the high-interest centre and the consequent pressure of the demand to buy spot and sell forward currency on the latter centre. Force of competition between investors, should the volume of available funds be large or the interest margin of profit be considerable, will cause the net difference between the percentage gain in interest and the percentage loss in the forward margin to become so narrow as to represent a minimum margin of net profit. Thus, taking the interest rates quoted above and working on a spot franc rate of 13·28, the gross interest gain of 1 per cent per annum is equal to $\frac{1}{4}$ per cent for an investment of three months, and $\frac{1}{4}$ per cent for three months is equal to three months forward margin on the spot rate of 13·28 of 3·32 cents. Therefore, an investor who purchased French francs spot at 13·28 and sold them three months forward at 13·3132 would lose on the exchange transaction the equivalent of 1 per cent per annum or $\frac{1}{4}$ per cent for three months. (Sterling is dearer forward —each pound spot realizing 13·28 francs whereas to purchase three months forward each pound will cost 13·3132 francs.) Under these circumstances the additional interest gained by transferring funds from London to Paris is completely nullified by the loss in the exchange transaction. However, should the forward spread be $2\frac{1}{2}$ cents only this is equivalent to approximately $\frac{3}{4}$ per cent per annum so that the net additional return on the investment in Paris would be $\frac{1}{4}$ per cent per annum. An investor may consider that this additional return makes the operation worthwhile.

Other Factors affecting Forward Margins

Apart from the effects of differences in interest rates on the forward margin, other factors may arise to cause offerings of or demands for outright forward currency which may then cause variations in the forward margin as based on the interest differential. For example, if, under the conditions given above, London financial interests had reason to suppose that funds would be strongly wanted at home in the course of three months or so, those houses having funds in Paris might wish to make sure of retransferring them to London by the time the need arose, and so might be good sellers of forward francs against sterling. The resultant demand for forward sterling against francs would tend to send the forward margin, a discount on the French franc, even higher, and if such demand were strong enough, it might overwhelm the interest basis and send the discount to 4·15 cents for the three months, equal to a loss of $1\frac{1}{4}$ per cent per annum. On the other hand, if the spot rate were 13·53, investors might take the view that this rate was so near the present upper "official" limit for the French franc/sterling exchange that the risk of exchange loss on an investment would be negligible, while speculators for a rise in the value of the franc would be ready to buy forward francs at a few points above the spot rate and just below the official maximum of 13·54232 for three months ahead outright. This would mean that the forward margin would stand at, for example, under $\frac{1}{2}$ cent discount, equal to approximately $\frac{1}{8}$ per cent per annum in spite of the interest margin of 1 per cent per annum.

In general, therefore, it may be stated that the margin between the spot and forward rates for any currency *will be at a premium on spot when the rate of interest here is higher than that ruling in the foreign centre, and will be at a discount over spot when interest rates in the foreign centre are higher than those ruling here for similar classes of securities,* but the percentage per annum equivalent of the forward margin will fall short of the full percentage per annum difference in the rates of interest.

Between the two wars, however, the normal rules for calculating forward margins went by the board owing to the enormous and sudden movements of capital from one centre to another, the prevalence of restrictions on exchange dealings, the activities of speculators, etc. This again provides another instance of the moderating influence of effective gold points. As long as gold can move freely at fixed prices between two centres, capital-owners feel secure, there is no need for any artificial control of exchanges, and there is very little margin for exchange fluctuations of which speculators can take advantage. But at the first hint that one or other country may be forced to suspend gold payments, capital takes fright and "flight," the resulting strain on the exchanges leads to government control and the imposition of exchange restrictions and often precipitates the actual event which it is the object of such capital to avoid, while speculators are in their element and "bear" the doubtful currency and "bull" some supposedly safe currency for all they are worth.

Under such conditions forward margins cease to be governed by any recognized factors, and it may eventually become impossible to deal in forwards at all. Since foreign exchange is the *exchange* of currencies, no currency can be sold without another being bought, and a "flight" of capital from one centre or a "bear" speculative movement against one currency must result in a demand for another currency or currencies. Where capital is invested in bills or securities which have to be realized, some delay may take place before that capital is rendered liquid and capable of being exchanged for another currency. Consequently, the owner, under conditions which have caused him to lose confidence, will sell forward the currency at present held (in the expectation of his funds having become liquid by that time) against a forward purchase of some more desirable currency. It should be clear that to an owner of capital who is seeking to avoid a capital loss of 25, 50 or more per cent, the percentage cost per annum of a forward margin is a matter of small importance, and the movements in forward margins in the currencies concerned can be as wide and as frequent as those in the spot rates.

Similarly, a speculator against any currency is necessarily looking for a heavy depreciation in the exchange value of that currency. If he expects a capital profit of perhaps 50 per cent in six months, he will disregard entirely the ordinary relationship of the forward to the spot rate since he must use the former to finance his operations. The usual *modus operandi* of the speculator is to sell "outright" forward at every opportunity but, as these are infrequent, to first buy spot and sell forward, for as far ahead as can be arranged, in the currency to be attacked, against some more stable currency. He then sells the spot so purchased and leaves himself short of the forward, this constituting his "short position," while in the "safe" currency he arranges to remain "long" of forward. The spot sale of the "doubtful" currency is made against a spot purchase of the "safe" currency, which cancels out the spot side of the "swap" in the "safe" currency and leaves the operator long of the forward purchase of the "safe" currency against his short position forward in the "doubtful" currency.

For example, suppose that an operator wishes to "bear" French francs and "bull" U.S. dollars. The conditions ruling at the time are that the U.S.A. has firmly re-established herself on gold, but France has had difficulty in balancing her Budget, has lost large quantities of gold, and is not so firmly anchored to a gold standard as she was; also, interest rates for prime three-months paper are 1 per cent per annum in New York, 1 per cent per annum in London, and 3 per cent per annum in Paris, while the exchange rates are $5 per £, fcs. 76 per £, fcs. 15·20 per $; three months forward margins in London are on Paris 25–35 c. discount, and on New York 4½–5 c. discount (owing to a previous "flight" from the dollar now stopped owing to returning confidence).[1]

The operator first commences to buy spot and sell three months forward francs and to sell spot and buy three months forward dollars. Since the conditions posed above indicated probable loss of confidence in France and increasing confidence in the U.S.A., bids for forward francs and offerings of forward dollars will be limited to current trade needs—a most inadequate counterpart to the sums in which the exchange speculator wishes to deal. Being concerned with a large capital profit, the operator is not disposed to haggle over a few centimes or cents in the forward margins as long as he can rapidly provide himself with the sinews of war in the shape of a "long" franc or a "short" dollar spot position and can get in before the man next to him. Consequently, he presses both his "swaps" in the world's markets at steadily cheaper prices, i.e. he offers increasingly large discounts on his sale of forward

[1] All these rates are imaginary and are used as a simple illustration.

francs and will take a successively smaller discount on his purchases of forward dollars against spot. At various stages he will encounter buyers of forward francs and sellers of forward dollars, each against spot, in the shape, on the one hand, of people who are willing to lend francs against sterling or dollars for three months for the sake of the interest yield shown by the forward margin and, on the other hand, by those who are prepared to borrow dollars against sterling or francs for the sake of the comparative cheapness shown by the reduced discount on the forward.

Eventually, these operations (probably multiplied many times over by those of other speculators) may result in the discount on forward francs reaching even fcs. 1·75 for three months and that on forward dollars being reduced to $\frac{1}{2} - \frac{3}{4}$ c. for three months. At these rates the forward franc margin bears no relation to the comparative interest rates, while the forward dollar margin is much nearer to its proper level. On the interest rates given, investors should be disposed to buy spot and sell three months forward francs until the margin represents nearly 2 per cent per annum, i.e. $\frac{1}{2}$ per cent for the three-months period, which, on fcs. 76 per £, was approximately correctly represented by the former margin of 25–35 c., whereas a margin of fcs. 1·75 for three months represents a giving away of interest at the rate of over 9 per cent per annum. On the other hand, the former distrust of the future of the dollar was shown by the forward margin of $4\frac{1}{2} - 5$ c. discount for three months, which is at the rate of 18 – 20 c. for one year, which on a rate of $5 is equal to giving away interest at from $3\frac{3}{4}$ to 4 per cent per annum. The eventual margin of $\frac{1}{2} - \frac{3}{4}$ c. is equal only to a giving away of interest at the rate of either side of $\frac{1}{2}$ per cent per annum, and is much more in relationship with the relative interest rates. Our speculator at last, or concurrently, proceeds to sell out his spot francs and buy in his spot dollars, and again the size of his operations overwhelms the normal demand for and supply of these currencies. Francs tend to depreciate and dollars to appreciate, and most probably these movements tend to enhance the existing lack of confidence in France and increasing confidence in the U.S.A. Eventually, the speculator's anticipations may prove to be correct. France has to raise her price for gold, thus devaluing the currency, and francs become permanently cheaper in terms of other currencies. Assuming that only a moderate devaluation of, say, 20 per cent is necessary, i.e. an increase of 25 per cent in the gold price,[1] our operator will find the

[1] If, for instance, a monetary unit is said to contain 100 grains of gold but is devalued by 20%, it will then only contain 80 grains and it will take 1·25 of the new units to purchase 100 grains of gold, i.e. a rise of 25% in the price of gold.

new level for francs is about fcs. 91 per £, and fcs. 18·25–·30 per $, with the dollar still at $5 per £. He can, therefore, close out his short position in francs and long position in dollars (obtained by leaving uncovered his forward sales of francs and forward purchases of dollars) and after some oscillations due to these covering operations, the rates will settle down around their new parities. There being no further inducement to "bear" francs, the pressure to sell forward francs will subside, and the forward margin will narrow in towards its proper level on an interest basis. This description illustrates speculation in exchange and its effects at their simplest, but in actual practice the repercussions are much more complex and widespread as all allied exchanges, both spot and forward, become involved, e.g. Belgium, Holland, and Switzerland in the instance given.

While, therefore, the relative interest rates in two centres is the basis of calculation of the forward margin in the exchange between them under stable conditions, this basis ceases to exert any influence as soon as conditions become abnormal, and indeed for the past few years the abnormal has been so much in evidence as almost to have come to be regarded as the normal. In the instance given above, if the operator loses, on the average, 8½ per cent per annum on his franc "swap" and gains ½ per cent per annum on his dollar "swap," this represents a net loss of 2 per cent on the three-months period. If he has to renew his "swaps" for a further three months, should events not have progressed as rapidly as he expected, he is still losing only 4 per cent on his capital for a six-months speculation, and if at the end of that time he makes a gross profit of 20 per cent, his net profit will be about 15 per cent on the amount of currency he has dealt in, even after allowing for the 4 per cent cost of his "swaps" and all other expenses. No rules can be laid down for the calculation of forward margins under such conditions, as the extent of their fluctuations is governed only by the estimate of the speculator as to the probable capital profit on his operations and the extent to which he is prepared to deal.

A further incalculable factor exists where official restrictions are imposed either on dealings in exchange or on the granting of overdrafts and credits. In the ordinary way, if an exchange dealer can obtain an overdraft or clean credit in a foreign centre at, say, 6 per cent per annum, he will be prepared to use such facilities to enable him to sell that currency on the spot and buy it back forward if the discount offered on the forward, plus the profit on the use of the home funds which he will receive, shows him a greater yield than the cost of borrowing the funds abroad. For example, if a London operator can obtain an overdraft in Switzerland at 6 per cent per annum and a "bear" movement against the Swiss franc is taking place causing forward Swiss francs to be offered at 20 c. for three months with a spot rate of Sw. fcs. 10·36 per £, and three-months bills can be purchased in London to yield 1 per cent per annum, the operator can make profitable use of his overdraft facilities in Switzerland. He borrows Swiss francs for three months at 6 per cent per annum, which costs him $1\frac{1}{2}$ per cent on his capital. He sells these francs as spot, against sterling, and buys them back three months forward, thus covering his exchange and showing him a profit of 20 c. for the period, which is nearly 2 per cent on his capital. In addition he has the use of the sterling equivalent of his spot sale of francs until it is needed to pay for his forward purchase. This sterling he can use at 1 per cent per annum, which gives him $\frac{1}{4}$ per cent on his capital for the period. He therefore makes $2\frac{1}{4}$ per cent gross on his capital against a cost of $1\frac{1}{2}$ per cent, showing him a profit of $\frac{3}{4}$ per cent, which is at the rate of 3 per cent per annum, neglecting expenses.

Where official exchange restrictions have been imposed, however, overdraft and credit facilities for financial purposes are usually unobtainable. Under British Exchange Control regulations existing at the time of writing, and even after the considerable relaxations which have taken place since the end of 1951, banks are still restricted as to the amounts in "specified" currencies which they may hold abroad as working balances or as spot cover for forward sales, while the amount of any "uncovered position" which may be outstanding at any time is severely limited, as is the period of its duration. In addition, British banks may not arrange to take overdrafts from their correspondents in non-sterling countries, nor may they extend overdrafts or any other form of credit facility to non-sterling correspondents or customers without the specific permission of the Exchange Control. This can create, and has in fact created, quite artificial conditions in forward quotations as the ability to switch funds from one centre to another in accordance with current interest yields is completely lacking.

Similar restrictions exist also in other countries. In France, for instance, banks are not allowed to cover abroad any forward operations except those relating to permitted commercial or financial transactions, and then only if it is found impossible to find cover on the French Foreign Exchange Market. This restriction prevents French banks from accepting forward deals, either outright or against spot, which may be offered to them from abroad because such deals would not be based on a French commercial or financial transaction. In consequence, at a time when there was considerable distrust of the French franc for political and economic reasons in the early summer of 1954 there was strong speculative forward selling of French francs from many quarters, notably Switzerland and the U.S.A., which swamped the available commercial counterparts. These sales could not be carried out in France and were mostly offered in London, with the result that French francs for delivery in one and three months were offered at 15 fcs. discount and 27 fcs. discount, respectively, without bringing out buyers. At the same time business was being done in Paris in sterling for forward delivery at a premium (representing the reciprocal of the discount in London on forward French francs) of only 7 fcs. and 12 fcs. for the one and three months positions respectively. Any restrictions of such a nature hamper the efficient working of the foreign exchange markets of the world and are a more or less severe handicap to the commercial community according to the degree of distortion which takes place.

The most unfortunate aspect of a general loss of confidence in a currency or of official restrictions on exchange dealings is the effect on the forward market, which usually at once becomes almost nominal with a corresponding handicap to traders who are genuinely in need of forward exchange facilities to cover imports or exports. It is no part of the business of a trader to speculate in exchange. If he contracts to buy or sell goods from or to a foreign country in terms of the foreign currency, he should do so because he already has, or his experience tells him he will shortly have, a profitable counterpart to such a deal in terms of some other currency. Since trade must be anticipatory, merchants must deal in goods for future delivery, and it should be the business of the financial community to provide the merchant not only with the finance needed to carry part of his stock, but also with the exchange facilities he requires in order that he can fix at once the cost or yield of any foreign currency with which his trading involves him, both spot and forward. Under normal conditions the banking world supplies such facilities with freedom—perhaps too freely—but they should not be allowed to lapse almost entirely during a time of crisis, as is usually the case. It should be the concern of every State Bank to afford such credit and overdraft facilities to approved banking agents as would enable the latter to provide even restricted forward exchange facilities to genuine commercial interests, where bona fides could easily be proved by the production of contracts or shipping documents. Unfortunately, it seems that financial interests have now everywhere come to overshadow commercial interests, and in the consideration of the colossal amounts of non-productive financial debt, the claims of the more modest but far more essential commercial items are made the subject of nationalistic negotiation.

How Banks Cover Forward Dealings

Where, say, an importer who will have to pay in a foreign currency at some future date for the goods which he has purchased, buys that currency forward from his bank, he is thereafter no longer affected by any movements which may take place in the spot rate for that currency, but when the maturity date of the forward contract arrives, he need only pay over the sterling equivalent of the foreign currency at the rate of exchange fixed when the contract was made, and will then receive the amount of foreign currency contracted for. The contracting bank has made itself liable to pay over the stated amount of foreign currency at the rate agreed upon, and, as banks in this country do not take up "open positions" in exchange, i.e. do not speculate on the possible future rate, it must conduct some other operation at once in order to cover itself, in turn, against the risk of an adverse movement in the spot rate by the time the forward contract matures.

Such covering operations may be carried out in several ways, which may be summarized as follows—

(a) In the case of a forward sale, the bank can lay down funds in the other centre immediately by means of purchases of T.T.s, M.T.s, cheques, or any other credit instruments payable at sight or at short sight. As the forward margin is normally based on the difference in interest between the two centres, and as the variation from the T.T. rate in the price of the other short-dated instruments is based on the value of money as used in their purchase, this method should show a reasonable profit on an interest basis, and is the one used whenever conditions permit, especially as banks usually need funds in other centres in order to maintain balances with their correspondents there. When the outstanding balances become larger than is necessary for this purpose, the surplus funds can be used in the foreign Call Money or Stock Markets, or loaned to first class borrowers for the period until the maturity of the forward contract. The limit to this form of covering is the amount of sterling which any bank is prepared to lock up in the shape of foreign currencies, and must be taken in conjunction with the other methods which involve the immediate use of sterling. It is also affected by any official restrictions on such operations.

In the case of a forward purchase, the bank may be able to use some of the funds it has acquired as cover for its forward sales, or which it holds for account of its customers, and can sell T.T.s, M.T.s, or cheques as cover for its forward purchase. The use of this method will depend on the rates of interest which can be obtained for the foreign currency in the other centre, and for the sterling which a sale of the currency would produce. It must be borne in mind that the bank will not receive the sterling for a forward sale, or pay out the sterling for a forward purchase, until the contract matures, and in its covering operations it must be guided by the relative cost in interest of using either sterling or the foreign currency which it holds. If sterling is more valuable, from an interest bearing point of view, than the foreign currency, it will endeavour to cover forward sales by some method other than one involving an immediate sterling outlay, while it will cover forward purchases as far as possible by disposing of its available funds in the foreign currency so as to have the use of the resulting sterling.

(b) To cover forward sales a bank may buy long bills on the foreign centre to mature immediately before the date on which it is under contract to provide the foreign currency for its customer, *if such bills can be obtained.* Here, again, an immediate sterling outlay is involved and the use of this method will depend on the rate of interest ruling in the foreign centre for the class of paper in question (which is the rate of interest which will be shown by the purchase of such paper), compared with the rate of interest which could be obtained by using the sterling in other ways at home or in other centres.

More usually, a bank will cover purchases of foreign bills at tenor by a forward sale of the currency concerned, rather than the reverse, as it is seldom possible to obtain foreign bills for the approximate amount and for a near enough maturity date to cover any given forward sale just at the moment when they are needed.

Frequently, indeed, a bank will find itself forced to quote for the purchase of foreign long bills on the basis of the forward rate and on an allowance for the interest value of the sterling used, plus cost of stamps and expenses, rather than on the basis of the foreign interest rate for that class of bill. This means that instead of being able to use sterling at the foreign rate, which is probably higher than the home rate, it must use it at the home rate only as, were it to quote on the usual basis, the customer would refuse the rate and would sell the currency "outturn" of the bill forward to the bank, taking an advance at home rates against the security of the bill to provide himself with the sterling in the meantime.

As banks in this country never draw and sell long bills, and never resell foreign bills from their portfolios, a bank will never cover a forward purchase of currency by a sale of long bills in that currency.

(c) In the case of both purchases and sales forward, a bank can communicate at once with a correspondent abroad, either in the centre concerned or some other, offering to buy from or sell to the agent sterling against the foreign currency concerned, and this may be done either in the shape of a spot transaction or as an outright forward deal for the same date as the contract with the home customer. As banks abroad "run open positions" to a much greater extent than do banks here, it is often possible to find a bank abroad willing to buy or sell its own currency forward as a speculation or in anticipation of some possible adverse or favourable factor which may have come into effect by the time the forward contract matures, and which may cause the spot rate to move in the right direction for the speculator to an extent sufficient to enable him to cover his open position at a profit by means of a spot deal at the then current rate.

(d) In addition to the possibility of finding an outright buyer or seller abroad of a currency "forward," a fairly active market in outright forwards for most currencies exists in London, and a bank will frequently attempt to undo a forward deal carried out with a customer here by means of a reverse outright operation in the London market. Having based its rate to the customer on the margin prevailing at the time in the market here, the bank is often able, after some haggling, to find a counterpart in this market, and can cover an outright forward sale by an outright forward purchase from some other member of the market, and vice versa.

Where, however, the spot rate for the currency concerned is fluctuating with any rapidity and to any extent, it is not safe to spend time in seeking an outright counterpart while the spot rate is perhaps moving adversely, as the forward margin seldom fluctuates to the same extent as the spot rate even when speculators are active. Thus if the spot rate for Swiss francs is 10·35–36, and the three months forward margin is 10 to 8 c. under spot, a bank might sell francs for delivery in three months fixed at an outright rate of 10·20, and would consider itself fairly safe to cover at a profit. If the dealer concerned begins to send his brokers round the market to try to buy three-months francs outright at the middle prices (9 points under 10·35½, making 10·26½ outright), he may find that the spot rate is suddenly moving owing to a buying order having come into the market, and is being quoted as 10·20–22. Even should he then find a seller of three-months francs at 9 points under spot, and can even find the spot at 10·21, the resulting outright price would be only 10·12, showing him a loss of 8 points per £ if he had to cover at this price.

Consequently, a dealer will usually cover himself at once in a moving market by buying or selling T.T. at the current rate against a forward sale to or purchase from a customer respectively. By this means he makes sure of his basic rate of exchange and can then look round for the "swap" at his leisure, since he is then merely in the position of needing to sell or buy T.T. against buying or selling for the forward date, respectively, and the forward margin can usually be relied on to remain within a few points of the original quotation, no matter to what extent the spot rate has moved in the meantime. In the case quoted above, for instance, if the dealer covered his forward sale by an immediate purchase of T.T., even at the "bottom of the market," viz. at 10·35; and then, later, paid the full "swap" margin of 10 points to sell the T.T. and buy the forward, he then secures his outright forward at 10·25 as against his sale at 10·20, and is unaffected by the subsequent adverse movement in the spot rate.

When dealing with "broken dates" or "option forwards" granted to his customers, the exchange dealer is faced with some difficulty. While it is often possible to deal in a "broken date" in the market and so secure the exact cover needed, it is very rarely that "option forwards" can be obtained as a market deal. Dealers consider that they have quite enough trouble in "matching up" options which they are compelled to grant to their own customers without further increasing disparities of value dates in their books by granting options to other members of the market who should be quite capable of looking after themselves!

Normally, a dealer is always prepared to have funds standing to his credit abroad and will cover a sale of a "long" forward by a purchase of T.T., M.T., or a "short" forward. Only under conditions of unrest does he cut down his foreign balances to a minimum, and it is at such times that the forward market is most difficult and may even become nominal. Whenever possible, then, the dealer maintains spot balances as cover for his short position in forwards. If he finds himself being asked to buy more forward currency than he is asked to sell, he straightens his book by a "swap" in the market, buying in spot and selling out forward for the date on which he has become too overbought. Again, this operation is simple when "fixed" forward dates are concerned, but it becomes much more complicated when "option" forwards have to be covered.

Sales of "options" by a dealer are nearly always covered by a purchase for the *earliest* date on which the customer can demand delivery, as any delay in taking delivery will merely leave the dealer with an increased balance abroad which he can probably use to advantage by "swaps" of T.T. against M.T. or in "day-to-day swaps" of the foreign currency for sterling. In many cases a customer will purchase a total amount of foreign currency forward at his option over a stated period and then will demand delivery in a series of smaller amounts from time to time. As long as the total is not too large, the dealer is quite prepared for this, and will cover for the total amount for the earliest date. In the case of large total amounts, however, the dealer will spread his covering operations over the major part of the option period. For example, if a dealer sells to a customer on 28th February, 1970, $100,000 for delivery to the customer at his option over April, May, and June 1970, the dealer will probably cover his risk in three parcels. The one, two and three months forward dates would be 2nd April, 2nd May and 2nd June, while the customer cannot demand delivery before 1st April of any part of his purchase. The dealer will therefore probably carry out three swaps (having covered his exchange risk by an immediate purchase of T.T.), and will sell, say, $50,000 spot against one months, $25,000 spot against two months, and $25,000 against three months, or such other proportions as the existing state of his forward "book" may show to be desirable. By this method he ensures that he will have available, by the earliest date necessary, sufficient currency to meet all probable requirements of his customer for a month of the option, and this without either using too much sterling in the purchase of spot or of having too large an amount of foreign currency standing to his credit abroad. At the same time, his purchases of two and three months forward ensure that such depletion of his available foreign balance as may have taken place will be made good in time to meet further withdrawals under the option until both balance and option are exhausted or the former at least reduced to normal proportions.

Where a dealer has failed to spread his covering operations evenly or has taken too optimistic a view of the date when a customer who has purchased foreign currency for delivery at his option over a period may demand delivery, he may find that withdrawals by the customer under his option are producing an overdraft on the bank's account in the foreign centre. This is a state of affairs which London banks endeavour to avoid, and the dealer will at once adjust the position by a "short swap" in the market, i.e. he will buy spot and sell forward for the nearest date on which he has already arranged for cover to come in. For instance, if in the example given above the customer asked for delivery of $80,000 on 14th April, the dealer has only provided $50,000, and his own credit balance is probably not more than $5,000, so that he will become overdrawn by $25,000 until 2nd May, when his next forward purchase matures, assuming

156   A MANUAL OF FOREIGN EXCHANGE

that no other operations exist. He must, therefore, buy spot for 14th April and sell 2nd May in $25,000, and any cost to him in the shape of a discount on the forward will, of course, reduce the profit he had expected to make on the deal. Where the forward margin is at a premium the dealer will probably cover the major portion of his sale by a forward purchase for the earliest date on which the customer can demand delivery so as to give away as little by way of premium on the forward as possible, though he will have charged his customer the maximum premium for the latest date of the option.

In the case of forward purchases by a dealer at the option of the customer, he follows the same method of spreading his risk and, after an initial sale of spot to cover at once his exchange risk, will proceed to buy in spot and sell forward for dates more approximating to the middle and end of the option period than to the beginning. This is because, should the customer deliver the currency earlier than anticipated, the dealer will then merely be left with a temporarily over-large balance to his credit, pending the maturity of his own sale forward, while if the dealer sells forward for an early date of the option and the customer does not deliver until much later in the period, the dealer may again be faced with an overdraft and have to carry out a "short swap" at a loss to adjust the position. These observations are, of course, entirely general in view, and no hard and fast rules can be given for covering any class of forward operation, as the actual form and date of the covering must depend not only on the state of the dealer's "book" and on his facilities or arrangements with his correspondent abroad, but also on his own view of possible movements in the spot rate and forward margin of the currency in which he has dealt.

"Swaps"

Operations consisting of a simultaneous sale or purchase of spot currency accompanied by a purchase or sale, respectively, of the same currency for forward delivery, are technically known as "swaps" or "double deals," as the spot currency is "swapped" against the forward. This is the type of operation carried out by a short-term investor in order to secure himself against loss in exchange during the period of investment. Such transactions consist of a spot purchase of the currency in which it is desired to invest, together with a forward sale of the same amount of currency for a forward date to coincide with the estimated maturity date of the investment. The rate of reconversion of the foreign funds into home currency is thus secured, and the investor can calculate his profit on the basis of interest and capital appreciation, if any, of his investment. The purchase of the spot foreign currency gives the investor immediate funds in the foreign centre of which he can dispose as he pleases. In some cases a foreign bank will have need of sterling for a certain period and will make an offer to a London bank to sell to it the foreign currency on the spot, against sterling, and to buy it back forward, also against sterling, at a margin to be agreed upon; at the same time the foreign bank will offer to take the foreign currency on deposit with itself at a stated rate of interest so as to offer the London bank employment for the foreign funds which it will obtain if it carries out the "swap." Such an operation is known as a "swap and deposit," both the swap and the deposit being carried out with the same bank abroad by the London bank. The desirability of the operation depends upon (a) the standing of the foreign bank, as the London bank will be entrusting it with the deposit, (b) the forward margin proposed, and (c) the relative rates of interest ruling in the two centres. For example, if the foreign bank is of sufficiently good standing to warrant the deposit being made with it, the profit to be made by the London bank will depend on the difference between the interest which it will lose on its sterling, and the interest which it will receive on the foreign currency deposit, *plus or minus the interest equivalent of the forward margin.* Thus, if money is worth $2\frac{1}{2}$ per cent per annum for three months in London, and a German bank offers a three-months swap in marks at a margin of 2 pfennige discount (a *premium* on forward marks in London turns into a *discount* on forward pounds in Berlin), coupled with an offer to take the marks on deposit for three months at 4 per cent per annum, the London bank, should it accept, would make a net interest profit of $1\frac{1}{2}$ per cent per annum for three months, plus 2 pfennige per pound on each pound's worth of marks dealt in, which represents an interest profit of about $\frac{3}{4}$ per cent per annum (2 pfennige for three months is at the rate of 8 pfennige for 1 year; 8 pfennige for 1 year on a spot rate of about 8·86 equals about 1 per cent for the year), so that its total profit would be at the rate of about $2\frac{1}{4}$ per cent per annum for the three months. If the operation were for D-mks. 450,000 (which is roughly £50,000), the profit for the three months operation would be $2\frac{1}{2}$ per cent per annum for three months on £50,000, or about £312.

Another and a more usual form of this operation is that in which an investor (whether a bank, firm or individual), wishing to have funds available in another centre for a limited time, purchases the required currency "spot" and simultaneously arranges a forward sale of the same amount of currency for a future date when he expects the use of the funds abroad to be at an end. The purchase of spot currency gives him funds immediately available in the foreign centre, against payment of funds in his home currency, while the forward sale fixes at once the rate of exchange at which he will eventually be able to reconvert the foreign currency into home funds. The currency abroad is thus at his disposal during the period before the forward contract matures, and he can use it in any fashion he pleases. He can place the money on fixed deposit with a bank in the foreign centre or with a bank in some other centre which is willing to borrow that particular currency, e.g. he can buy spot U.S.A. dollars against a forward sale and lend the dollars for the period to a German bank, or he can use the funds in the foreign Call Money market or in loans on the foreign Stock Exchange, or he can buy bills or short-dated investments in the foreign centre, or he can use the funds for operations in securities or commodities, or in any other way in which he thinks a profitable return can be obtained. Such operations are known as "swap and investment," and their desirability depends on the profit which might have been obtained on the funds by keeping them in the home currency and the profit to be made by employing them abroad, making allowance for the cost of the "swap," i.e. the discount gained or the premium to be given away in order to sell the currency forward.

As an example of such an operation, if London bills of three-months tenor can be purchased in the London market at a discount rate of 6⅞ per cent per annum, while similar bills in the New York market can be purchased only at a discount of 4 per cent per annum, then New York banks and financial houses wishing to invest funds temporarily in three-months bills will endeavour to do so in London as long as the cost of buying spot sterling for dollars and reselling it forward for dollars does not absorb too much of the gross interest profit. If the T.T. rate on London in New York is 2·40 dollars per £, and the three-months forward margin there is 1½–1⅜ discount on the forward sterling, a New York bank can buy spot sterling only by giving 2·40 per £, and will receive only 2·38½ per £ (2·40 less the buying discount on the forward sterling of 1½ c.) for each pound he resells forward. He thus loses 1½c. per £ over the three months, which is at a rate of 6 cents per £ for one year, which on 2·40 is about 2½ per cent per annum. As the gross gain in interest is at the rate of 2⅞ per cent per annum, the net gain, neglecting expenses, is at the rate of ⅜ per cent per annum, or 3/32 per cent *ad valorem* for the three months; therefore on an investment of $250,000 (which is just over £100,000) the profit would be, in sterling, 3/32 per cent of £100,000, that is £97.

The student should note these methods of working out approximate profits, and more particularly *the methods of expressing a fraction in the rate of exchange over a given period as a percentage per annum on that rate, and vice versa.*

It should also be noted, however, that the working in all the above examples is only approximate and is not arithmetically correct. To arrive at an exact result in any calculation of a percentage on a foreign *currency* exchange rate, one must *work on what the rate has become, not on what the rate was at the beginning of the calculation.* For example, if the dollar-sterling rate falls from $5 per £ to $4 per £, the appreciation in the dollar is not $1 on $5, or 20 per cent, but $1 on $4, or 25 per cent. This is proved by the fact that, in New York, sterling will have depreciated from 4s. per dollar to 5s. per dollar, which is again 25 per cent. Similarly, if the spot rate for French francs is fcs.980 per £ and three months forward is fcs.50 per £ discount, this latter would be at the rate of fcs.200 per £ for a full year or, apparently, at an interest rate of over 20 per cent per annum. Actually, however, a person selling fcs.980,000 for spot at fcs.980 per £, thus receiving £1,000 and buying them back for delivery in twelve months time at fcs.1,180 per £, would then have to spend roughly £830, which would show him a profit of £170, which is only at the rate of 17 per cent per annum. It is always the new rate which must be used, therefore, as the basis of calculation and not the former rate.

CHAPTER XI

OTHER METHODS OF ELIMINATING EXCHANGE RISKS, AND THE COLLECTION AND NEGOTIATION OF FOREIGN BILLS

Exchange Clauses on Foreign Bills; a "Flat" Rate of Negotiation
for Bills in Sterling on Foreign Centres Bearing an Exchange
Clause; Marginal Deposits; Foreign Currency Accounts

THE early practice of merchants in this country of buying and selling internationally in terms of sterling led to the development of certain recognized forms of wording being included in bills drawn in sterling by creditors in this country on other countries, so as to ensure that any exchange risk was thrown on to the foreign drawee and that the English drawer should receive the full sterling amount due to him.

In addition, clauses were gradually introduced to provide, in some cases, for the payment of interest by the drawee, and in other cases for payment by the drawee in sterling according to the customary usance in his centre, or again, that a bank should act as the arbiter of the rate of exchange at which the bill should be paid in local currency by the drawee.

Exchange Clauses

An "Exchange Clause" may therefore be defined as a clause included in the wording of a bill which fixes the *method* of arriving at the rate of exchange at which the drawee must pay the bill. The principal exchange clauses still in use in this country are dealt with below, but it must be understood that they apply to *bills drawn on foreign centres in terms of sterling* by creditors in this country.

In every case, however, an exchange clause should only be included in the wording of a foreign bill *with the prior and complete consent of the drawee*. If possible, the use of an exchange clause in specific terms should be included as part of the contract for the sale and purchase of the goods covered by the bill; otherwise, there is always the possibility of the bill being dishonoured by the drawee on the grounds that he had not authorized and was not prepared to allow the exchange clause included in the wording of the bill to be used. As the relative goods will by that time have been dispatched, considerable trouble and expense can be occasioned in such circumstances.

"EXCHANGE AS PER ENDORSEMENT"

This clause is used, often with others, in sterling bills drawn on European and Middle East Countries, Australia, New Zealand and South Africa. Other clauses are used for bills on India, the Far East and Latin-America, and these are treated later.

The following is a specimen of a bill bearing the "exchange as per endorsement" clause—

£200

London,
27th June, 1954.

Ninety days after sight of this first of exchange (second and third of same tenor and date unpaid) pay to our order the sum of Two hundred pounds for value received, exchange as per endorsement, which place to account as per advice.

JOHN BULL AND CO.

To Messrs. DEUTSCH AND CO.,
Berlin.

The effect of this clause is to enable the bank in this country to whom the drawer sells the bill, to fix the rate of exchange at which the draft will become payable in terms of the foreign currency. It is not necessary that the draft should be sold by the drawer immediately. It may be sent abroad for acceptance and return, and may be sold only a few days before its eventual due date. When it is actually offered to a bank for purchase, the bank dealer will have to pay the drawer or holder the face amount of the bill, and so must allow in the rate of exchange for all expenses of collection, foreign stamp, any loss of interest, and his profit. He must therefore fix a *tel quel* rate of exchange, and this rate he includes in his endorsement of the bill, which will read thus—

"Pay A.B. Bank or order at the rate of..........for £1 sterling."

On the face of the bill, this rate is written above the sterling amount, together with the resulting equivalent in foreign currency, and the bill then ceases to be a sterling bill and becomes a bill for that amount of foreign currency.

It is always customary for the drawer, as soon as he has sold the bill, to advise the drawee of the rate fixed by the purchasing bank so that the drawee will know exactly how much local currency he will have to provide to meet the bill on its presentation. In some cases, the purchasing bank will quote a rate but will require the drawer to include this rate in his first endorsement and to convert the sterling amount on the face of the bill into the foreign currency at that rate; this is in order that the bank shall not be involved in any dispute between the drawer and the drawee regarding the rate. The clause "exchange as per endorsement" therefore *results in the negotiating bank here being empowered to fix a "tel quel" rate of conversion of the sterling amount of the bill into foreign currency and the bill is thereafter treated as a bill for that amount of foreign currency.* The bank dealer is therefore required to purchase foreign currency from the holder, and he must arrive at his "all in" buying rate by taking the rate at which he is prepared to buy T.T.s in that currency and adding to it (*a*) interest at the foreign discount rate for such paper from the date of purchase until the estimated date of payment and credit of proceeds, (*b*) the cost of any foreign stamps and any collection charges made by the foreign agent, and (*c*) a reasonable margin of profit. On concluding the purchase, the bank dealer will have bought the resulting amount of foreign currency and must cover this by a sale of "spot" or "forward" T.T., or cheque, etc.

"PAYABLE WITHOUT LOSS IN EXCHANGE"[1]

This clause also has the effect of ensuring that the drawer in this country shall receive the full sterling amount of the bill under discount, but only after deduction of all collecting charges and the cost of any foreign stamp. Such bills are purchased by the bank here for their face value, less discount at the rate applicable to such paper from the date of purchase until the estimated date of the arrival of the return remittance, and less the bank's collecting charge (where this is not allowed for in the discount rate) and less any foreign stamp duty. The collecting bank abroad acting as agent for the London bank must eventually forward to its principals a sight draft on London for the face amount of the bill less its own collecting charge and the cost of any foreign stamp. The foreign drawee will have the bill presented to him for payment by the collecting bank, *converted into local currency at a rate of exchange fixed by the collecting bank, which will be the rate at which the latter is prepared to sell sight drafts on London.*

The drawee, however, is not bound to accept this rate and to make payment of the equivalent of local currency so obtained, *but can tender in payment a sight draft on London for the sterling amount of the bill, issued by any local bank whose name the collecting bank is ready to take,* which he may have purchased elsewhere at a better (for him) rate of exchange. In this latter case the collecting bank would be deprived of the opportunity of selling a draft on London and so would lose its possible profit on such a transaction.

[1] The use of this clause is now infrequent.

"PAYABLE BY APPROVED BANKERS' CHEQUE ON LONDON FOR FULL FACE VALUE"[1]

This clause is exactly similar in effect to the one above. The collecting bank will endeavour to sell its own cheque on London to the drawee, but must accept any approved local bank cheque on London, in sterling, for the face amount of the bill, if such is tendered by the drawee, in payment. It should be noted that, in both the last two clauses, *neither the negotiating bank here nor the collecting bank abroad is empowered definitely to fix the rate of conversion of the sterling amount into local currency*, though the latter bank may be able to do so if the drawee will accept its quoted rate.

"PAYABLE AT $\frac{\text{BANKERS'}}{\text{X BANK'S}}$ $\frac{\text{SELLING}}{\text{DRAWING}}$ RATE FOR $\frac{\text{DEMAND}}{\text{SIGHT}}$ DRAFTS ON LONDON ON DATE OF PAYMENT"

This is the usual clause for bills drawn on Far Eastern Countries and on the South American States. The wording and type of return remittance required is varied to suit the customary usance of the drawee country, and instead of "sight" or "demand" drafts, may read "Telegraphic Transfers." The effect of any such clause is *to empower either the named bank, or the bank shown by the last endorsement as being the agent for collection, to fix a rate of conversion into local currency at which it is ready to sell a remittance on London of the type specified in the clause. The drawee has no alternative but to accept the rate so fixed*, and any such clause, therefore, means that the collecting bank sells to the drawee a remittance in sterling on London of the stated type for the face amount of the bill at its own rate. The collecting bank will deduct the cost of any foreign stamps both on the original bill and on the return remittance, and will forward the net proceeds to its principal by a remittance in the form prescribed by the clause. It is not usual for the collecting bank to make a charge for the collection of bills so claused as its profit is taken in the rate at which it sells the sterling to the drawee in exchange for local currency.

Another variant of this clause is, "*Payable at collecting bank's selling rate for sight drafts on London.*"

CLAUSES ON INDIAN AND FAR EASTERN BILLS

Trade custom between these countries and the United Kingdom has led to the general adoption of an exchange clause of which the

[1] The use of this clause is now infrequent.

wording differs but slightly from that of the last two clauses given above, and it usually reads as follows: *"Payable at the* $\dfrac{X \text{ bank's}}{\text{current}}$ *rate of exchange for demand drafts on London together with all collecting charges."*[1]

It will be noted that the first part of this clause either empowers the local collecting bank to fix the rate of conversion into local currency and gives the drawee no option but to pay at this rate, or, alternatively, allows the collecting bank to fix a rate of conversion, but gives the drawee the option of tendering an approved sterling draft by way of payment, which he may have purchased elsewhere on terms more advantageous for himself. Should the drawee adopt this latter course, the collecting bank will lose the profit which presumably it would have made by selling him its sterling draft on London. This clause contains an important addition in that it requires the drawee to pay not only the face amount of the bill in sterling but any additional amount which may be added thereto both by the negotiating bank here and by the collecting bank in the foreign centre on account of their respective charges for collection. This means that in the case of a bill for £100 on which both the negotiating bank and the collecting bank wished to charge ⅛ per cent for the service of collection, the negotiating bank here would forward the bill to its collecting agent in the foreign centre with instructions to forward a return remittance for £100 plus commission of 2s. 6d., making £100 2s. 6d. in all. The collecting bank, on receipt of the bill and these instructions, will add also its own commission of 2s. 6d., and will write over the amount on the face of the bill "Collection charges 5s.," thus making the bill payable for a total amount of £100 5s. It will then convert this amount into local currency at its selling rate for demand drafts on London and will affix any necessary local stamp, but this latter item it will charge against its principal, as the drawee is not asked to pay this charge. The drawee can either pay over the required amount of local currency which is the equivalent of the total sterling amount at the rate fixed by the collecting bank, or, if the wording of the clause permits him to do so, tender an approved bank demand draft on London for £100 5s. in discharge of the bill. This draft will be forwarded to the London principal by the collecting bank, who will either debit the cost of stamp and charges to the principal's local currency account or will ask for credit in its own sterling account. The drawer of such a bill can therefore, by negotiating it, obtain the full amount of his bill less only interest

[1] If the drawer is prepared to bear the collection charges, the last five words should be omitted.

from the date of purchase by the negotiating bank here to the estimated date of the arrival here of the return remittance, and less any foreign stamp, as the collection charges are all paid by the drawee.

THE INTEREST CLAUSE

Also in connexion with bills on India and the Far East, the custom has grown up of including an even more comprehensive clause in such bills with the object of passing on to the drawee not only all the collection charges but also the interest charged by the negotiating banker which would otherwise fall on the drawer.

This clause is known as "the interest clause" and reads as follows:

"*Payable at the* $\dfrac{X \text{ bank's}}{\text{current}}$ *rate of exchange for a demand draft on London, together with interest at......per cent per annum from date hereof until approximate date of arrival of return remittance in London plus all collection charges.*"[1] The rate per cent at which interest must be paid by the drawee is fixed and usually filled in by the negotiating bank here, and is based on the rate for bank advances to customers *in the foreign centre*. The negotiating bank here will then calculate the amount of interest at this rate for the estimated period and will add this sum, together with its collecting charge, to the amount of the bill, which then becomes payable for the resulting total amount. The collecting bank on receipt will add its own collecting charge, and will demand payment of the resulting total sterling amount, either in terms of local currency at a rate of conversion fixed by itself or by approved banker's draft in sterling for this amount where the drawee has the option of paying in this manner. It will also have affixed any necessary local stamp, and the cost of this will be deducted from the total sterling amount claimed by the principal, the return remittance being for the resulting net amount.

As the negotiating bank eventually receives the amount due to it by way of interest, and also its collection charge, when the return remittance arrives, the only charge which falls on the drawer is the cost of any foreign stamp. Consequently, when the drawer of such a bill presents it for negotiation to his bank here *he receives at once the full face amount of the bill less only the very small cost of any foreign stamp, and there is no question of the bill being "discounted" by the negotiating bank*, as it will collect the interest on its money from the drawee. Should such a bill be dishonoured and returned unpaid, the

---

[1] If the drawer is prepared to bear the collection charges, the last four words should be omitted.

drawer must then submit to having his account debited with the face amount of the bill plus interest at the rate stated in the bill and for the full period which has elapsed since date of purchase and plus all collecting charges, stamps and expenses. He must then take whatever action is open to him to recover the amounts from the drawee.

When goods are invoiced on the following terms the relative bill usually bears the interest clause—

    1. C.I.F. (Cost, Insurance and Freight)
    2. C. & F. (Cost and Freight)
    3. F.O.B. (Free on Board)
    4. C.I.F. & C. (Cost, Insurance, Freight and Commission).

Occasionally sales are made on C.I.F.C.I. terms and the goods invoiced at a price to include collecting bank's charges plus interest from the date of the bill to the approximate date of arrival of proceeds in London. In these cases the bill usually bears a rebate clause authorizing the collecting bank to allow the drawee, if payment is made before maturity of the bill, a rebate for the number of days between the date of payment and the actual due date.

The interest rate for bills drawn on places in India, Pakistan and Burma is fixed by the Eastern Exchange Banks' Association from time to time.

CLAUSES ON AUSTRALIAN BILLS

Other slight variations of some of the above clauses are to be found in bills on Australia, New Zealand and Fiji. The usual clauses are as follow—

"*Payable at banker's drawing rate for demand drafts on London, plus stamp duty,*" the first part of which is equivalent to the "payable without loss in exchange" clause, and the second part of which requires collection of the cost of any local stamp from the drawer;

"*Payable at the current rate of exchange for demand drafts on London, together with all collection charges,*" which has the same effect as that above, except that the charges made by the banks on both sides are collected from the drawee, but not the cost of any local stamp;

"*Payable with exchange and stamps for negotiating bills on Australia (or New Zealand) as per endorsement,*" which is used only on bills which are to be negotiated here by the drawer and which has the same effect as the simple "exchange as per endorsement" clause in that the negotiating bank quotes a "flat" rate of negotiation, i.e. it allows for exchange, stamps and its own and the agent's charges in the rate which it endorses on the bill; the amount of the bill is then converted into Dominion currency at the endorsed rate, the resulting equivalent is written above the sterling amount, and the bill then becomes one for this amount of Dominion currency. The collecting bank will collect this amount, deduct its own commission, and will credit the account of its principal in its own books with the resulting net amount of Dominion currency.

BILLS ON SOUTH AFRICA

While several of the clauses given above are often included in bills drawn here on South Africa, there is no special clause in general use. The "Interest Clause" is seldom used on bills drawn on South Africa from this country, but is occasionally used in bills drawn from the U.S.A. on South Africa.

In many cases the drawer will allow for the exchange in his invoice, and will then draw his bill for the resulting amount in South African rands. In other cases any one of the recognized exchange clauses, either with or without the additional demand for the payment of collection charges and stamps, is included in the bill by arrangement between drawer and drawee.

Finally, it should be noted that the inclusion in the wording of a bill of any exchange or collection of expenses clause should be arranged for in the original contract between seller and buyer, i.e. the drawer should have obtained the agreement of the drawee to the inclusion of any such clause in the bill. The "exchange as per endorsement" clause cannot accompany any other clause which shows that the bill is eventually to be paid in sterling, as once a rate of exchange has been endorsed on a bill under this clause the bill then becomes expressed and payable in terms of the foreign or overseas currency. Also no exchange clause can appear on a foreign currency bill when the currency is that of the drawee's country. It is possible to draw a foreign currency bill when the currency is that of a third country, however, as for example a bill of exchange for $1258·50 U.S. currency drawn on an importer in Caracas, Venezuela, by a British exporter bearing the clause "payable at collecting banker's selling rate for sight drafts on New York."

Collection and Negotiation of Bills

Where a bank here merely undertakes the *collection* of a bill on behalf of a customer, it acts only as an agent, and will not pay over to or credit the account of the customer with the proceeds until it receives either a return remittance from its agent or advice that it has received credit for the proceeds in the books of its agent.

Where a bank agrees to *negotiate* a bill for a customer, it acquires full rights in the bill and, in most cases of documentary bills, a right to the property in the relative goods, since it purchases the draft for its "present value," i.e. discounts it, and so becomes a holder for value and usually a holder in due course.

The customer for whom the bill is negotiated receives payment or credit of the sterling equivalent immediately, and is thus actually the recipient of an advance from the bank of the full amount of his bill, less interest and charges against the security of the draft and/or documents.

Should the draft eventually be returned unpaid, the customer must refund to the negotiating bank the amount paid to him, plus interest for the intervening period and plus all charges and expenses. The bank must have a reasonable certainty of the ability of a customer to do this, if necessary, before it negotiates his draft, and the "limit" or "sanction" is fixed by the management in respect of this class of business for any customer in accordance with the estimate of his stability in this regard.

A "FLAT" RATE OF NEGOTIATION FOR BILLS IN STERLING ON FOREIGN CENTRES BEARING AN EXCHANGE CLAUSE

In the case of a foreign bill drawn in sterling and bearing one or other of the various "exchange clauses," which require a "return remittance" to be made also in sterling, the banker negotiating (or discounting) such an instrument is using sterling funds for a certain time which will eventually come back to him in the form of sterling. He is, therefore, in effect making a sterling advance to the customer against the security of the bill until he receives the "return remittance" in the shape of a sterling T.T., sight draft, or M.T., according to the wording of the clause, and it is customary for him to work out a "flat" or "all-in" percentage rate for the purchase, "with recourse," of such instruments.

The "flat" rate of negotiation is a rate per cent *absolute*, i.e. an *ad valorem* percentage and not a percentage per annum. The buying banker considers that he will be making an advance in sterling against the bill at the appropriate rate per cent per annum for the period from the date of purchase until the "return remittance" arrives back in London and is either immediately payable or is at once accepted and so becomes discountable. He therefore begins by calculating an *absolute* or *ad valorem* percentage on this basis. He must first have regard to the tenor of the draft he is buying and then to the time which it will take for the bill and, subsequently, the "return remittance" to pass by telegraph or air or sea mail between the two centres. This will give him the period in respect of which he must allow for loss of interest *at the rate ruling in the foreign centre*,[1] because that is where he would have to rediscount the bill at the interest rate current there should he wish to obtain early reimbursement of his advance. Unless the "return remittance" is to be by T.T. he must allow for the number of days which would be taken up in the course of mail—by air or surface means as the case may be. He must then allow for the foreign stamp duties which he will have to pay, collecting agent's commission and his own profit, and he can then arrive at the "flat" or "all-in" rate which he will apply to the negotiation of the draft.

MARGINAL DEPOSITS

Where a bank does not wish actually to negotiate for their full "present value" the drafts on other centres of a customer, it may arrange to pay over or credit him with a proportion only of the "present value" of each draft. The methods employed by the various banks differ either because of their own preferences or because of the practice of the particular area of the world involved. Nevertheless, the effect is that the bank pays over, or credits the customer with, a percentage only of the face amount of the draft. Once again it is impossible to be precise, but the current practice with U.K. banks is that the marginal deposit is likely to be between ten and twenty per cent.

When the final proceeds of the draft are received the bank accounts to the customer for the difference which is due.

Foreign Currency Accounts

Finally, a method of occasionally eliminating the risk of loss in exchange is that by which a creditor accepts payment in terms of the currency of his debtor and converts the foreign currency into his own at a suitable opportunity or uses the funds in the purchase of goods in the foreign country or in a third country. The elimination of eventual loss in exchange depends, in the first case, on the possibility of eventually converting the funds into home currency at a rate of exchange which shows the holder no loss on the whole transaction and which depends in turn on the movements which take place in the exchange value of the currency concerned. In the

[1]The rate applicable would be that for the particular type of sterling paper.

second case, the elimination of exchange loss depends on whether the funds have been used abroad as profitably as they could have been at home and on whether the eventual "outturn" from the goods purchased or the profit made on any other use to which the funds may have been put, coupled with the rate of exchange obtained when they are eventually brought home, shows no loss on the original transaction. An example of this latter case occurred during the heavy depreciation in the Australian exchanges when many creditors of Australian debtors had the Australian funds placed to the credit of a Foreign Currency Account, i.e. held for them in terms of Australian pounds, and used such accounts to pay for purchases of Australian produce. This produce was brought home and sold, and the eventual "outturn" in many cases was greater than if the original debt in Australian pounds had been sold as currency at the current market quotation.

Foreign Currency Accounts, however, cannot be considered to provide an absolute safeguard against risk of loss in exchange, as is the case with the exchange clauses or in dealing forward, and their utility is limited to those who are able to operate expertly in exchange, when an element of speculation enters, or who are able to make profitable use of a foreign currency in their normal trading or financial activities. Moreover, at the present time British residents need the special permission of the Exchange Control to maintain a "Retained Currency Account" with their bankers at home or abroad in any "specified" currency, and such permission is granted only in special cases and for specific purposes in view of the continued need to conserve and to use to the best advantage the national reserves of foreign currencies.

CHAPTER XII
THE EURO-CURRENCY MARKET

Definition of Euro-currency; The Market Structure; Source of Funds;
Interest Rates; Use of Euro-currencies; Euro-currency Operations;
Euro-bonds; Recognition.

THE Euro-currency Market is now of such magnitude and international importance that for these reasons, apart from any other
considerations, it warrants individual attention. The term "Euro-
currency" is somewhat of a misnomer because it implies that the
currencies used are deposited by, or on-lent to, other countries in
Europe whereas, in fact, participation is world-wide. One view of the
origin of the term is attributed to a bank which had the word "Euro"
in its title and which, on behalf of a depositor, undertook an operation
for political reasons which proved to be the foundation of the
present market. Another is that it is because the market for the
depositing and lending of the funds is in Europe only.

Whatever view is held it started only a few years ago but development has been so rapid that the Euro-currency market is now the
largest international deposit money market in the world. Without
doubt, although it is international, London is by far the most important centre for its operations. Because of the volume and nature of
the business and because there is no central control it is virtually
impossible for statistics to be obtained which would reveal the full
extent of the market. However, the Bank for International Settlements has, from time to time, published its estimates of the size
of the Euro-dollar market. In these estimates the bank has en-
deavoured to avoid the duplication which arises from the redepositing
between banks. Even after this they have estimated in their thirty-
ninth Annual Report that the market's gross liabilities expanded
from $9,000 million at the end of 1964 to $25,000 million at the end
of 1968. With the massive increase of business in London alone
during 1969, where other reports indicate that this was in the region
of 75 per cent, it can only be assumed that the total amount must be
very impressive.

Definition

As indicated above, the Euro-currency market is still comparatively
young but even over the few years of its existence there have been

several definitions of a Euro-currency. Because the market was still developing these definitions suffered because they were too restrictive. It is reasonable to assume that conditions within the market have now settled to such a degree that a definition for general purposes can be given which will hold good throughout the foreseeable life of the market in, what appears to be, an established state. The definition is: *A Euro-currency is a currency which is available for deposit or loan in a country in which it is not the domestic currency.* For example, for banks in the United Kingdom—including not only U.K. registered banks but also the U.K. offices of overseas banks— Euro-currency business comprises deposits and lending in currencies other than the pound sterling. At the time of writing it is practice that only foreign currencies are applicable and does not include those currencies of other countries of the sterling area.

The definition given above embraces all currencies for "Euro" purposes but such is the omnipotence of the U.S. dollar that the market itself is often referred to as the Euro-dollar market. The currencies next most dealt in are the Deutschemark, The Swiss franc and the pound sterling. The major Western European currencies are all dealt in to varying degrees and occasionally other currencies are found suitable.

It must be understood that the market is essentially a deposit market—*there is no buying or selling of currencies.* The periods of time for the deposits most commonly range from call to six months although some business is concluded on periods of up to three years or even longer. The market in London is conducted in a very similar manner to the London Foreign Exchange Market with all the actual dealing being by means of private telephone lines between broker's offices and the banks' dealing rooms and direct by means of telephone and, particularly, telex with overseas operators. The only difference from the position as explained in Chapter IX from the brokers' point of view is that there has been no formal division of currencies although, as a result of affiliations and connections with particular overseas locations, some brokers do tend to "specialize" in particular currencies. The other major difference that, of course, affects the market as a whole is that the "price" is quoted not for buying and selling purposes but on a deposit and loan basis so that it is an interest rate per annum.

The Market Structure

A report which has been issued by the Bank of England shows that at the end of 1963 three groups of banks together accounted for two thirds of the business done in the London market; these were the

American banks and the British overseas and Commonwealth banks (each accounting for about 25 per cent of the total) and the accepting houses (rather less than 20 per cent). With the great increase in the borrowing of Euro-dollars by banks in the United States, which has been effected mainly through their branches in London, the share of these branches in the London Euro-currency market rose substantially over the years to stand at 54 per cent at the end of 1969. Over the same period the number of branches of American banks in London rose from nine to twenty-nine. The share of all other groups of banks fell, and in particular the accepting houses now account for only 8 per cent of the market total.

The Euro-currency operations of the U.K. deposit banks, comprising primarily the London clearing, Scottish and Northern Ireland banks, have always been comparatively small. Most of these banks conventionally maintain cash and liquidity reserves in respect of their total deposits, in both sterling and foreign currency; this makes it difficult for them to compete in the Euro-currency market. The deposit banks have surmounted this particular obstacle by operating through their subsidiaries, which are not required to observe the same liquidity conventions.

American banks have changed from being net lenders of the currency equivalent of £22 million to the U.K. interbank market at end-1963 to net borrowers of the currency equivalent of £677 million at end-1969. They used these funds, together with others, principally to lend to their head offices. The Japanese banks in London were also heavy net borrowers from other banks in the United Kingdom, lending the funds to their head offices to support domestic advances. Most other groups of banks borrowed large amounts from overseas and lent the funds to the American and Japanese banks through the inter-bank market.

Since May 1966, some of the banks in London have issued certificates of deposit denominated in U.S. dollars. The practice was slow to develop at first, but during 1968 and 1969 the rate of growth increased appreciably; by the end of 1969 there was the dollar equivalent of over £1,537 million of certificates of deposit outstanding, representing some 9 per cent of total gross foreign currency liabilities of the London banks. There is an active secondary market in certificates of deposit now operated by seven institutions (there used to be eight), mostly discount houses. The number of issuing banks has risen to fifty-two, but ten of these accounted for the dollar equivalent of £1,043 million, or over two thirds of total certificates outstanding, at the end of 1969.

The growth and popularity of the Euro-currency market can be attributed to certain factors which could be described as being almost indirect although they contribute directly to its efficacy. The market is able to operate on a much smaller margin between borrowing and lending rates than is usual in domestic banking systems. One reason for this is that the market deals only in large amounts whereas, in domestic business, banks also have to allow for the handling of much smaller sums. In addition, domestic banks are often subject to regulations which limit the rate of interest which may be paid on deposits. Domestic banks under the majority of systems at present in force are subject to reserve requirements in one form or another the return on which is, at best, comparatively low. These restrictions do not usually apply to Euro-currency business and, also, the market itself is not subject to any exchange or other controls. It may be that lenders and borrowers of funds are subject to such controls under their own countries' regulations.

Source of Funds

As stated previously, the statistics available in relation to the Euro-currency market tend to be rather sparse and, in addition, the existence of the market may allow anonymity should a holder of a foreign currency prefer not to place it directly with the banking systems of the country of the currency involved or the funds may have been the subject of a series of redepositing. However, it would appear that Western European countries supply just over half the London market's overseas deposits. The U.S.A. and Canada together account for little over twenty per cent and the overseas sterling area supplies almost ten per cent. Other sources of any note are Latin-America, Eastern Europe, the Middle East and Japan.

It is possible for United Kingdom residents to deposit funds in the Euro-currency market occasionally. It is, of course, necessary for exchange control approval to have been obtained to hold foreign currencies. For example, as has been explained elsewhere, much direct investment by U.K. companies in non-sterling countries is now financed by borrowing foreign currencies in London or abroad, and, pending investment, the borrowed funds may be redeposited. Similarly, U.K. financial institutions may be allowed to borrow in the Euro-currency market to finance portfolios in foreign currencies. The liquid portion of these portfolios may be redeposited with the Euro-currency market. At a time of disinvestment, the funds, pending re-investment, are often placed in the Euro-currency market. Another major contribution to the U.K. source of funds supply to the market is the foreign currency holding of the insurance market and to a lesser extent those of trading and commercial companies.

Interest Rates

In the same way that rates of exchange for the foreign exchange market are published in the national press the rates of interest obtaining in the Euro-currency market are also published. The following is an example which was taken from *The Financial Times* of 27th May, 1970.

U.S.$ IN LONDON			£ IN PARIS		
Call notice 8–8½	7 Days notice 8–8½	3 mths 9¼–9¾	2 Days notice 8½	Month 9¼	3 mths 10

The interpretation of this table is that, in every case, the dealers in the market are prepared to pay interest on a per annum basis at the lower rate and to lend similarly at the higher rate. This is strictly an inter-bank relationship and private customers that wish to borrow will be required to pay a margin over the inter-bank rate which is assessed according to the standing of the customer and the risk involved.

For a purely historical note, the rate for three months' Euro-dollar deposits in London at the end of 1963 was about 4¼ per cent per annum which had risen gradually until in August, 1968, it stood at around 6 per cent per annum. Thereafter, in order to alleviate liquidity shortages, the American banks borrowed Euro-dollars so heavily that the rate in London had risen so that by June, 1969, it was standing at almost 13 per cent per annum. Since that time the Federal Reserve Bank of the U.S.A. has introduced requirements that limit, to a certain extent, the effectiveness of the U.S.A. banks in the London Euro-dollar market and rates of interest have resumed a more normal pattern. Nevertheless, the rates at present in operation do reflect a pattern of dearer money throughout the world.

Euro-dollar rates tend to influence domestic interest rates, because differences between them significantly affect the movement of over-seas funds into or out of the United Kingdom. Depending mainly upon the state of confidence in sterling, the comparison between Euro-dollar and domestic rates might often be made after taking account of the cost of forward cover. Various domestic rates might be chosen for this comparison. Those payable in the interbank sterling market would sometimes prove the most suitable, and for some purposes the deposit rates paid by hire-purchase finance houses would be relevant. But the most widely used comparison is with the rates paid for short-term funds by local authorities. A comparison of the three months' Euro-dollar rate with the return on U.K. local authority deposits of the same term, adjusted to allow for the cost of forward cover, shows that the yields were nearly the same for most of the time up to the devaluation of sterling in November, 1967, save for two short periods around May, 1965, and September, 1967. This near identity of covered yields was almost entirely attributable to the fact that between November, 1964, and devaluation the authorities supported the rate for forward sterling, keeping the discount to a very small figure. Since devaluation the rate for forward sterling has been allowed to find its own level, and has fluctuated a great deal, the cost of three months' cover has ranged between over 8 per cent per annum and as little as $\frac{1}{8}$ per cent per annum. For much of this period, Euro-dollar rates have yielded substantially more than local authority deposits, after allowing for the cost of forward cover. Indeed, as a result of the steep rise in Euro-dollar rates in 1969, three months' deposits of Euro-dollars have, since May, 1969, given a higher return than U.K. local authority deposits even on an uncovered basis.

Banks in the United Kingdom will take account, among other things, of the comparison between Euro-dollar rates and the covered return on funds employed in the United Kingdom when judging whether to convert foreign currency assets into sterling, or to convert back into currency amounts previously switched into sterling. But they have little scope for employing their own funds in the Euro-currency market, because the size of the net currency assets they may hold either uncovered or against forward liabilities is restricted by foreign exchange limits fixed by exchange control. These limits are very small in relation to the banks' total foreign currency operations. During 1964 and 1965, the banks consistently employed in sterling part of the foreign currencies deposited with them; the net amount converted into sterling reached a peak of over £300 million during the early months of 1965. The position later changed, however, and at the end of 1969 the banks had net currency assets of nearly £60 million.

In conclusion, with regard to interest rates, it is obviously very difficult, if not impossible, for any market to operate completely independently and ignore outside influences so that those influences exert no pressures on that market. Nevertheless, the Euro-currency market is as near perfect in that respect as one could reasonably expect in the present day circumstances of immediate communications. The market is governed almost purely by the rules of supply and demand. The supply or demand may, of course, be influenced by circumstances outside the market.

Use of Euro-currencies

Indications have been given earlier that U.K. residents employ Euro-currencies for direct overseas investment in non-sterling countries and for portfolio investment in foreign securities. Another very important use at the present time is for what has become known as "front-end" finance. Although, technically and practically, the borrower is the overseas resident the object is to foster U.K. exports and many export contracts would not have come to fruition without the added facility of front-end finance. Front-end finance covers that portion of the total cost of an overseas export contract or project that does not come within the scope of the preferential rate of interest finance which is afforded by the U.K. Clearing and Scottish banks in conjunction with a direct bank guarantee of the Export Credits Guarantee Department.

However, the majority of borrowing in the London Euro-currency market is on behalf of overseas residents. The uses to which it is put are various but in general categories they may be described as being for liquid working capital, a temporary form of capital of a more permanent nature to be replaced by a recognized form of permanent capital at an auspicious moment, the purchase of a capital asset where it is anticipated that future profits will cover the cost thereby avoiding any alteration in the current capital structure. By way of country, at the end of 1969 the London market position was that the U.S.A. was borrowing about half of the funds available, Western Europe came next at around a third, and was followed, although for considerably less amounts, by Japan and Latin America.

Euro-currency Operations

The Euro-currency market proper has been stated earlier as being a deposit market. This applies in its entirety provided that all obligations are met. In other words, when a deposit is made it is in a currency, for example U.S. dollars, and when the time for repayment arrives this will be made in the same currency, in the example, U.S. dollars. When a borrowing is effected exactly the same principle applies. In consequence, in its pure state the market does not incur or acknowledge any exchange risk. However, in practice there is always the possibility that a borrower may be unable to repay and a dealer who has borrowed in the inter-bank market in order to on-lend to a commercial customer may be faced with having to buy the currency in order to meet the obligation to the depositor. This risk element will obviously be taken into account when the on-lending bank assesses the margin over the interbank rates of interest to be charged to the customer.

Another way in which Euro-currencies come on to the ordinary foreign exchange market is where the borrowing is in a currency different from that which is required by the borrower. The borrowing may be in U.S. dollars but the borrower requires pounds sterling. Obviously the borrower sells the U.S. dollars and thereby obtains the required sterling. This is a perfectly normal foreign exchange transaction. At maturity of the borrowing repayment must be in the currency, U.S. dollars. The dollars for this repayment could normally have been anticipated in one of three ways. The first is that the borrower could have expected U.S. dollar earnings from commercial transactions. The second is that the borrower, at the time of selling the borrowed dollars, could have arranged a normal forward exchange contract in order to purchase the dollars to meet the repayment. The third method is that the borrower could have awaited the repayment date and then bought the dollars at the then spot rate. The first method incurs no exchange risk; the second, again, incurs no exchange risk but entails the cost of the forward cover; the third leaves the borrower with a full exchange risk and he is completely at the mercy of any fluctuation in the rate of exchange. The first two methods may be subject to national exchange control. For example, at the time of writing, a U.K. borrower would require permission to maintain a Retained Currency Account for the first method; and for the second, forward exchange cover is restricted to the last quarter of the term of the loan but with an absolute maximum of six months.

It is often said that a characteristic of the Euro-currency market is that the operators borrow short and lend long. Current statistics evidence that in a general sense this is the case. However, from the commercial borrowers' point of view although he may be assured that the Euro-currency will be left with him for his use for the previously agreed term, which may even be for several years, it is most unlikely that he will know in advance the rate of interest that will be applied throughout. In other words, it is now unusual for a fixed rate of interest to be agreed. The procedure is that a margin over the inter-bank deposit rate is agreed and this is applied to one of the normally dealt-in deposit periods, usually the six months' rate. Under these circumstances the rate of interest payable is liable to change at the beginning of each new six-monthly period. This has become known as being on a "roll-over" basis. By way of example, a borrower who has agreed to a margin of $1\frac{1}{2}$ per cent per annum above the six month London inter-bank deposit rate may take delivery of the currency on 15th June. The appropriate inter-bank rate is $8\frac{1}{4}$ per cent per annum, the agreed margin is $1\frac{1}{2}$ per cent per annum; the borrower pays interest therefore at $9\frac{3}{4}$ per cent per annum until

14th December. The appropriate inter-bank rate for the next period which commences on the 15th December may have risen to $9\frac{1}{2}$ per cent per annum. Under these circumstances the borrower pays interest at 11 per cent per annum for that period. It is emphasized that, although the rate of interest changes periodically, the bank effecting the lending is committed to keep the currency available throughout the whole of the agreed period of the loan.

Euro-bonds

Euro-bonds fall outside the scope of this manual except in their relation to the Euro-currency market. In some instances the amount and period for which a borrowing is required is too great and too long for a normal Euro-currency operation. When this is so a bond issue is arranged in much the same way as a capital loan raising is effected on a stock exchange market in the country of the borrower. Euro-bonds are all bearer securities and Issues are usually underwritten by an international syndicate and sold in a number of countries. The tendency with these bond issues has been for them to carry a fixed rate of interest but recently there has been an issue which has a variable rate on the same basis as the roll-over procedure previously described. Normal straight issues, i.e. fixed repayment dates, soon became unpopular and now almost invariably bonds carry some form of conversion rights to enable purchasers to gain access to the equity of the company should they so desire.

Recognition

Over the past few years, and particularly in 1969, the Euro-currency market has expanded greatly. It has become an established source of providing additional liquidity during strict credit restriction periods at the same time providing a means for surplus funds throughout the world to be employed profitably. Despite certain disturbances throughout the world's foreign exchanges the Euro-currency market remained remarkably little disturbed. It would appear that this market is here to stay for very many years. Support is readily added to this view when it is realized that the Bank for International Settlements occasionally puts funds into the Euro-currency market in order to alleviate temporary disturbances and thereby assist in the maintaining of a stable market. Additionally, it would appear that the international recognition of the value of the market is such that very firm action would be taken, if necessary, to ensure its continuation.

CHAPTER XIII

EXCHANGE RESTRICTIONS

Clearing Arrangements; an Outline of the British Exchange and Trade Control System

TRADE depression and financial crises have occurred from time to time over the whole period of the world's history and, no doubt, to each successive generation the current crisis appeared to transcend any which had gone before. The complexity of the modern economic structure, however, has created a tendency for any disaster to produce effects much more far-reaching than was formerly the case. A comparison of the effects of an earthquake on the western seaboard of America a thousand years ago with the effects of such a happening today, with all its concomitants of escaping gas and water, cutting-off of electricity, shortage of the necessities and the decencies of life, etc., will serve to illustrate the point. Man's belief in himself being boundless, many and varied efforts have been made in the course of the succession of post-war crises to stem the current of events and to stop, or at least to palliate, the normal working of economic forces. The problems which have arisen and the attempts which have been made to cope with them are too vast and too widespread to be examined under any one head, and yet they are so closely interlocked one with the other that the consideration of any one facet inevitably leads to other facets thrusting themselves into prominence.

Since the term "economics" is nowadays made to cover every form of social activity, it is customary to refer to all troubles connected with such activities as "economic problems." Whether the trouble is a strike of coal miners in Fifeshire, or a default in the interest payments on its external debt by a small South American State, an "economic problem" arises, and it is a fact that cause and effect seem to be mixed so inextricably that an unbroken circle, "vicious" or otherwise, seems to be presented. In this chapter an attempt is made to explain and classify certain conditions which have resulted from the efforts made to cope with one aspect of the diversity of problems. It is impossible to treat in a few paragraphs of the world-wide series of events and mistakes which led to the taking of such steps, and it is even impossible to deal in detail with the actual steps, since these are themselves continually being revised and amended. It is proposed, therefore, to deal only with what are known as "exchange restrictions" from a general viewpoint, and to state broadly their causes, operations, and effects.

In the first place, the primary law of modern social existence may be stated that we must produce in order to consume, and that we must sell in order to buy. This should mean, *ipso facto*, that the interchange of commodities and services should everywhere be made as simple and as easy as possible. International trade demands not only that the passage of goods and services between nations should be facilitated but that the means of payment for such goods and services should be freely obtainable. In other words, the economic ideal is "free trade" in both commodities and services and in foreign exchange. The balance of payments between the nations of the world on trading account must tend to cancel out within a little. Young undeveloped countries may trade at a loss for a time through their need to import the means of development before the growth of their ability to export. Older countries can trade at a profit by importing raw materials or supplies and exporting finished products, but they must develop their potential markets by judicious loans to other countries out of their trading profits. The progress of the world depends upon the steady accumulation of savings and the investment of those savings in the further development of the more backward parts of the globe. It is of the first importance that the invested savings should be used productively, either directly or indirectly, and of equal importance that consuming power should keep pace with increased production.

The external consuming power of any country depends upon its supply of foreign exchange which, in turn, depends upon the proceeds of its exports and its ability to borrow from other countries. A country which has borrowed in the first place to enable it to develop must eventually become self-supporting, if it is to continue to exist, and as a result it tends to become less of a borrower and more of a lender. If general progress is to continue, fresh lendings must be directed towards fresh territory, and original borrowers must not be shut out of new markets or they will find no outlet for their produce, and so be unable to repay their borrowings. It is of no use to lend a man money with which to start a business and then to place every obstacle in the way of that business. Also, it is useless to lend money to a man who is already in debt if he proposes to use the loan for some purpose which is not connected with his business and will not increase his earning capacity. What applies to the individual applies also to communities or nations. Borrowings can be repaid only out of income, and any lender should first consider whether his loan is likely to increase the income of the borrower to the extent necessary for the payment of interest on and capital repayment of the loan. Increased income can result only from increased sales of products—whether of goods or services. If the borrower is in any way prevented from disposing of an increase in his output or if his borrowings are used in a manner which does not increase his output, his income will prove insufficient for the discharge of his debt, and the lender will be the ultimate loser.

When a country incurs a debt abroad, that debt can be discharged only out of the available supply of foreign exchange. Normally, the nationals are taxed internally in terms of the home currency and the proceeds are used in the purchase of the necessary sum in foreign exchange. For such a purchase to be possible, the country must be a creditor on trading account, and the surplus due to it is absorbed by official purchases of foreign currencies on debt account. Where the total debt incurred has grown too large for the country to support or where the existing load of debt is rendered too heavy by a falling off in exports or by a fall in the world price for such exports, then drastic measures must be taken to restore equilibrium between income and expenditure.

Exchange Control and Exchange Restrictions

The external value of a currency, i.e. its exchange value in terms of other currencies, depends normally on the relation between the world demand for and supply of that currency. Where a country has a credit or debit balance on trading and financial account over a period the resulting steady excess of demand for or supply of that currency will cause its exchange value to move accordingly. As long as the country is a member of a gold group, gold will move to or from that country and others within the group, and the balance of payments can be thereby adjusted. If the country is a consistent creditor or debtor, either so much gold will flow to it as to drive weaker members of the group off gold or so much gold will leave it as to force it off gold itself. The only preventive of such ultimate effects is a steady flow of loans for productive purposes from established creditor countries to younger and less-developed countries. There is, therefore, a rigid control of exchange fluctuations between countries on a full metallic standard of the same metal, but the extent of this control is limited as to time by the relative balances of indebtedness compared with the relative stocks of gold.

Where a country abandons any tangible base to its currency that currency becomes "free" and, in the absence of any official steps, "uncontrolled," and its value in terms of other currencies is left to be determined by its relative purchasing power. The most usual causes of the abandonment of a metallic or "currency exchange" base to a currency are—

(a) Official borrowings from abroad or any enforced contraction of external debt, e.g. reparations, too heavy for the normal resources of the country. The service of such debts in the shape of interest and capital repayments creates a demand for foreign exchange in excess of the ability of the country to supply either by way of a favourable balance of payments or by exports of precious metal. The stocks of the latter steadily become depleted until there is an insufficient or no backing to the currency. The metallic standard is perforce suspended.

(b) An excess of production of staple commodities at a time when general consuming power abroad is contracting. If such disparity between supply and demand is general, a fall in world prices must follow, with the result that the income accruing to the exporting countries is materially reduced, their balance of payment is seriously disturbed, and an outward flow of gold as in (a) will occur, with similar results. Under such conditions the Government will often try to bolster up prices by "rationalizing" the industry, or by raising a fund to buy up and destroy the supposed surplus or by payment of "bounties" to producers out of new taxation. Most of these artificial measures have always failed, however, and the only cure, in default of steps being taken universally to increase the general purchasing power, seems to have been the operation of the somewhat harsh law of "the weakest to the wall," i.e. allowing the price to fall until those producing at a loss are forced out of production, and the total supply thereby reduced to a nearer accord with the effective demand.

(c) Bad or extravagant internal financing, unbalanced budgets, industrial unrest or inefficiency, are all likely to lead to a "flight" of capital from the country. This once more results in an undue strain being placed on the available supply of foreign exchange and on the stock of gold, with similar results to those given in (a). It is usually in the effort to prevent the abandonment of a metallic standard that exchange restrictions have been imposed, and these have been continued in conjunction with a greater or less degree of official "control" over the exchanges when such abandonment has finally taken place.

(d) A state of national emergency, such as a major war which demands the complete mobilization and State control over national resources of all kinds, whether financial, material or human. In addition to imposing measures which give the State complete control over all the external resources of the country, further measures to control the volume and direction of both import and export trade will be introduced, so as to conserve national resources by preventing unessential expenditure abroad and to ensure that only goods surplus to the national war effort are exported, and then only (as far as possible) to countries from which essential purchases must be made and for which the export proceeds can be used in payment.

Forms of Exchange Restrictions

Exchange dealings being dealings in currency and it being part of the duty of a Government to safeguard the currency, all restrictions on exchange dealings are originally imposed with the object of preserving currency stability. Such restrictions may be only moderate in their inception, but they tend to become more and more onerous and drastic as their contractive effect develops. All systems of import and export licences, "quotas," etc., are in the nature of exchange restrictions, as their object is to reduce the effective home demand for foreign exchange, and/or to increase the supply by artificial measures. It cannot be too strongly emphasized that State interference with trade or exchange is nearly always due to a too heavy load of unproductive debt having been incurred, the service of which is too great a strain on the normal exchange resources of the country. In the effort to compromise with its creditors, the debtor State will first make strenuous attempts to meet its obligations, then offer part payments in foreign exchange and part in terms of the home currency (with restrictions on how these shall be used) and probably in the end will ask for or be forced to declare a moratorium, or cessation of debt payments.

The expression "exchange restrictions" is applied not only to official regulation of dealings in foreign exchange, but also to any disabilities attaching to the ownership of certain forms of the home currency. In their early form, exchange restrictions usually consist of regulations requiring importers to apply for licences authorizing them to purchase in the open market the foreign exchange needed to pay for their imports. This is very similar in operation and effects to a system of licences for the goods themselves. The next stage is for the State to require all exporters of home produce to sell only in terms of foreign currencies, and to hand over the eventual proceeds in such foreign currencies to the Government banking agent, which will pay out the equivalent in home currency to the exporter at the "official" rate of exchange. These combined restrictions give the Government complete control over the foreign exchange resources of the country. It buys up all the exchange available at an arbitrarily fixed price, which probably bears little or no relation to the actual international value of the currency, and retains for its own purposes such quantity of this "pool" as it may require. Only the balance is available to importers for purchase under licence, and then either at a price which shows a handsome profit to the Government or by tender, which means that the highest bidder stands the best chance, i.e. that the currency tends to depreciate further through more and more home units being offered by eager importers in the endeavour to obtain the foreign units desired.

Each of the main methods is capable of refinements. An exchange "quota" system may be introduced, allowing the purchase at the official selling rate of a monthly allowance of exchange based on the average over a previous period; arbitrary "rationing" of exchange to buyers may be resorted to; exporters may be required to hand over only a proportion of the proceeds in foreign currency of their exports, leaving them free to dispose of any balance in whatever manner they choose, etc. Again, import and export restrictions and official control of exchange dealings are usually combined, and may be reinforced by regulations against the granting of "clean" credits or overdrafts to foreigners (to prevent outside speculation against the currency), by the enforced surrender on the part of home owners of any assets which they may hold abroad, usually at an arbitrarily fixed price, and by the prohibition of the export of capital in any form. All such restrictions entail the appointment of a Government banking agent or the creation of some special body to handle the State monopoly in exchange, such as the Exchange Control Commission in the Argentine, the Spanish Foreign Exchange Institute in Spain, or the Exchange Equalization Account working through the Bank of England in this country.

All these restrictions are fairly simple both to operate and to understand. The serious complications arise when restrictions are placed on the actual use of certain funds in the home country. Since the object of the Government when imposing any trade or exchange restrictions is to reduce the demand for and increase the supply of foreign currencies against the home currency so that a larger balance of foreign exchange shall be available for Government purposes, it follows that this object would be defeated if foreign owners of capital were able to withdraw that capital from the country at will, or if foreign exporters were allowed to take payment from home importers in terms of the home currency and then offer that currency for sale in the exchange market, or if existing home debtors to foreign creditors could have any pressure brought to bear on them by the latter to discharge such debts immediately in full either by payment in home currency (no foreign exchange being available) or in goods, services, or securities.

To prevent such possibilities, the restrictions on trade and exchange are frequently reinforced by restrictions on the working of foreign-owned accounts, either banking or trading, by restrictions as to the uses which may be made of the proceeds of specified operations in trade and finance, and, more drastic still, the declaration of moratoria on certain forms of foreign debt. These latter may be entered into with the more or less reluctant consent of the main creditors, in which case the stigma of complete refusal to pay by the debtors is modified by using the term "Standstill Agreement." This means that, there being no method of putting a nation into bankruptcy, realizing its assets and generally "winding up" its affairs, the creditors have to accept such arrangements for the repayment of their dues as the debtors think fit to offer. This will eventually prove to be the minimum possible without doing irreparable damage to the future borrowing powers of the debtors. Invariably a large proportion of the original capital will have to be written off as a dead loss by the creditors, and this will induce a general reluctance, for some time following, to subscribe to any "foreign" loans, no matter for what purpose they may be issued. Since most of the debts covered by the moratorium will have been incurred on account of financial operations or of unproductive Government borrowings, while the cessation of foreign lendings will operate against the development of world trade in general, commercial interests are likely to suffer still further constriction owing, indirectly, to the overwhelming weight of "credit money" created during and since the war, which is continually seeking employment as a commodity instead of performing its proper function as the hand-maiden of the exchange of goods and services.

The first step under a moratorium on exchange dealings is to forbid the transfer out of the country of any sums in the home currency owned by foreigners. Such balances are then described as "frozen" and, in many cases, further additions are continually being made to such balances, as through the operations of a foreign-owned trading concern, e.g. a railway, which likewise become "frozen." The remittance outward of profits due to the foreign owners becomes impossible, and the pent-up demand for exchange eventually reaches a point which is impossible of satisfaction out of any likely resources of the country. Such debts have then to be capitalized and their redemption spread over a long period, but this again adds to the total burden of external debt due by the country, and its ultimate liquidation presupposes an increase in its net income which can be possible only if its trade is allowed to increase—a doubtful possibility in these days of universal restrictions and nationalism.

The same principle is applied to financial debts. Where credits have been granted by other countries to home nationals for trading, financial or stock exchange operations a purchase of foreign exchange must be made eventually in order that the home debtor may discharge his debt to the foreign creditor. Such credits may have been running for years, being carried on by a series of periodic renewals of the bills drawn under them, and the funds raised through the original drawing of bills will have been remitted to the borrowing country long since. Should a moratorium on foreign debts be declared by that country, the foreign grantors of such credits will be compelled to renew them, fully or in part, for an indefinite period, since the foreign exchange needed to pay them off cannot be obtained by the debtors. Such debts are usually made the subject of a "standstill agreement," under which very small percentages of the amounts outstanding are paid off periodically, the remainder having to be renewed by the creditors or written off as a loss, while the creditors will usually place restrictions on the utilization by the debtors of any existing "credit lines" which have not been fully availed of or of any fresh "credit lines" which might conceivably be granted. The renewals of acceptances drawn under such agreements in respect of outstanding engagements are known in the market as "standstill bills," and command a somewhat worse rate of discount than does home commercial paper.

The emergency of war, demanding the complete mobilization and State control over national resources of all kinds, usually results in even more drastic restrictions being placed on the use of foreign-owned assets within the country. Assets belonging to residents of enemy countries will, of course, be sequestrated by the State and used eventually to discharge debts due by enemy residents to home residents, and should there be a surplus, it will be taken over as an instalment on account of whatever reparations may be demanded from the enemy after the conclusion of hostilities. As regards the liquid balances and investments of all kinds in the ownership of residents in allied or neutral countries, these become immediately subject to strict control. In the most drastic cases withdrawals from liquid balances are limited to maximum amounts within a given period, and even where no such restriction is placed on these liquid balances, the purposes for which they can be used and any change of ownership of the funds are strictly controlled. This is essential in order to safeguard the official exchange rates. If a foreign country is piling up balances in the home currency owing to the need to purchase from it various essential commodities, it would obviously be bad policy to allow the owners of those balances to transfer them at will to residents of some other foreign country, because they would tend to do so at exchange rates increasingly adverse to the home country through whatever "free" world exchange markets remained open, thus causing a divergency from official exchange rates and undermining world confidence in the home currency. It was this consideration which led the British Treasury to create so many bilateral types of sterling in the early stages of the last war and to which more detailed reference is made later in this chapter.

It has now become an established practice under any extensive system of exchange and trade control for foreign-owned investments within the country to be "blocked" in a greater or lesser degree. The argument is that if the country was regarded as good enough to invest money in before the occurrence of the emergency which required the imposition of such controls, it should be regarded as capable of eventually surmounting the emergency and so good enough for foreign investments to remain there during the intervening period. In most cases it is only the sale of the investment and the repatriation of the sales proceeds to the foreign country or the transfer of the investment to a resident in another foreign country which are prohibited. Wherever possible the remittance of all income from such investments is allowed to be made to the owner in his normal country of residence in order to preserve as far as possible the financial reputation of the home country. Similarly, legal obligations undertaken before the emergency are usually allowed to be implemented for the same reason: the proceeds of maturing insurance policies, securities due for repayment under fixed redemption arrangements, royalties and licence fees payable under pre-emergency contracts, and similar recognized contractual liabilities are allowed to be remitted to the foreign owner in his normal country of residence. Circumstances may, however, prove too adverse for such concessions to remain in force. Bad internal administration and severe inflation within a country may so denude it of external resources that it can hardly find sufficient foreign exchange with which to pay for its minimum essential purchases abroad and is quite unable to find the foreign currency required to meet financial remittances of this nature. In such cases, it is usual for debtors of this kind in that country to be required to pay their liabilities in local currency into a bank account in the name of the foreign creditor, with a guarantee to be responsible for any additional payment required by an adverse movement in the exchange rate pending the eventual allocation by the State authority of the required amount in foreign currency. These local currency accounts are usually "blocked" against the foreign owner, but in some instances he may be allowed to use part of such balances to meet expenses in the course of a business or pleasure visit to the country, or for the upkeep of dependants living in the country, or similar personal expenditure. Experience has shown that the "unblocking" of investments or local currency balances is a painful and lengthy process for all parties, but it is a rather curious psychological fact that where the fortunes of a country seem to be improving to the stage where the release of "blocked" assets can safely be undertaken, foreign investors, so far from making plans to repatriate their outstanding investments, are more inclined to place further capital in the debtor country in view of the flourishing state of its economy.

Methods of Exchange Control

Any form of official interference with the freedom of dealings in foreign exchange is, of course, a form of exchange control. Normally, a form of control over fluctuations in exchange rates is exercised by the working of the gold standard. Such control is automatic as long as free gold markets are maintained, and is also rigid for all practical purposes. Where a currency is divorced from any international common denominator, as where a gold standard country suspends gold payments, it must be left to find its own level in terms of other currencies, in which case it will fluctuate continuously with every change in the temporary international balance of payments and with the operations of exchange speculators, or else some official action must be taken to "control" the exchange value of the currency, i.e. to prevent or at least to limit wild and constant fluctuations in exchange rates.

The most drastic form of official action is that by which all exporters are compelled by law to sell only in terms of the currencies of buying countries and to hand over to the home Central Bank or State Bureau the entire proceeds of such sales. Such foreign currency will be purchased from the exporter by the central authority only at an arbitrarily fixed "official" rate of exchange in terms of the home currency. At the same time importers wishing to buy goods from abroad must first apply for a licence to import and must also apply to the central authority for the allocation of the necessary foreign exchange. This latter will only be sold to them at another arbitrarily fixed "official" rate (which may bear little relation to current market quotations), and which even then may only be obtainable in a series of small amounts. It is under such conditions that clandestine dealings in exchange take place that lead to the creation of a "Black Bourse" or illegal exchange market. Such markets have persisted under these conditions in spite of rigorous attempts to suppress them, as the prospects of large profits for the operators appear to outweigh the fears of fines and imprisonment. A slight relaxation of this form of control is to be found when the central authority is permitted to offer specified sums of foreign exchange for sale by tender to prospective buyers who already hold the necessary licences, instead of "rationed" sales at the "official" rate.

A variant of this system, practised in some of the Latin-American countries, marshalls all imports according to their priorities. Products such as capital goods required for the industrial development of the country are given top priority, then come necessities of various kinds such as materials for industry and essential foods not obtainable from indigenous sources, lower down the list come other imports in different categories until non-essential and luxury items are reached at the end of the table. Then a sliding scale of exchange rates is fixed to give importers preference according to the type of merchandise they bring into the country. In the hypothetical case of a country using a monetary unit called a "peso," a rate of ten to £1 is applied when importers of the highest priority goods wish to pay for their purchases; various higher rates (more pesos per pound) are fixed for goods lower down the scale, until one gets to luxuries where the rate is, say, fifty pesos to the pound. In order to maintain flexibility, the allocation of goods to categories is varied from time to time by the controlling authority according to changing needs, and the rates of exchange are altered in response to balance of payment criteria. When a favourable tendency is in evidence, the control relaxes the high rates for non-essential imports; when the trend is unfavourable, the control raises these rates in order to conserve exchange resources by cutting down the amount of foreign exchange spent by importers on goods coming into these categories.

In a still more relaxed form, the duty of acquiring all foreign exchange from exporters and allotting it to importers may be handed over to approved home banks instead of being carried out by the State Bank or a State Bureau. Even so, it is usually stipulated that official buying and selling rates shall be fixed and that a stated percentage of all foreign exchange acquired by the banks shall be sold to the State at the fixed price.

Greater relaxation still is shown by the system under which approved banks are allowed to deal freely in foreign exchange, but must submit periodical summaries of their transactions to a Government department or to the State Bank. Any bank which is considered by such authority to have dealt unwisely or to have facilitated speculation in the currency may be reprimanded, and is liable to have its freedom of action curtailed or even withdrawn. As mentioned earlier, a ban on the granting of overdrafts or "clean" credits to foreigners is also nearly always imposed under all these conditions, and this is sometimes reinforced by a ban on the public issue of loans for foreign account.

Finally, there is the method by which the Central Authority endeavours to prevent, or to limit, fluctuations in the exchanges by entering the market as a seller or buyer of other currencies as the need arises and according to the requirements of the market, which otherwise is left completely free to deal as it chooses. Given a high degree of efficiency in operation, this method would be by far the most satisfactory of any system of "control," since it imposes no hindrance on either trade or financial activities, but allows the normal economic life of the country to proceed as usual. Its drawback lies in the fact that, while the Central Authority can always sell the home currency and accumulate a stock of other currencies, it cannot buy its own currency indefinitely in exchange for others unless it possesses ample balances or credits abroad on which it can draw, or an ample stock of gold at home. A country which has had to render its currency temporarily inconvertible, to produce the need for exchange "control," is not usually in a position to command any resources in gold or foreign assets or credits, since these must have been utilized before the currency was allowed to become inconvertible. It is quite possible, however, for such steps to be taken as will prevent exceptionally wide and rapid fluctuations in the exchanges without hoping to arrest completely a definite world trend either for or against the home currency.

Clearing Arrangements

Another form of exchange and trade control which does not require constant official intervention in the exchange market is the establishment of an "Exchange Clearing" under a bilateral agreement between two States. It usually forms part of a comprehensive Trade and Payments Agreement which provides for an estimated volume of trade in a stated range of commodities between the two countries, for which payment will be effected each way through the Clearing. A temporary "swing" one way or the other is allowed for, and each country agrees to hold at any one time a maximum sum in the other currency. The Agreement may provide that balances in excess of this sum shall be discharged in gold or in U.S. dollars, or it may provide that exports from the creditor country shall be slowed down until the arrears have been overtaken. In some cases official exchange rates are fixed in each country for the currency of the other, while in others a unit, usually known as a "Clearing dollar"—theoretically the equivalent of the U.S. dollar—is used as the unit of account. For example, if an "Exchange Clearing" is set up between countries A and B, with official exchange rates for each currency on either side, a par rate of exchange is agreed upon for the two currency units— let us say 2·50 of A for 5·00 of B. Official buying and selling rates will then be fixed in each country. A will probably fix a rate of $49\frac{1}{2}$ – $50\frac{1}{2}$ of A units per 100 B units, while B will probably fix a rate of 199–201 B units per 100 A units. This means that a resident of A who has to discharge a debt to B will have to pay in local currency to his own authorities at the rate of $50\frac{1}{2}$ local units per 100 B units, while a creditor in A will receive $49\frac{1}{2}$ local units for each 100 B units due to him. Any B debtors will have to pay their debts at the rate of 201 local units per 100 A units, while creditors will receive 199 local units for each 100 A units due to them. This profit margin between the official buying and selling rates is used to cover the expenses of the Clearing.

Where Clearing arrangements are based on a "Clearing dollar," nominally equal in value to the U.S. dollar, each country uses the official parity between its currency and the U.S. dollar as the value of the "Clearing dollar" in terms of local currency. If a resident in country A buys goods from a resident in country B, the seller will convert his invoice price in terms of his own currency into "Clearing dollars" at the official rate fixed by his own authorities. To meet this invoice the buyer will then have to pay into the Clearing Office at his end an amount of his own currency sufficient to purchase the required amount in "Clearing dollars" at the official rate fixed by his own authorities. If, for instance, the two countries are both members of the International Monetary Fund, with which A has a declared parity of 5 local units per \$1 and B of 625 units per \$1, and an "Exchange Clearing" using a "Clearing dollar" is set up between them, these parity values will be used to calculate the value in "Clearing dollars" of debts due either way. If A buys from B, the seller will invoice in local currency and convert the total into "Clearing dollars" by dividing by 625. The buyer in A will then have to pay into the Clearing Office 5 units of his own currency for each "Clearing dollar" required. In addition the Clearing Office at each end will make a charge for their services by adding a commission to the amount to be paid by the buyer in local currency at the one end, and by deducting a commission from the amount paid over to the seller in local currency at the other end.

The working of these systems is quite simple. The Central Bank in each country opens an account in terms of local currency in the name of its counterpart, and Clearing Offices are opened in all the principal centres in both countries, each of which keeps an account in local currency with its Central Bank. Creditors in each country present their claims, properly documented, to the nearest local Clearing Office, which thereupon forwards them direct, or through its Central Bank, to the Clearing Office in the other country nearest to the debtor. This Office then presents the claim to the debtor, and on receiving the equivalent in local currency pays it over to its Central Bank and notifies its opposite number of the amount so credited. The original collecting Office will then, or at some later date, be advised by its own Central Bank that its account has been credited with the equivalent in local currency of the amount received in the other country, and it then pays out to the creditor the amount of his original claim in local currency, less any deductions which may have been made by the debtor (the correctness of which must be thrashed out between the two parties) and any official commission which may be chargeable.

It can easily be seen that unless trade between the two countries is more or less in equilibrium over a period, one or other of the two Central Banks concerned will accumulate a balance in the other currency against which it has to create an overdraft in terms of its own currency for its counterpart. It is the size of these excess credit balances and overdrafts that is limited as a rule by the terms of the relative Trade and Payments Agreement and, when the limits are reached, either the creditor country must cut down its exports to the debtor or the debtor must redeem the surplus by paying over gold, or some currency acceptable to the creditor, equivalent to the amount of the excess. While arrangements of this nature can be of considerable temporary use to countries with only small reserves of gold and "hard" currency, they have, of course, a restrictive tendency in that buyers in each country may be forced to purchase essential goods in the other country at uneconomic prices because their authorities cannot provide them with the foreign exchange needed to cover purchases in cheaper markets. It is now generally recognized that all types of bilateral Trade and Payments Agreements are restrictive and that international trade must be liberalized on a multilateral basis if the full benefit of potential world production is to be attained and enjoyed by the human race as a whole.

The British Exchange and Trade Control System

Although on previous occasions the British Government has assumed control of, and responsibility for the exchanges with certain currencies, beginning with the 1914–18 war, and again in 1932, following the suspension of gold payments in September, 1931, no measures had ever been taken prior to the outbreak of war in 1939 to introduce a comprehensive system of control over both the foreign exchanges and foreign trade. The enormous disruption of the economy which another world war would cause had, however, been foreseen some time in advance, and detailed plans had been formed to cope with any such emergency in regard to finance and trade. When war was plainly imminent, legislation permitting these plans to be put into operation was immediately passed by Parliament in the form of the Emergency Powers (Defence) Act, 1939, of 24th August, 1939. This general Act gave power to the Crown to issue Defence Regulations by Order in Council, which would have the force of law, and one widely-drawn section gave the powers necessary to institute exchange and trade control. The first Defence (Finance) Regulations in the form of Statutory Rules and Orders were issued immediately and required U.K. residents to declare their interests in securities payable in certain foreign currencies. With the actual outbreak of war on 3rd September, 1939, further Defence (Finance) Regulations were issued in a steady stream and were interpreted by the Bank of England Exchange Control, as agents for H.M. Treasury, by means of Notices to Banks and Bankers. The story of the principles and practices of the British Government in regard to these matters is told in the late H. E. Evitt's *Exchange and Trade Control in Theory and Practice,* and it is not proposed to deal here in detail with the inception, waxing and waning of the British system. The following, however, is the broad outline of the subsequent course of events.

As a first step on the financial side, control was assumed over all dealings in gold and all the major foreign currencies. Any resident of the United Kingdom was placed under a legal obligation to offer through his bankers for sale to the Treasury, at an official fixed price, all gold in bars or coin (except collectors' pieces) in his possession, or in his ownership, or under his control. This obligation did not apply to silver, but dealings in that metal were confined to recognized brokers and members of the jewellery trade. A similar obligation rested on U.K. residents who held or owned or had control of any of the foreign currencies over which official control had been assumed and for which official buying and selling prices against sterling were fixed by the Bank of England. These currencies were, and still are, known as "specified currencies," and the official list of such currencies as in March, 1970, is given in the Appendix to this book. While the Bank of England was the principal Treasury agent, it was given power to appoint sub-agents, and a number of banks and finance houses were at once designated as "authorized dealers in exchange" or, more shortly "authorized banks." Additions were steadily made to this list of sub-agents, and it now comprises almost every commercial bank and finance house in the country. It is these sub-agents who actually carry out the day-to-day exchange dealings with their customers, who are responsible for examining much documentary evidence, and who are the channel of communication between the public and the Exchange Control. In fact, with recent relaxations in Exchange Control regulations and the very wide powers now delegated to these sub-agents, they can almost be said to constitute the Exchange Control!

When fixing the official prices for gold and for the "specified" currencies, the authorities had to have regard to several considerations. The gold price had to be based, within a little, on the world price in order to discourage smuggling, but the exchange rates were affected by different factors. The authorities had to decide—

(a) from which other countries the most essential goods and services, e.g. shipping, would have to be obtained;

(b) the probable maximum value of exports which this country could provide, having regard to the vital importance of war production, and which the foreign country concerned would accept and absorb at a given rate of exchange;

(c) what rate of exchange would give the maximum impetus to such exports without unduly raising the cost of essential imports;

(d) what would be the reaction of the foreign country concerned to any proposed rate of exchange, because too great a cheapening of sterling in terms of one foreign currency as against another might well provoke hostility in the first country because its non-essential exports would be made too dear for the British buyer, and in the other country because its essential imports from Britain were not being made cheap enough;

(e) for how long national resources, when mobilized, would be sufficient to bridge any gap between the probable cost of imports and the proceeds of exports at the proposed rates of exchange; and

(f) which foreign currencies were of such prime importance as to demand immediate State acquisition and the fixation of official buying and selling rates, which currencies could be left for the time being but were likely to be subject to similar action in due course, and which were of so little importance as to render the need for State acquisition improbable, so that the exchange rates with sterling could be left to the normal operations of the open market.

The skill and vision with which these decisions were taken is shown by the fact that the exchange rate for the U.S. dollar was unchanged at 4·03 from September, 1939, to September, 1949.

The development of the group of countries known as the "Sterling Area" has been dealt with in Chapter VI, and all the independent Commonwealth countries and the foreign countries who joined the group voluntarily, introduced similar measures and have kept in step all the time with the British Exchange Control. The Colonies and Mandated Territories fall, of course, under British jurisdiction, and the same system was also applied to them.

MOBILIZATION AND CONTROL OF EXTERNAL RESOURCES

The mobilization of and control over the external resources of the United Kingdom itself was accomplished by the following measures—

(*a*) The compulsory surrender by all U.K. residents to the Treasury of all existing liquid balances held abroad in any of the "specified" currencies over which the resident had control, and by the similar surrender of all sums in such currencies over which control was subsequently acquired by the resident.

(*b*) The registering with the Bank of England by U.K. residents of particulars of all securities under their control, of which the interest or repayment of capital could, under the terms of the issue, be claimed from the borrowers in terms of any of the "specified" currencies. From time to time Orders were issued vesting the property in certain of these securities in the Treasury and requiring the U.K. resident who had registered these securities with the Bank of England immediately to take steps to effect the legal transfer of the securities to that Institution. Official prices were fixed for the purchase of these "vested" securities based within a little on current market quotations. In some cases the British owners of foreign subsidiary companies were required to dispose of these subsidiaries to the best possible advantage in terms of the relative "specified" currency and to surrender the proceeds at the official exchange rate.

(*c*) To conserve foreign exchange resources to the greatest possible extent, no British resident could arrange for payment to be effected to a non-resident, either in foreign currency or in sterling, without obtaining official approval to an application in writing on an appropriate Exchange Control Form for permission to do so. Expenditure on imports was kept to a minimum by an extensive system of import licencing operated by the Board of Trade, the effects of which are dealt with in a later paragraph. Payments ancillary to imports, such as freight, insurances, transhipment charges, commissions, etc., were allowed if adequately documented, but personal payments were severely restricted.

(d) With the dual purpose of securing the homeward remittance of the foreign exchange proceeds of exports and of preventing exports of capital in the shape of goods, a system of export licensing was gradually introduced commencing on 8th March, 1940, with export control over whisky, furs, tin, rubber and jute. The detailed effects of this step are also given later.

(e) Realization of existing capital investments in this country by non-residents and the repatriation of the proceeds was prohibited. Transfers of securities between residents of the same monetary area could be carried out under special licences issued by the Bank of England, but the sterling proceeds of any outright realization of such investments could only be placed to the credit of a "blocked" sterling account in the name of the foreign resident and could only be used by him for further investment in this country. "Blocked" sterling accounts were also created out of sterling assets owned by persons leaving this country that were in excess of the amounts they were permitted to take with them. In the early stages, persons who had come to this country as refugees from Nazi oppression and who, in many cases, had brought with them substantial sums of money, were, at first, allowed to take with them their entire assets if they decided to move on to some other country, such as Brazil. By the middle of 1940, however, it was evident that this concession was proving too costly and the amounts which emigrants were allowed to take with them were steadily reduced to a figure of £5,000 for countries outside the Dollar Area and to £2,000 for Dollar Area countries. These capital sums, however, could only be withdrawn by equal instalments over a period of four years, and during this probationary period the emigrant remained a "resident" for Exchange Control purposes. At the end of that time he was officially recognized as permanently resident in his new country, his banking account was given this designation, and he was allowed to receive all subsequent income accruing to him in this country. His remaining capital, how- ever, whether liquid or invested, became "blocked." In August, 1954, the probationary period of four years was abolished, so that emigrants could at once receive the full permitted capital allowance in their country of destination, of which they became immediate residents for official purposes. Any subsequent sterling income could be remit- ted to them as it accrued. Finally, in February, 1959, the allowance for the Dollar Area was raised to £5,000. This figure still obtains but any excess amount is "restricted" for four years after which it becomes subject to the regulations then in force.

CONTROL OF IMPORTS

The procedure for the control of imports was simple, but effective, and that part of it which concerns Exchange Control is still in force. A wide range of commodities can now be imported under Open General Licence, but for others a special Import Licence must still be obtained by means of an application on an official form to the Import Licensing Department of the Board of Trade. This enables the authorities to regulate both the volume and source of imports, It has been a basic principle of the British Exchange Control, in contrast to many other similar Controls, that permission to import goods automatically carries with it permission to pay for them in an appropriate manner. The granting of a special Import Licence, or the admission of goods under an O.G.L., is sufficient for the importer to be allowed to purchase the requisite foreign currency or to make a sterling payment to an appropriate foreign account.

Where merchandise is imported from any other sterling country, there is of course no exchange control formality. But where the goods originate from outside the area, which will involve the importer in paying sterling to a non-resident or payment in non-sterling currency, it is necessary for the importer to produce certain evidence to his bank when arranging for payment to be made. The formalities vary according to whether the amount does or does not exceed £2,000, or the equivalent in foreign currency. In the case of a single payment in full and final settlement not exceeding the figure mentioned, no Exchange Control form need be completed; the importer produces to his bank a copy of the settlement invoice, and the bank marks this document to indicate that payment has been made; but if the goods have not arrived, then the importer must show the bank evidence of the purchase and value of the goods and the definitive import licence where this is required for goods of that class. When the amount to be paid in full and final settlement exceeds £2,000 (or equivalent in foreign currency), if the goods have arrived and have been passed through customs, the Customs will have issued a "Customs Entry Form" with a copy marked "Exchange Control Copy" and this latter document must be handed to the bank— there is no exchange control form to be filled in except in certain very special circumstances; if, however, the goods have not arrived and thus have not been passed through customs, the importer must complete an exchange control form as well as showing the bank evidence of the purchase and value of the goods (form E for payment in foreign currency, or Sterling Transfer Form when paying in sterling). When the arrangements between the importer and his foreign supplier involve multiple payments the procedure is slightly varied, and when the debtor who wants to make payment is not himself the importer he must get the Exchange Control Copy of the Customs Entry from the actual importer, always supposing the amount to exceed £2,000.

The procedure outlined above represents a simplification of that which earlier applied. Indeed, it can be truly said that the complications of form-filling for parties engaged in foreign trade are now being made less and less onerous as time passes.

CONTROL OF EXPORTS

An equally simple procedure was evolved to control both the volume and direction of exports and to ensure that the sales proceeds of exports were brought home to this country within a reasonable time, so as to prevent the export of capital in the form of goods. The procedure originally involved a form in duplicate called "C.D.3" for exports to destinations outside the sterling area. The minimum amount for which form-filling was required was progressively raised, until in December, 1963, the form was superseded by a much simpler form called "C.D.6." This is a single sheet which has to be completed by the exporter of goods going outside the sterling area, when the f.o.b. value of the goods is £2,000 or more, or equivalent in foreign currency. The same form is employed for certain other purposes, such as gifts of a value exceeding £100 in value.

It should be clearly understood that no exporter avoids the responsibility for securing payment in what the Act calls "an approved manner," even if he does not have to fill in a form; this basic requirement of the Exchange Control Act, 1947, is interpreted to mean payment in sterling from an external account, or payment in any specified currency, or by International Money Order, or (in practice, and by a special dispensation) payment in any currency which is freely convertible into sterling, as further explained in the next section of this chapter.

All exports are "entered to customs" at the port where they are loaded on the export vessel (or aircraft). This is a process by which the shipper, or an agent acting for him, submits a customs form within six days of the departure of the vessel; these forms become the basis from which are compiled the export statistics of the country; corresponding statistics are compiled for imports, thus enabling the Customs to arrive at the balance of trade as explained in Chapter 11. The form C.D.6, referred to above, has to be submitted to customs at the time of customs entry.

If there are some special circumstances, the exporter is required to apply for permission before the goods are sent off to any destination outside the Scheduled Territories, and form C.D.6 can be used for this purpose. "Special circumstances" in this connexion arise when the exporter is to receive less than full value in payment, when payment in the prescribed manner is not contemplated by the parties, when more than six months' credit is being given to the foreign importer, where the goods are being exported on consignment, or if the export arises from a contract of hire. The form C.D.6 has to be submitted to bankers by the exporter for permission before the merchandise is shipped, or sent by parcel post, or air-freighted to the destination outside the Scheduled Territories.

An interesting development is worth mention here, though not connected with exchange control. This is the simplification of all documentation after the bill of lading by using a recently designed "aligned series" of forms, including the commercial invoice, certificate of origin, port note, customs entry form and the C.D.6, all of which are made out from one "master." This makes the documentation much simpler, since it cuts out much of the preparation and checking of different forms, and in effect concentrates all the effort into a single operation.

PAYMENT FOR EXPORTS

Recent relaxations in Exchange Control requirements have simplified greatly the payment problems of the exporter. During the period when a variety of types of bilateral sterling existed, the methods by which an exporter could accept payment from a foreign buyer were extremely limited and special permission had to be obtained from the Exchange Control before any other form of payment could be accepted. When practically all the sterling accounts of foreign countries outside the Dollar Area were merged into one type of sterling (which was designated "Transferable Sterling") in March, 1954, the methods by which exporters could accept payment and the sources from which it could be obtained were appreciably enlarged. In December, 1958, all current sterling balances of "non-residents," i.e. resident outside the sterling group of countries, were merged into one type of sterling, with limited convertibility, which was designated "External Sterling," and all foreign sterling accounts were designated "External Accounts." This further simplified the position of the exporter in regard to the forms of payment which he might accept and an official notice of April, 1968, sets out the prescribed manners of payment for exports from the United Kingdom to the Non-scheduled Territories, i.e. all countries outside the sterling group of countries. These prescribed manners of payment

for exports, as current at the time of writing, are as follows—
(a) In sterling from an External Account or in any foreign currency.

(b) From funds due to a non-resident. The exporter must satisfy an "Authorized Bank" that, as a result of some previous transaction, he is indebted to a non-resident for a specific sum in sterling, of which, because of the nature of the underlying transaction, the "Authorized Bank" would have power to approve the transfer to an External Account. If the sterling debt has arisen as the result of the import of foreign goods into the United Kingdom, it can only be used in settlement for an export if the imported goods have, in fact, already arrived in the United Kingdom.

(c) By international money order.

(d) By funds credited to a Retained Currency Account. In certain cases, and for certain well-defined purposes, a British resident may be authorized by the Exchange Control to maintain an account abroad in a "specified" currency, and such accounts are known as "Retained Currency Accounts." An exporter who has received permission to maintain such an account, and who is prepared to accept payment for an export to a foreign buyer in terms of the currency in which that account is maintained, is allowed to do so.

The sales proceeds of exports can be accepted by any one of these methods under the General Authority conveyed by the official notice but, if it is desired to accept payment by any other method, an application must be made to the Exchange Control for a special permit. Now that only one type of international sterling exists for use in the settlement of all current transactions, it is no longer necessary for an exporter to obtain payment by any one of the approved methods direct from a foreign buyer. A British exporter may, for instance, ship goods to Spain and receive payment from Holland, or Switzerland, or the Argentine, as long as payment is made by one of the approved methods. An importer in Hungary can arrange with a West German agent to effect payment to the British exporter, for his account, in External Sterling or in Deutschmarks, or by any other approved method. The method of payment must, of course, be described fully on the relative Form C.D.6 where applicable, and the supervision of an Authorized Bank is required.

EXPORTS OF CAPITAL

In addition to preventing withdrawals of foreign-owned capital by requiring non-residents to retain in this country their existing invested capital, the British Exchange Control also had to prevent the export of capital by residents, so as to retain within the country the maximum of capital resources. The complete control over all payments from resident to non-resident accounts provided the necessary administrative power, and for a long period no new investments of British capital overseas of any kind were authorized. With the gradual return to economic strength and the official policy of the removal or relaxation of controls of all kinds, however, some capital investments abroad are now being allowed, but subject to certain conditions. The would-be investor must be able to show that the proposed investment will be of benefit to British economy, particularly in furtherance of the export drive. For example, a British firm might find its finished products shut out from a foreign market by tariff or other conditions, and therefore propose to establish a subsidiary in the foreign country which it would supply with technical information and a certain quantity of semi-finished products or finished parts which the subsidiary would incorporate into the finished product with the aid of local labour and the other necessary materials. This would preserve the identity and trade name of the British product and would permit continuance of at least a part of former British exports. Again, a British firm using a certain product, either primary or manufactured, as an essential part of its output, might be allowed to invest in a foreign company from which the product was obtainable in order to preserve continuity of supplies, if the product was not obtainable in this country. Where permission is given and the investments meet certain criteria the financing is allowed through the official foreign exchange market or investment currency otherwise it must be by loan in foreign currency.

On the subject of subsidiary companies, the policy of benefit to the British economy is applied in reverse to projected investments of foreign capital in British industry. All such investments would naturally be made with a view to receiving a profit and unless, as a result of the proposed investment, some industry or process is developed in this country which is superior to any existing method, and which will consequently extend British export markets in areas which will bring in foreign exchange, the investment may not be accepted by the authorities. There have been many instances where American firms have wished to set up subsidiary companies in this country with the object of manufacturing an American patented article for sale to other Scheduled Territories countries into which the product is not admitted owing to the enforced discrimination against unessential dollar goods. Such proposals are invariably rejected because the gain to British export trade would be largely in "resident" sterling, while royalty fees and the share of profits of the British subsidiary payable to the American interests would cost dollars.

Similar considerations apply to royalty agreements in which a British firm would acquire manufacturing and selling rights under foreign-owned patents. All such agreements must be submitted to the Exchange Control for approval before they can legally be signed by the British firm concerned, and it will again have to be shown that the acquisition of the rights will benefit British economy and that sufficient of the resulting product will be exported to foreign markets to more than compensate for the loss of foreign exchange arising from the payment of royalties and licensing fees. Royalty agreements with American firms in particular must show a sure prospect that a dollar income will result from eventual exports more than sufficient to cover the royalty payments in dollars.

"Frozen" Sterling Balances

There is a clear-cut distinction between "blocked" and "frozen" sterling. The term "blocked" applied only to sterling funds already in the United Kingdom for account of residents of countries outside the Scheduled Territories which, by a ruling of H.M. Treasury, were not allowed to be transferred out of the country, but were eligible only for investment in specified securities. The causes which gave rise to the creation of "blocked" sterling have already been mentioned. The creation of "frozen" sterling balances arose from very different causes. During the war our productive capacity was almost wholly devoted to war production, and the surplus available for export grew steadily less. Our mercantile marine was mainly engaged in fetching and carrying war supplies, so that our "invisible" income from shipping fell to a small percentage of the normal, while the general contraction of international trade reduced our insurance income, and the closing of the commodity markets and the great reduction in other forms of "invisible" services cut our receipts to a minimum. At the same time we were forced to purchase heavily from certain overseas countries essential supplies of foodstuffs, armament materials, etc., for which their accounts were credited in sterling. Normally they would have used this sterling to purchase commodities within the Sterling Area or elsewhere to meet their current needs. The available surplus of the Sterling Area was, however, quite inadequate to absorb the large credit balances which these overseas countries were accumulating, while the restrictions on the international transfer of sterling, which the exigencies of war had compelled this country to impose, prevented the expenditure of these sterling balances in foreign countries. In some cases, such as India and Egypt for example, these balances were further swollen by local expenditure for the upkeep of the Armed Forces and their bases abroad. At the end of June, 1947, Indian sterling balances amounted to no less than £1,160 millions, while Egypt had accumulated about £400 millions.

Even before the end of the war it was apparent that the economy and productive capacity of this country would be quite inadequate to redeem these accumulated balances by taking them in exchange for current production of goods and services, even over a period of years. Our own current needs, combined with the almost total exhaustion of our external resources, imperatively demanded that our maximum current production should be devoted towards providing the means of payment for current essential purchases. We simply could not afford to spare any of our current production as an unrequited export for the discharge of old debts. The British Government, therefore, had to announce to each of the countries concerned that its sterling balance in excess of a stated sum, which was to remain freely usable as a working balance, must be regarded as "frozen" and as completely unusable until mutually satisfactory arrangements for their release could be made. In conformity with that part of the Anglo-American Loan Agreement of 1946 which required this country to arrange for the releasing, funding or writing off of "frozen" sterling balances as soon as might be practicable, discussions with the various creditors were commenced early in 1947.

The first agreement was made with the Argentine and was exceptional. Her "frozen" balances amounted to nearly £140 millions, and out of this sum it was agreed that £125 millions should be released for payment to British residents in return for acquisition by the Argentine Government of the vast railway system in the Argentine, which was originally developed and financed by British capital. Somewhat similar arrangements were made with Brazil and Uruguay, but the agreements with India, Egypt and Iraq, and subsequently with Pakistan, provided for the release of agreed amounts annually. As previously mentioned, this type of sterling no longer exists.

BILATERAL TYPES OF STERLING

Traditionally a holder of sterling anywhere in the world was at liberty to transfer it at will to any other party, or to exchange it for any foreign currency of his own choosing, or even for gold. This is true convertibility, of which more is said in the final chapter. As has already been explained, however, the heavy reduction in our exportable surplus and the vast increase in our essential imports threw our external balance of payments into chaos. Had we allowed foreign holders of sterling to transfer it freely between themselves, and to exchange it for other currencies as and when they wished, a state of exchange rates totally out of line with the official rates fixed here would quickly have been established in the neutral exchange markets of the world, with dire consequences for the external purchasing power of sterling. Consequently, control was instituted over the transfer of sterling from one foreign account to another in addition to the control already exercised over transfers of sterling from resident to non-resident account. Bilateral agreements were also gradually concluded with all the allied and the neutral countries, which provided that sterling (or, in some cases, the currency of the country concerned) should be used only for the settlement of transactions between that country and the whole of the Sterling Area and that transactions between the country concerned and other foreign countries could only be settled in sterling by permission of the British Authorities. These agreements, of course, resulted in the creation of a large number of bilateral types of sterling which were not automatically interchangeable and which replaced the former single and internationally accepted type of pound sterling.

In June, 1940, a new type of "Special" sterling account was introduced which was gradually extended by agreements with several countries, mainly in South America. Transfers of sterling between these Special Accounts were allowed freely so that sterling became transferable between the members of this system, but not between the members and other foreign countries. Further attempts were made on a minor scale to permit the transferability of sterling between other small groups of countries, but the first step of this nature on a major scale was taken in February, 1947, again in conformity with the requirements of the Anglo-American Loan Agreement of 1946. A new type of sterling account, known as "Transferable Sterling Account," was introduced, and the system at first comprised only five countries, including Canada and Newfoundland, but by 15th July, 1947, the scheme had been extended to quite a number of countries. The important feature of this new system was that sterling held on Transferable Sterling Accounts was made interchangeable with sterling on American accounts, so that in effect Transferable sterling was made convertible into dollars. The provisions of the Loan Agreement required that within twelve months of its coming into force *all* sterling acquired by non-residents as a result of any current transactions should be made freely convertible into dollars, and the operative date for this obligation was 15th July, 1947. On the eve of that date still more countries were admitted to the Transferable Account System, and the Special

Account System was brought practically to an end by the inclusion of its remaining principal members in the American Account System. This gave a widespread "limited" type of convertibility to sterling and meant, in effect, that sterling had to bear the burden of the dollar deficit of a number of other countries as well as the overall deficit of the Sterling Area with the rest of the world because any Transferable Account country which had a trading surplus with the Sterling Area, and so acquired a surplus of sterling, would immediately convert it into dollars. Out of the original American loan of about £940m. which had been made available on 15th July, 1946, an amount of nearly £600m. had already been used to meet the net adverse dollar balances of the Sterling Area and the countries which were then members of the Transferable Account System by 15th July, 1947. This left only a little more than £350m. out of which to meet the continuing Sterling Area dollar deficits and the conversion of sterling into dollars from the extended Transferable Account System, although the original loan had been intended to last until the end of 1951. In consequence, the experiment in convertibility which was launched so bravely on 15th July, 1947, lasted only until 21st August, 1947. During this period of less than six weeks an amount of over £250m. had been converted into dollars out of the remaining balance of the dollar loan, and it was evident that the small remainder would be absorbed in a matter of days. The facility for the conversion of Transferable sterling into dollars was therefore withdrawn, and sterling once more became inconvertible, although a degree of international transferability remained.

GRADUAL MERGING OF STERLING ACCOUNTS

Although, for the next few years, the Transferable Account System was gradually expanded, there were still a number of countries whose sterling accounts were operated under bilateral arrangements, while the accounts of countries in the American Account Area formed another segregated group, and Canadian sterling was a type of its own. In 1953, Canadian and American sterling accounts and their respective currencies were made interchangeable, but the next great step towards consolidating the various types of non-resident sterling was taken in March, 1954. Under this general reorganization practically all the bilateral types of sterling account were merged in the Transferable Sterling Account System, while a new type of account was introduced to facilitate dealings in gold in the London Bullion Market by foreign residents, and this was designated a "Registered Sterling Account." Apart from "blocked" and "frozen" sterling accounts and some unimportant private accounts which were not officially recognized, this reorganization reduced foreign sterling accounts to the following types—

(a) American Sterling Accounts, applying to the sterling accounts of residents of all countries of the American Account Area with banks in the United Kingdom. Transfers could be made without formality between these accounts and Canadian and Registered Sterling Accounts and to, but not from, Transferable Sterling Accounts. Payments or receipts in respect of dealings in American or Canadian dollars with Authorized Banks in the United Kingdom, or of gold transactions with the London Bullion Market, could also be passed across these accounts without formality.

American Sterling Accounts could only be opened by British banks for residents of countries in the American Account Area (commonly called the Dollar Area). This group included the following countries—

U.S.A. and U.S. Dependencies	Dominica	Mexico
Alaska	Ecuador	Nicaragua
Bolivia	El Salvador	Panama
Colombia	Guatemala	Philippines
Costa Rica	Haiti	Puerto Rico
Cuba	Honduras (Rep.)	Venezuela
	Liberia	

(b) Canadian Sterling Accounts, which covered all the sterling accounts of residents of Canada with banks in the United Kingdom and which could be used in the same way as American Accounts.

(c) Registered Accounts, which were intended to provide a kind of free gold and dollar account for residents of countries outside the Scheduled Territories and the Dollar Area. They could be opened by Authorized Banks only for such foreign residents and were created by sterling resulting from a sale of gold or of U.S. or Canadian dollars in this country by the account holder, or by a transfer from an American or a Canadian Sterling Account. Registered Accounts could be used in settlement of dealings in gold in the London Bullion Market or of dealings in U.S. or Canadian dollars with Authorized Banks, and could be credited without formality with transfers from other Registered Accounts or from American or Canadian Sterling Accounts, and vice versa.

(d) Transferable Sterling Accounts, which were the sterling accounts with British banks of residents of all foreign countries outside the Scheduled Territories and the Dollar Area, with the exception of a very few "unclassified" countries such as Afghanistan and Nepal. These made sterling a multilateral medium of exchange which could be used by all foreign countries outside the Dollar Area. Sterling payments between Transferable Accounts could be made without formality and they could receive freely any payments from American, Canadian or Registered Sterling Accounts, but could not be used to make payments in the reverse direction.

A few "private" accounts remained in existence, but could be used only for personal payments in this country by the account holder. Following the "Suez incident" in 1956, all the Transferable Sterling Accounts of Egyptian residents were "blocked" and payments into and from these accounts were rigidly controlled. This situation continued for over two years but in March, 1959, an official notice was issued under which all Exchange Control restrictions imposed on Egyptian accounts of residents of the Egyptian Monetary Area in July, 1956, were removed and in which instructions were given that all sterling accounts of residents of the Egyptian Monetary Area with banks in the United Kingdom should be redesignated as External Accounts as from the date of the notice. This last instruction was in conformity with the next great forward step towards complete freedom for sterling which will now be described.

The Final Merging of Sterling Accounts

In December, 1958, the British Government announced that the sterling accounts of all residents of countries outside the Scheduled Territories would thenceforth be merged into one type of non-resident account to be designated an "External Sterling Account." This removed all distinctions between the accounts of non-residents, and American, Canadian, Registered and Transferable Sterling Accounts all became External Sterling Accounts overnight. As an essential part of this merger, the new type of External sterling was given the attribute of convertibility in that any foreign holder of an External Sterling Account could make or receive payments to or from any other External Sterling Account without formality, or could use the balance on that account to purchase any foreign currency in any foreign exchange market, or to purchase gold in the London Bullion Market which he could either have held in safe deposit in this country or which he could have shipped, without special permission, to any other country of his choice. External Sterling Accounts can be used by the holder for the settlement of any current commercial or financial transaction, either with another foreign resident or with residents of the Scheduled Territories, but payments to External Sterling Accounts by residents of the Scheduled

Territories are still subject to control and must be approved either by Authorized Banks under the general powers granted to them or by the Bank of England, Exchange Control, if the stated purpose of the payment is not covered by the powers held by Authorized Banks. The only foreign-owned accounts which were not converted into External Sterling Accounts were those attaching to a very few countries and which were known as "undesignated non-resident accounts," and the few private accounts known as "special resident accounts" to which reference was made earlier.

This great step forward affected only foreign-owned sterling resulting from *current* commercial and financial transactions. No change was made in the regulations governing "blocked" and "frozen" sterling accounts. The first type arises from capital transactions, and the second from special circumstances relating to past transactions. A series of relaxations in the regulations governing the use of "blocked" sterling resulted in its becoming available for the purchase of securities quoted on any Stock Exchange within the Scheduled Territories (Sterling Area), provided that the security was not redeemable within five years from the date of purchase. If and when such securities were sold, the proceeds became known as "security" sterling because they were immediately available for re-investment on the same terms. In 1955, the regulations were relaxed still further to allow foreign-owned sterling securities to be transferred freely between non-residents, even if the transferee was resident in the Dollar Area, and "security" sterling was given similar freedom of transfer. With the creation of "external" sterling, it was widely assumed that within a comparatively short time "security" sterling would also be merged with it, but this assumption ignored the essential difference between sterling resulting from current transactions and sterling representing an investment of foreign capital. The total value of foreign-owned sterling assets (many of which had been in foreign ownership since before the second world war) was not known in 1955, and is still an unknown quantity; it must run into many millions of pounds. If "security" sterling had been merged with external sterling in 1955, all these assets could have been realized if the foreign owners had so desired and the proceeds withdrawn from this country. The central reserves would have been inadequate to meet such a drain, though some people thought that a merging of the two kinds of sterling would have created such confidence that large-scale withdrawals would not have taken place. Some measure of confidence is inherent in the quotation for security sterling, at a small and decreasing discount against external sterling over the succeeding decade. The merger has now taken place without any immediately noticeable drain on the reserves.

IMPORT AND EXPORT OF STERLING BANK NOTES AND FOREIGN CURRENCY

There is no restriction on the import into the United Kingdom of notes expressed in any currency (sterling or foreign).

Permission is required for the export from the United Kingdom of sterling notes, Guernsey notes, notes expressed in foreign currencies and currencies of the Scheduled Territories other than the United Kingdom, bills of exchange, promissory notes, drafts, travellers' cheques, letters of credit and similar documents which are expressed in a foreign currency or are of a kind intended to enable the person to whom they are issued to obtain foreign currency, and postal orders and assurance policies. Certain general authorities are in operation but otherwise permission for export must be obtained by an application on Form X to the Bank of England through the medium of the applicant's bankers and, if the application is approved, a Certificate C, which is valid for one month from date of issue, will be issued covering the items which it is desired to export.

There are certain exceptions to these regulations. Sterling notes, Guernsey notes, notes expressed in foreign currencies and currencies of the Scheduled Territories other than the United Kingdom in any amount may be carried by travellers proceeding direct to a destination in Eire or may be sent by post to Eire. Notes expressed in the currency of a Scheduled Territories country other than the United Kingdom may be sent by post to that country up to any amount. Any instrument or document enabling the person to whom it is issued to obtain foreign currency which has been issued by an authorized bank or otherwise with permission, and any traveller's cheque or letter of credit brought in and taken out again by a traveller who is a non-resident, is also exempt from these regulations. Postal orders may be taken or sent to a country within the Scheduled Territories, and assurance policies expressed in sterling or in a currency of the Scheduled Territories may be taken or sent to a country within the Scheduled Territories as also being exempt from these regulations. Authorized banks have also been given exemption for certain purposes as regards applications on Form X for Certificate C.

STOCKS AND SHARES

Owing to the technical nature of dealings in securities, the Exchange Control regulations covering such dealings by both residents and non-residents are somewhat difficult to describe in outline. Broadly speaking, however, residents may not make fresh investments without official permission, but if they already hold overseas investments they may switch from one investment to another over a fairly wide field, including American and Canadian securities. Non-residents can invest freely in sterling securities and in securities issued and quoted in other Scheduled Territories countries and can, without difficulty, obtain a licence which is valid for an indefinite period and which allows them to realize the investment at any time and to repatriate the proceeds to the same type of account as that from which the original investment was made.

Certain securities, which are mainly bearer securities and securities on which interest or dividends are payable by coupon, and registered certificates issued by a registrar outside the United Kingdom, whether such securities are payable in sterling or in any other currency, are subject to special control. If such securities are physically held in the United Kingdom, no matter in whose ownership they may be, they must be deposited with what is known as an "Authorized Depositary," and if they are held abroad, but are under the control of a resident of the United Kingdom, they must be held by the local foreign agent of an Authorized Depositary to the order of that Depositary.

An Authorized Depositary is a body corporate or a firm or a person authorized by H.M. Treasury so to act. All the authorized banks and a number of finance houses have been officially appointed as Authorized Depositaries. Deposited securities may be freely transferred from one Authorized Depositary to another, and in order to facilitate dealings in securities an Authorized Depositary is permitted to release deposited securities for technical purposes, such as to a stockbroker or a lawyer, who is also recognized under the regulations as an Authorized Depositary for such purposes. In the case of all other securities quoted on the stock exchanges in this country, dealings on behalf of non-residents as well as residents are carried out normally, but a declaration has to be completed on the eventual transfer deed as to the country of residence of both buyer and seller. Once again the formalities have been made as simple and as least troublesome as possible.

INVESTMENT CURRENCY

The demand for foreign currency securities is usually so strong as to ensure a premium on investment currencies over the official rate for T.T. This premium is quoted daily in the press at the head of the stock exchange table, and, as might be expected, it fluctuates with demand and supply. Because of the nature of the turnover in this market, there are not only fluctuations, but sometimes quite wide ones; on one day early in 1965 the premium was over 12 per cent, but within two days it had fallen back to a little over 8 per cent. It has not been unusual to see the premium exceed 30 per cent in recent years. Although the investor has to pay the premium when putting up his capital, any interest or dividend he receives can only be converted to pounds at the official rate—it cannot be sold in the investment currency market.

On the supply side, the market is fed by investors selling out foreign currency securities. For some years, further supplies came from accruals to residents in various ways, such as legacies, gifts, restitution payments from Germany and Austria, and assets brought into the country by new United Kingdom residents. But whereas these could then be sold in the investment currency market, the Budget of April, 1965, withdrew authority for this to be done. From then on such recipients of foreign exchange were required to sell it to an authorized dealer at the current official rate in the market.

A further change brought in by the Spring budget of 1965 requires United Kingdom residents who sell foreign currency securities to surrender 25 per cent of the proceeds in specified currency in exchange for sterling at the official rate, leaving them only 75 per cent on which to obtain the investment currency premium.

The demand side of the market comes from investors wishing to purchase foreign currency securities. These investors may be private residents, investment trusts or unit trusts buying securities quoted on Wall Street, or Continental bourses or other stock exchanges. Such holdings are called "portfolio investments."

Both demand and supply are fed from certain industrial types of investment ventures. If a United Kingdom manufacturing company had applied to the Exchange Control for permission to make a capital transfer so as to set up a company outside the Scheduled Territories to make its brand goods there, and the Exchange Control had refused to allow normal exchange for the purpose, in certain circumstances approval may be given for the currency to be obtained through the Investment Currency market. If later the institutional investor had sold out his foreign investment, then this would be done again in investment dollars, subject to the 25 per cent; meantime, any profits or dividends earned would have to be sold as ordinary exchange, not qualifying for the premium. During its life, any share certificate or other document of title would have to be held by an Authorized Depositary.

PROPERTY CURRENCY[1]

Another type of currency exchange arises from measures introduced by the Budget of April, 1965. As from then, any resident of the United Kingdom wishing to buy property outside the Scheduled Territories can only do so by first purchasing this property currency, and the only sources of supply are from sales of property outside the Scheduled Territories by U.K. residents. For some weeks after the introduction of the new regulation, there was no supply, mainly because sales of houses, villas and other property takes some time to go through, especially in such countries as Spain where it may take six months. Before the pool can start to operate, somebody has to sell his foreign property and get the money transferred to his bankers. In addition, the exchange dealers had to master the details of procedure laid down in the regulations and obtain Exchange Control permission. When the market settled down, a premium of some twenty per cent appeared to be the "middle rate," but there is no risk in forecasting that there will be a wide spread between buying and selling rates and fluctuations will certainly occur.

FOREIGN TRAVEL

Control has, of course, been exercised over the expenditure of United Kingdom residents travelling abroad since the inception of Exchange Control. For a long time no funds available in foreign countries were provided for purely pleasure travel. Funds required for business journeys were allotted on a somewhat meagre scale and, very exceptionally, allotments were also given to individuals who could show that it was imperative for them to go abroad for a certain period for health reasons. After the war, however, what came to be known as "Tourist Allowances" began to be made in increasing amounts and over an extending list of countries. In February, 1970, the latest in a series of Notices to Travellers was issued by the Bank of England. Briefly this shows that the current allowance for private journeys is £300 per person in respect of any one journey. For business travel the allowance is £40 per day per person subject to a maximum of £2,000 for any one journey. For amounts in excess of this approval must be sought. These allowances do not include the cost of fares and travel services which may be paid in sterling in the United Kingdom.

Under the impact of war or any other grave emergency numerous ancillary controls have to be introduced, such as control of overseas

[1] Since writing the above the Property and Investment Currency Markets have been merged in order to make more funds available for property purchase but, otherwise, the conditions are unchanged.

transport and of immigration and emigration, and even control over private communications by means of a cable and postal censorship. British psychology, however, is always resentful of such interference with the liberty of the subject and the Authorities take care to remove such controls at the earliest possible moment. In general, it can be said that the British Exchange and Trade Controls have operated with the maximum of efficiency and the minimum of interference with normal trade and personal relationships. Their administration has been above suspicion and has been conducted with scrupulous fairness—dukes and dustmen being treated alike. Thus controls which the Government has evidently felt it essential to retain are likely to be with us for some time. Control over exports of capital will have to remain until our external balance of payments is sufficiently in surplus to permit capital at present invested in this country and future savings to be diverted for investment in foreign countries. As long as this need exists it will be necessary to retain control over payment for imports and all other types of payments to foreign countries in order to prevent money being withdrawn from this country on the pretext that it is required to meet a debt due to a foreign country, whereas in reality the funds are intended for investment abroad. Control over the repatriation of the proceeds of exports must also be continued for similar reasons. The formalities connected with these controls have now, however, become such a matter of habit as to have been incorporated into ordinary business routine.

All these restrictions and official requirements were originally introduced under the provisions relative to Exchange and Trade Control which were included in the Emergency Powers (Defence) Act, 1939. This Act was repealed in 1947 and was superseded by the Exchange Control Act, 1947, which is dealt with in the next chapter. The Act gives wide powers to H.M. Treasury to withdraw, as well as to impose, control regulations and would appear to be a permanent piece of legislation. All alterations in Exchange and Trade Control requirements are effected by the issue of Statutory Rules and Orders and Statutory Instruments under the Act of 1947.

N.B. In several instances throughout this chapter reference has been made to conditions ruling at the time of writing. On every occasion it must be noted that the political circumstances with regard to Southern Rhodesia require that special arrangements always are applicable. It is not pertinent for the special arrangements to be mentioned throughout the text because of the very exceptional circumstances.

CHAPTER XIV

THE EXCHANGE EQUALIZATION ACCOUNT AND WORLD INSTITUTIONS

The Birth of the Exchange Equalization Account; the International Monetary Fund and the International Bank for Reconstruction and Development; the Organization for European Economic Co-operation and Development; the European Payments Union and the European Monetary Agreement

To understand the reasons which led the British Government eventually to engage actively in dealings in foreign exchange, it is necessary to recall some of the monetary history of the inter-war years. Prior to the First World War such business in foreign exchange as was done in London and all dealings in bullion were left to the operation of the open markets. The Bank of England was the unofficial custodian of the gold reserves of the country but was under no legal obligations whatever to expand or contract its gold holdings according to circumstances. It tacitly assumed this responsibility, however, and used Bank Rate as the means of checking an excessive outflow or inflow of gold. Exchange movements between gold standard countries were limited by the "gold points," but even then gold movements were left largely to private enterprise, and only occasionally were there direct dealings between the Bank of England and foreign central banks. This situation continued for several months after the outbreak of the First World War, but on 6th January, 1916, the Government announced that the sterling-dollar exchange rate would be "pegged" at $4·76½ per £ and that the Bank of England, as its financial agent, would be prepared to supply the foreign exchange market with dollars at this price. Import and export trade had already been placed under control, and other measures were taken to minimize the dollar drain. This official rate was maintained until 20th March, 1919, when the "peg" was removed and the open market was left to its own devices. The rate fell steadily for the next twelve months until it reached the then lowest record of 3·20½ in February, 1920. By this time, however, our industrial productivity was recovering, deflation was being achieved by heavy taxation, and an annual Budget surplus was being established. As a result, the external value of the £ steadily improved until, by 1923, it was in the region of 4·70. Apart from seasonal depressions, the rate was maintained at this level and in the Budget of 1925 it was announced that the £ would be restored to a gold bullion standard instead of the former gold specie standard and that the Bank of England would be placed under the legal obligation of dealing in gold in unlimited amounts, but in minimum quantities of 400 fine ounces, at officially fixed prices. As the price of gold in America had remained unchanged, this immediately restored the former gold parity of $4·86⅝ per £ and similarly revalued the pound in terms of all other currencies. The wisdom of this step has since been seriously questioned, and the late Lord Keynes held that, as a result, sterling had been over-valued externally by at least 10 per cent and that the consequent damage to our export trade was the direct cause of the unemployment and distress which led to the General Strike of 1926.

Matters gradually righted themselves, however, until the repercussions of the disastrous financial crisis in America in 1929 made themselves felt in Europe. The losses suffered by financial interests and by industry in consequence of the general fall in values and the severe business recession grew steadily worse during 1930, and the first rumblings of the European storm were heard in May, 1931. A leading bank in Austria found itself unable to meet its liabilities. This caused what amounted to a panic in bank circles, and a general repatriation of capital commenced. London had been "borrowing short and lending long," in that she had been accepting short-term sterling deposits from foreign lenders, such as the U.S.A. and France, against which she had made loans to Germany and Central Europe for capital projects which could not become immediately self-liquidating. The hurried and heavy withdrawals of short-term deposits threw a heavy strain on the Bank of England's gold reserve, and to provide some immediate reserves of foreign exchange, the Bank borrowed £25m. each from the Bank of France and the Federal Reserve Bank on 1st August, 1931. In the meantime, to protect their sterling interests, a powerful group of British insurance companies had mobilized their American security holdings and borrowed dollars against them which it had been selling in the open market in the hope of stemming the tide. Even these two sources of supply, however, were quickly absorbed, and on 28th August, 1931, the Treasury announced that it had arranged for the sale in America of British Government Dollar Treasury Bills to a total of $200m. Against this, however, the Treasury had to "earmark" a corresponding amount in gold out of the reserves. These reserves stood at about £133m. at the end of July, 1931, but had become pledged as security to the extent of £50m. by the Bank and a further £80m. by the Treasury, so that it was impossible to borrow further foreign exchange because no acceptable security remained. Speculation against the pound redoubled, and the final borrowings were exhausted within three weeks. On 19th September, 1931, therefore the Government was compelled to announce the suspension of gold payments as from Monday, 21st September, 1931.

This left sterling as an inconvertible paper currency of which the international exchange value had to be determined by the effective demand for and supply of sterling against other currencies. Its real international value as a purchasing agent was, however, greatly obscured by the current volume of speculation. Further capital withdrawals and "bear" speculation caused a fall in the sterling-dollar rate to $3·40 by 25th September, 1931, but at this level "bear" covering commenced, and the commercial demand revived so that within a fortnight the rate had improved to $3·90. At this level the Bank of England appeared as a buyer, and later in the month the first signs of a "two-way" control were seen as the Authorities made tentative sales of dollars whenever the rate fell below $3·83. An attempt was also made to curb speculation by the introduction of forms of declaration to be issued by a bank to any person wishing to deal in foreign exchange and to be signed by that person with a statement as to the purpose underlying the proposed exchange deal. The banks themselves were also required to render returns to the Authorities of the state of their accounts in foreign centres and details of any other foreign assets and liabilities, and to supply bulk figures of their dealings in foreign exchange. With certain variations, this system of returns is still in force. In spite of all these measures, however, the usual autumnal pressure against sterling proved too strong for the meagre official resources, particularly as a start had been made on the repayment of the earlier borrowings. Official support for sterling had therefore to be withdrawn, and the rate fell steadily until it touched a low point of $3·23 on 8th December, 1931. A recovery then set in which carried the rate up to $3·50 by the middle of January, 1932, and the Authorities then recommenced purchases of dollars for the dual purpose of trying to maintain a reasonably stable exchange and of accumulating funds for the repayment of the balance of the earlier borrowings. With the exception of a bond issue in French francs to the equivalent of about £25m. which did not mature until 10th September, 1932, the other borrowings were all repaid by the end of March, 1932, by which time the dollar rate had risen to $3·80 in spite of these official operations.

From the figures of the Bank Return and official statements in the House of Commons, it appears that this country lost over £200m. in gold and foreign exchange during the three months prior to the suspension of gold payments, but that during the following six months nearly £150m. in gold and foreign exchange had been acquired by the Authorities, leaving a balance of about £50m. in hand after the debt repayments. The very forces which pushed us off gold in 1931 would, therefore, have pushed us back again in 1932 had not official action been taken!

The Birth of the Exchange Equalization Account

During this initial period the Bank of England had conducted these official operations on behalf of the Treasury, but out of its own resources, and it was evidently felt that the new experiment in the management of external currency matters ought to be placed on an official basis. In his Budget speech in April, 1932, the Chancellor of the Exchequer announced that the Government proposed to take steps for the regulation of the exchanges by the establishment of a fund to be known as the "Exchange Equalization Account." The initial assets of the Account were to be a sum of about £25m. in U.S. dollars which the Treasury had accumulated towards one of the periodical repayments of war debt to the U.S.A., together with an undisclosed amount in gold which the Treasury had purchased from time to time in the open market since the suspension of gold payments. These assets were supplemented by an authority for the Account to raise a sum of £150m. by borrowing, which, in practice, was carried out by the issue of Treasury Bills by the Treasury to the Account. These bills were discounted with the Bank of England or in the Discount Market as and when the Account needed sterling to finance its operations. Finally, the Account took over the current foreign exchange holding of the Bank of England against, of course, a sterling payment to the Bank, but also assumed the liability for the losses sustained by the Bank in its earlier operations on Government account. The foreign exchange borrowed in 1931 had, of course, been sold at the then current prices, while the foreign currency purchased subsequently and used for the repayment of these debts had necessarily been bought at the rates then ruling, which showed a heavy depreciation of sterling. These losses were estimated at about £28m. so that the net initial capital of the Account cannot have been much more than £175m. In 1933 the borrowing powers of the Account were increased by £200m. and in 1937 by a further £200m. With other small intervening increases and a final increase of £300m. in May, 1954, the total borrowing powers of the Account are now £975m. which, with its initial net capital, would give it total resources of about £1,000m. Since the beginning of 1953 the central reserves of gold and foreign exchange have risen from just over $2,000m. to nearly $3,000m., i.e. about £1,100m. These reserves must be financed by the Account and, in addition, it must always have in hand a working capital which it is safe to assume would be at least £100m. This means that apart from its initial net capital and its borrowing powers, the Account has also acquired at least £200m. of other resources which can only be the accumulated profits on its operations. When it is remembered that in addition to the fairly heavy exchange loss of 1931 and 1932, a much heavier loss must have been incurred as a result of the devaluation of sterling in September, 1949, and November, 1967, the fact that a net profit of at least £200m. now exists is a high tribute to the skill and foresight of those responsible for the conduct of the operations of the Account.

E.E.A. Operations in the Sterling Crisis of 1964–5[1]

During the late Autumn of 1964 it became apparent that a "run on the pound" was developing, following a period during which the increase in productivity in the United Kingdom had fallen behind the rate in many other leading industrialized countries. By the end of October, 1964, there were vague rumours that the pound would have to be devalued. Forecasts of the balance of payments deficit for the whole year were of the order of £800m. Importers and exporters at home and abroad started to sell sterling in exchange for foreign currencies, both spot and forward, in anticipation of normal settlements, whilst debtors and creditors on non-trade account such as those concerned with services also operated in anticipation—this was probably the best illustration ever of the effect of "leads and lags." At the same time foreign banks converted their holdings of sterling whilst foreign speculators sold sterling forward in exchange for their own currencies or dollars. The Exchange Equalization Account was thus faced with the task of holding the value of sterling with the help of its resources and credits from other Central Banks, subsequently covered through I.M.F. arrangements involving a total of $3,000m.—though this was not fully utilized. In the months that followed, the task was complicated by efforts on the part of the United States to correct its own adverse balance of payments, largely arising from over-liberal aid to needy countries.

Action taken by the "Authorities," as the financial press usually calls the E.E.A., was of three inter-related types; buying spot sterling offered in the markets; buying forward sterling whenever they thought this more appropriate than operating in the spot market; and either buying or selling whenever a momentary over-demand or over-supply seemed to be indicated as a passing phase. Thus, in November,

---

[1] 1964 was the year when the United Kingdom balance of payments deficit on current and long-term capital account was the largest ever recorded. Hence the interest of these operations.

sterling was bought in exchange for dollars on several different occasions at the rate of $2·78¼ to £1; this was not allowed to become a fixed limit however and in one or two instances the rate was allowed to slip below this level by a small fraction in order to squeeze the foreign "bears." In the forward market the E.E.A. bought sterling outright forward when considered appropriate, and especially when the forward discount on the pound rose above the interest parity with the U.S. dollar. On occasion, the operations in the forward market took the form of swaps, especially, early in 1965, when the original outright purchases at three months became due for delivery. On one or two days when there had been a reversal of sentiment and the market was squeezed for spot pounds and the dollar ran quickly up over 2·79, the authorities sold sterling (i.e. bought dollars) and thus recovered some of the funds by which its dollar resources had been previously depleted.

The Account does not, of course, operate in isolation but as part of an overall strategy of economic and monetary control. Whilst the Account was operating to support the pound in the exchange market, short-term and long-term measures were put into force to correct the underlying causes of sterling weakness. Bank rate was raised to 7 per cent in November, 1964, thus making the cost of bear operations against sterling more expensive and making London more attractive to foreign depositors, though in the event this produced no very marked inflow of funds. New measures were announced to make exporting more attractive by various means, especially the "Export Rebate Scheme," and to make certain imports dearer by means of a surcharge. Both the emergency budget in the late Autumn of 1964, and the April, 1965, one, were largely concerned with correcting the basic position of the pound, and relieving some of the strains on our balance of payments.

The Account and the Internal Credit System

Under the automatic operation of any form of gold standard an influx of gold broadens the credit base and provides an inflationary potential, while an efflux of gold narrows the credit base and almost inevitably causes a more or less severe deflationary movement in the internal credit system. It is this automatic impact of fluctuations in the external balance of payments on the internal economy to which so much exception is taken by the opponents of a Gold Standard. It is argued that the state of internal trade and employment should not be rigidly linked to our external fortunes, and that a business slump in a foreign country should not be allowed to create similar conditions in this country through internal deflationary action having to be taken as a result of adverse exchange rates. In principle, there is no difference between the support of sterling by the E.E.A. and an outflow of gold under a Gold Standard, or in sales of sterling on a bid market by the E.E.A. and an inflow of gold. In the first case the sales of foreign currency withdraw sterling from the accounts of the buyers into that of the E.E.A. and so reduce the credit base. In the second place the sales of sterling against purchases of foreign currencies transfer sterling to the accounts of the sellers from the account of the E.E.A. and so broaden the credit base. The technique adopted by the E.E.A. almost from its inception operates to insulate the internal credit system from external influences. It should be mentioned briefly that the Bank of England and the commercial banks always try to preserve a minimum percentage of liquid assets to liabilities. Their lending powers therefore depend on the amount of their liquid assets. Any extension or contraction of the credit base represented by these liquid assets means an expansion or contraction of the total volume of credit several times larger. Monetary policy therefore requires that the credit base should always be kept proportionate to the credit needs of the country and should be allowed to expand or contract only in conformity with those credit needs and not as a result of any other influences. The principles of credit management in relation to the foreign exchanges which have been developed over the past two decades can be described briefly as follows—

(a) In accordance with its obligations as a member of the International Monetary Fund, this country declared a parity for sterling against gold and the U.S. dollar which, after the devaluation in 1967, became $2·40 per £. Other member countries similarly fixed parities for their currencies, and these form the basis of the "cross rates" between all the member currencies. Also in accordance with its obligations, this country restricts fluctuations in exchange rates to within 1 per cent on either side of the declared parity or of the "mean cross rate." Consequently, the Treasury, through the E.E.A., has fixed minimum and maximum exchange rates at which it will either sell or buy unlimited amounts of the "specified" currencies until further notice. It reserves the right to intervene in the open market, either in spot or forward exchange, if it considers such action is necessary to prevent undue fluctuations in rates. For example, the minimum and maximum dollar exchange rates are 2·38 and 2·42 and at these levels the E.E.A. would presumably take a firm stand in selling or buying dollars respectively. On many occasions, however, it has operated in the open market in order to cushion the effects of seasonal influences and to minimize fluctuations which might be detrimental to commercial interests. Through international arbitrage, official control of the dollar rate is usually sufficient to produce corresponding effects on the other quotations but, if any of these show signs of moving unduly out of line, direct official action in that currency is taken. The E.E.A. also operates in gold in the London Bullion Market on similar lines, and if and when convertibility for sterling is introduced, no doubt official buying and selling prices for gold will be legally established at the same time.

(b) If the E.E.A. decides to buy foreign currency or gold against sterling, the foreign currency is paid over to one of its accounts abroad or the gold taken into its vaults, while the sterling purchase price is paid by the debit of its account with the Bank of England to the bank or broker or other intermediary in this country from whom the purchase has been made. In any case this payment increases the cash resources of the commercial banking system and so broadens the credit base. The E.E.A., however, must provide the necessary sterling on its account with which to make these payments, and this it does by discounting part of its holding (as capital) of Treasury Bills. By tacit agreement the banks or finance houses which receive the sterling proceeds of the sale of foreign currency or gold become the buyers of the Treasury Bills offered for sale by the E.E.A. The inflationary potential of the inflow of foreign currency or gold against the creation of new sterling cash balances is therefore completely damped out.

An influx of gold under the Gold Standard was taken over by the Issue Department of the Bank of England against an issue of notes to the Banking Department. Against this increase in its cash the Banking Department credited the deposit accounts of the commercial banks which were due to receive payment for the gold purchased. In consequence, the cash reserves of the Bank of England, as well as those of the commercial banks, were both increased by the equivalent of the gold inflow, so that the lending powers of both sections of the credit system were increased by about two-thirds in the case of the Bank of England and no less than ten times the cash increase in the case of the commercial banks. Under the present system, however, the Issue Department of the Bank of England is not affected at all, while the Banking Department merely makes a transfer from the account of the E.E.A. as one depositor to the accounts of others represented by the commercial banks. Its own credit base is not therefore affected. By requiring the commercial banks whose deposits with the Bank of England have been increased to absorb an almost equivalent amount of Treasury Bills issued by the E.E.A., the cash reserves of such banks are restored to their former level and the inflationary potential disappears. In effect the E.E.A. has bought foreign currency or gold against Treasury Bills.

(c) When the E.E.A. decides to sell foreign currency or gold, it receives payment in sterling from a bank or finance house acting as agent for the ultimate buyer. This payment is effected by a transfer of sterling from the deposit account at the Bank of England of the commercial bank concerned to the deposit account of the E.E.A. Again the cash position of the Bank of England itself is not affected, but the other part of the credit system has suffered a decrease in its lending base. To counteract the deflationary potential of this position, the E.E.A. proceeds to use the sterling resulting from these sales to purchase Treasury Bills, mainly from those banks whose deposits have been reduced through the payments in question. The cash reserves of the commercial banking system are thus built up again, and ultimately the E.E.A. will have sold foreign currency or gold against Treasury Bills. This contrasts with the effects of an outflow of gold under a Gold Standard. The gold purchases would be paid for by debiting the deposit account with the Bank of England of the commercial bank acting as buying agent. These funds would be withdrawn from the Banking Department in the shape of notes which would then be presented to the Issue Department for encashment against gold. The Issue Department would deliver the gold and cancel the notes, thus decreasing both its assets and its liabilities. The cash reserves of the Banking Department would have been depleted by the value of the gold purchased, and the cash reserves of the commercial banking system would have suffered a similar decrease. In both cases, therefore, the contraction of the credit base would mean a contraction of lending power, and loans would have to be called in and short-term securities allowed to run off for cash until the accepted ratios of cash reserves to liabilities were restored.

None of this happens under the new system of credit management, and the genius of the technique now employed lies in its simplicity. Even more than Exchange Control, planned management of the sterling exchanges interlocked with management of the internal credit system has become, and seems likely permanently to remain, a part of our national economy.

The Exchange Control Act, 1947

The powers of exchange and trade control conveyed by the war-time Emergency Powers (Defence) Acts were temporarily renewed under the Supplies and Services (Transitional Powers) Act, 1945, and were finally codified and revised in 1947 and incorporated into a special Act of Parliament. Statutory Instruments concerning exchange and trade control are now issued under this Act which actually came into force on 1st October, 1947, which is known as the "appointed day." The Act is in six Parts, containing in all forty-four Clauses, and it has six Schedules. Its provisions may be summarized thus—

Part I. Gold and Foreign Currency. This covers the declaration and surrender to H.M. Treasury on demand of all gold and "specified currencies" which are in the ownership or disposal of any resident of the United Kingdom, other than an "authorized dealer." It empowers the Treasury to fix the purchase prices without right of appeal. It brings certain credit documents within the definition of foreign currency. It requires gold and foreign currency held by a resident as bailee for a non-resident to be declared and deposited with a named bank in this country for safe custody. It forbids any resident, other than an "authorized dealer," to buy or borrow or sell or lend any gold or foreign currency from or to any other person, either in this country or abroad, other than from or to an "authorized dealer." This makes it illegal for any person in this country to deal in any way in gold or foreign exchange except through the intermediary of one of the banks and financial houses who have been appointed "authorized dealers."

Part II. Payments. This forbids transactions or operations of three kinds: first, in this country, no payment may be made to or for the credit of a person resident outside the Scheduled Territories nor, on behalf or by order of such a person, may any payment be made to or for the credit of a person resident within the Scheduled Territories nor may any sum be placed to the credit of a person resident outside the Scheduled Territories; secondly, no resident of the United Kingdom may make any payment outside the country to or for the credit of a person resident outside the Scheduled Territories; and, thirdly, no resident of the United Kingdom may make any payment outside this country to or for the credit of a person resident within the Scheduled Territories as a result of which any person receives a payment outside the Scheduled Territories, or acquires property situated outside those Territories, or has transferred to him, or has created in his favour, a right, whether present or future and whether vested or contingent, to receive a payment or to acquire property outside those Territories. This makes illegal any form of "compensation" arrangement between residents and non-residents.

Part III. Securities. This deals with the issue and transfer of securities and coupons, the duties of registrars of companies and the procedure in regard to securities which are required to be placed in the custody of an "authorized depositary." It also empowers the

Treasury to take special action in regard to securities on which the interest and eventual capital repayment can be required by the holder, under the terms of the issue, to be paid in any of the foreign currencies "specified" from time to time by law.

Part IV. Import and Export. This covers the import and export of currency notes, Treasury Bills, bills of exchange in general, securities, documents of title (except bills of lading) and gold. Clause 23 gives power to control exports and the repatriation of export proceeds within six months from the date of export.

Part V. Miscellaneous. This requires residents to secure prompt payment of any money due to them by foreigners, not to delay obtaining payment for exports and to ensure that imports for which they have been allowed to make payment shall actually be imported within the stipulated period. It also gives power to the Treasury to direct that specific rights, goods or property acquired in contravention of the provisions of the Act shall be disposed of or even vested in the Treasury. It deals with the transfer of assurance policies, annuities, pensions, etc., and settlements in favour of non-residents. Finally, it lays down the duties of residents or groups of residents who hold a majority interest in any foreign company or business, the restrictions on the acquisition by non-residents of a controlling interest in a British company or firm and prohibits the lending of money, Treasury Bills or securities by residents to any concern carrying on business in the Scheduled Territories and which is controlled by non-residents, unless Treasury consent is first obtained. This last provision is of great importance to banks keeping the accounts of British companies or firms in which the majority interest is held by non-residents.

Part VI. Supplemental. This gives power to the Treasury to grant exemptions from any of the provisions of the Act and authorizes the continuance of the system of "blocked" accounts. It also contains a number of minor clauses in regard to contracts, legal proceedings, the mechanism for the enforcement of the Act, its application to the Crown, i.e. to Government Departments, the making of Orders under the Act, etc. It covers also the residential status of emigrants and the estate of a deceased person, and gives a number of definitions and interpretations of the terms used in the Act, as well as extending it to Northern Ireland, the Isle of Man and the Channel Islands.

Schedules. The six Schedules apply each to one Part of the Act and amplify and extend the provisions of each of those Parts. The Scheduled Territories are defined in the First Schedule, and the

Treasury has power at any time and without notice to add to or subtract from the territories set out in the Schedule. Because of this method of definition and of publicizing the territories concerned, they were given the new title of "Scheduled Territories" instead of the former description of "Sterling Area."

World Institutions

The pattern of events after the First World War was more or less repeated after the Second. The League of Nations was replaced by the United Nations, and out of a spate of conferences a variety of "Charters" and projected world institutions were conceived. The Bank for International Settlements, which was promoted after the first war and which still functions actively as a clearing house and depositary for many Governments and central banks, was apparently considered to be too much of a European institution for American tastes. Instead of building up the resources and extending the powers of this existing and well-organized institution, it was decided to create two new world institutions, one of which was to regulate the monetary affairs and exchanges of its members, while the other was to finance world reconstruction and subsequent further development, particularly of the more backward countries. These decisions were taken and the framework of the two new institutions laid down by the United Nations Monetary and Financial Conference held at Bretton Woods, New Hampshire, U.S.A. from 1st to 22nd July, 1944. American insistence on stability of exchange rates, non-discriminatory trade practices, an unchanged gold price and complete orthodoxy in fiscal and economic policies by the nations of the world is very evident in both plans. The new gold price of $35 per fine ounce troy which had remained fixed in America since 31st January, 1934, was made the world standard of value regardless of the greatly increased money values of all other primary products, commodities and services. No amount of argument seemed able to alter the American view that it is a waste of manpower and material to dig up gold from one hole in the ground only to bury it in another at Fort Knox. Its interim use as a universal purchasing agent and the possibility that America may not always be the universal creditor to whom all the world's gold automatically flows seem to be ignored. On the other hand, both plans link currencies to gold and the "gold motif" runs through the whole of both schemes. The proposals were eventually ratified by a large number of Governments, but not by Russia, and the two institutions were brought into being. The following is an outline of their constitution and objectives—

INTERNATIONAL MONETARY FUND

This is the institution designed to secure the operation of common economic and fiscal policies by the member States and to make available to its members supplies of foreign currencies needed to adjust a *temporary* debtor position. Its constitution represents a new departure in the formation of an international organization. In order to arrive at a basis for the borrowing powers of each member country, a quota system of subscriptions to the Fund was evolved, the quota for each member being based on its pre-war average share in the total volume of international trade. Each member was required to subscribe its quota partly in gold and partly in its own currency. For original members the minimum gold subscription was either 25 per cent of the quota or 10 per cent of the net official holdings of gold and U.S. dollars on 12th September, 1946, whichever was less. The balance of the quota was subscribed by the member making available to the Fund an equivalent amount in its own currency. Voting rights are based on the quotas and, in addition to the permanent officers of the Fund, there are sixteen executive directors elected by leading member countries and by groups of the smaller countries. Each member also elects a governor to the board of the Fund.

The number of subscribing member countries in April, 1969, was 111. Each member has a quota and the quota unit is the equivalent of one U.S. dollar. A basic obligation laid on members of the Fund is that they shall establish and declare a par value for their own unit of currency with the Fund unit (which is, of course, equivalent to a parity with the U.S. dollar), but some member countries have still not yet declared a par value for their currencies. The par value is used to determine the amount of subscription payable in the member's own currency and any subsequent increase or decrease in a quota must be effected by the deposit or release of gold, or of gold and U.S. dollars, and of the member currency concerned at the fixed parity and in the same proportion as the original subscriptions. Cambodia and Switzerland are not members of the Fund.

Should a member, in agreement with the Fund, change the par value of its currency, its subscription to the Fund must be increased in the case of a currency devaluation by making available to the Fund an additional amount of its own currency to restore the gold purchasing power of its original quota deposit. If a currency is revalued upwards, the Fund will release to the member an amount of its own currency sufficient to restore the gold purchasing power of the remainder to its original level. The following is a summary of the obligations and privileges of members of the Fund—

1. PAR VALUES. Under the original Plan the par value of a currency was to be based on the rates of exchange prevailing on the sixtieth day before the entry into force of the Agreement for the establishment of the Fund. A member, however, was given the right to object to this basis of calculation and to agree with the Fund on a different parity. The Fund can also object to any proposed parity on the grounds that it could not be maintained by the member without undue recourse to the resources of the Fund. A change in the par value of a member's currency may be made only on the proposal of the member and after consultation with the Fund, and it must be demonstrated that the change is necessary to correct a fundamental disequilibrium in the member's external balance of payments. Where the proposed change does not exceed 10 per cent of the *initial* par value the Fund cannot object, but if the proposed change would cause a variation of more than 10 per cent of the initial par value, the Fund may either concur or object. If a member changes the par value of its currency without consulting or in the face of objections by the Fund, the member may be declared by the Fund as ineligible to use its resources and may eventually be required to withdraw from membership.

2. STABILITY OF EXCHANGE RATES. Once a parity for a member's currency has been agreed with the Fund, the member must take the following steps to ensure that, in practice, current exchange rates fluctuate only within a narrow margin around this parity.

(*a*) If gold dealings are permitted, official buying and selling prices must be fixed which do not exceed a margin, *prescribed by the Fund*, below and above the fixed gold parity.

(*b*) Fluctuations in the exchange rates for "spot" transactions with the currencies of other members must be limited to a maximum margin of 1 per cent on either side of the "cross rate" parity calculated on the respective parities with the Fund. In effect this means that the member State must undertake exchange operations at or within the 2 per cent "spread" to maintain exchange stability.

(*c*) For other exchange transactions, including of course "forward" dealings, in the currencies of other members, steps must be taken to ensure that they are carried out at a margin over and above the margin for "spot" exchange, *which is not more than the Fund considers reasonable*. As almost constant touch with the permanent officers of the Fund is maintained by most of the member countries, the extent of these margins can be subject to a day-to-day review, if necessary, in the light of current circumstances.

(*d*) No member or any of its fiscal agencies may engage in discriminatory currency arrangements or multiple currency practices. Nor, unless the approval of the Fund is first obtained, may they impose restrictions on the making of payments and transfers for current international transactions.

(*e*) The existence of exchange restrictions was, however, recognized but members are under an obligation to withdraw all existing exchange restrictions as soon as they are satisfied that they will be able, in the absence of such restrictions, to supply their balance of payments in a manner which will not unduly encumber their access to the resources of the Fund. It was originally intended that all exchange restrictions should be removed within the ensuing three years, or within five years at most, but circumstances, including the Korean, Indo-Chinese and Vietnam wars, have frustrated this ambition.

(*f*) Members undertake to maintain orderly exchange arrangements with other members and to avoid competitive exchange alterations. International transfers in respect of capital movements must be strictly controlled, and members may not make net use of the resources of the Fund to meet a large or sustained outflow of capital. They must, however, allow exchange freely to be bought or sold and transfers of funds abroad to be made in respect of—

(i) All payments due in connexion with foreign trade, other current business including services, and normal short-term banking and credit facilities.

(ii) Payments due as interest on loans and as net income from other investments.

(iii) Payments of moderate amount for amortization of loans or for depreciation of direct investments.

(iv) Moderate remittances for family living expenses.

3. THE USE OF FUND RESOURCES. As at 31st December, 1958, the total assets of the Fund amounted to nearly $9,213·4m., of which $1,531·6m. was in gold and $1,164m. in convertible currencies.

By 30th April, 1969, the total of all quotas of the 111 members amounted to $21,231 million. At that time the Fund held $3,371 million in the form of gold and $18,802 million in the form of national currencies. In addition, as from January, 1963, there is provision for up to $6,000 million in supplementary resources under an arrangement by which ten industrialized countries (Belgium, Canada, France, Germany, Italy, Japan, Netherlands, Sweden, The

United Kingdom and the United States of America) stand ready to lend
to the Fund, if it should prove necessary for them to do so, to forestall
or cope with any impairment of the international payments system.

Members have the facility of access to these resources to correct
any temporary adverse balance of payments and are allowed to purchase from the Fund the currencies of other members for an equivalent
amount of their own currency. It is accepted as a general rule that the
member currency so acquired by the Fund shall be repurchased by
the member against the foreign currency for which it was exchanged
or against gold or dollars within a period of from three to five years
unless the Fund's holding of the member currency has been reduced
in the meantime by the purchase of some of that currency by another
member.

In addition, the Fund will enter into "standby arrangements"
with a member which ensure that the member may draw upon Fund
resources up to specified limits and within an agreed period without
any further reconsideration of the member's position. These stand-
by arrangements are normally limited to six months, but the Fund
is now prepared to engage itself for longer periods. This might be
of great help to countries which intend to introduce general convertibility of their currencies. Standby arrangements are renewable
according to the merits of each individual case but, again, they are
not intended to be used to support an outflow of capital or to defend
a fundamental disequilibrium in external payments.

There are limitations on all these drawing rights which are
expressed in terms of the member's quota and by the Fund's holdings of the member's currency. Normally a member may only
purchase other currencies during a twelve-month period up to a
value of 25 per cent of its quota, and purchases must cease altogether
if the Fund's holdings of the member's currency exceed 200 per cent
of its quota. A service charge of $\frac{1}{2}$ per cent is made on all purchases
of other currencies from the Fund, and an additional charge is made
where, as a result of such purchases, the Fund's holdings of the
member's currency exceed 100 per cent of its quota. This charge is on
a rising scale based on the relation between the member's drawings
and its quota and the length of the period for which the Fund must
hold an excess of the member's currency. A charge of $\frac{1}{4}$ per cent per
annum is made for standby arrangements, but as soon as purchases
are made under such an arrangement this charge is merged with the
service charge for the purchase. In addition to the requirement that
currency acquired by the Fund as a result of purchases of other
currencies by a member should be repurchased by the member
within from three to five years, the member is also under an obliga-

tion to repurchase at least part of the Fund's excess holdings of its currency if its monetary reserves improve or if in any one year it draws on the Fund without drawing equal amounts from its own reserves. This obligation remains as long as the Fund's holding of the member's currency exceeds 75 per cent of the member's quota in the Fund.

Although conceived in 1944, the plans for the establishment of the Fund underwent a lengthy period of gestation, and the Fund did not actually commence business until 1st March, 1947. Through force of circumstances it has not so far been able to achieve the results for which its progenitors hoped. In spite of its gold and dollar resources, the world shortage of dollars would soon have swamped its lending powers, and for a long time it had to invoke the "scarce currency" clause in its constitution which enables it to ration its sales of any currency for which the demand greatly exceeds the supply. Of recent years, however, the Fund has played quite an important part in helping countries which, for one reason or another, have run down their gold and currency reserves or are in balance of payments difficulties. Not only has it allowed certain member countries to make cash drawings in dollars and other hard currencies in appreciable amounts, but it has also provided in several cases what are known as "stand-by" facilities under which a member is granted the right to draw up to a stated sum within a specified period. Britain herself had recourse to the Fund during the currency crisis which followed the "Suez incident" in 1956 and drew in cash a sum of $561½m., which was used to raise the central reserves from the low level to which they had fallen. She also arranged for a "stand-by" credit of a further $738½m. which she could withdraw in cash at any time during the following twelve months, either in part or in whole. The Fund is therefore playing an increasingly important part in world finance.

The growth of world trade and the steadily decreasing liquidity ratio of world finance led to intensive discussions for increasing international credit facilities. In October, 1958, at the Annual Meeting of the I.M.F. and the World Bank, it was decided to increase the Fund quotas by 50 per cent and to double the present subscription capital of the International Bank. At the same time, adjustments were made in the quotas of several member countries, notably Germany and Japan, and the result was to increase the Fund's holdings of gold and dollars by something over $2,000m.

4. SPECIAL DRAWING RIGHTS. In order to alleviate the problem of the decreasing liquidity of world finance and also to be of greater

assistance to members, it was proposed that the rules of the I.M.F. be amended so that members would be afforded special drawing rights. These have become known as S.D.R.'s and are often referred to as "paper gold". This proposal came into force on 28th July, 1969, when the requisite number of the Fund's members had formally expressed their agreement. The result is that the Fund now conducts two accounts, namely a General Account and a Special Drawing Account, with the original functions of the fund being passed over the first-named account and the new function over the latter account. The unit of value for expressing S.D.R.'s is 0·888671 grammes of fine gold which is equivalent to the gold parity of the U.S. dollar.

The basic principles for participation in and allocation of S.D.R.'s is similar to that of the general fund. The fund made an initial allocation of S.D.R.'s equivalent to $3,414 million on 1st January, 1970, to 104 participants. This allocation was made for the first year of a first basic period of three years to be followed by annual allocations on 1st January, 1971, and 1st January, 1972, to a total of $3,000 million in each year to give an overall total of about $9,500 million. S.D.R.'s are international reserves and are not for use in direct settlement of international transactions, but are transferable from country to country against currency convertible in accordance with the Fund's rules. Initially, therefore, the above-mentioned account will be available to allow a country, according to its allocation, to add to its reserves without putting pressures on other countries' balance of payments.

Much discussion and conjecture as to how effective S.D.R.'s will prove to be has taken place, but it seems likely that the growing climate of international co-operation will be a major factor in the development of S.D.R.'s. There is no doubt that developments will be watched by many interested parties.

5. THE STERLING CRISIS—WINTER, 1964–5. The sterling crisis has already been briefly referred to in connexion with the operations of the Exchange Equalization Account during the critical period mentioned. It remains to record the nature and extent of the aid received from the I.M.F. and related agencies.

On the 7th November, 1964, the "Paris Club" (otherwise known as the "Group of Ten," and listed on p. 229) agreed to activate the standing arrangements under the stand-by which the Fund made in 1962, and renewed annually thereafter, to provide resources to meet United Kingdom drawings.

On 25th November (following the increase in Bank Rate from 5 to 7 per cent on 23rd November), the Bank of England announced having arranged additional credits with other central banks—U.S.A., Canada, Japan and eight of the leading European banks—amounting to 3,000 million U.S. dollars, apart from the amounts to be drawn as itemized hereunder. Some of these credits were for three months; their renewal for a further three months was subsequently negotiated in February, 1965.

It was announced in December, 1964, that the following resources had been placed at the disposal of the United Kingdom, and had been drawn by them—

(A) From the Fund's existing resources—

In U.S. dollars	.	.	U.S. $200m.
,, Canadian dollars	.	.	,, 45m.
,, Spanish pesetas	.	.	,, 30m.
,, Japanese yen	.	.	,, 20m.
,, Austrian schillings		.	,, 20m.
,, Italian lire	.	.	,, 15m.
,, Belgian francs	.	.	,, 10m.
,, Swedish kronor	.	.	,, 5m.
Total under Item (A)	.	.	,, 345m.

(B) Under the Paris Club stand-by—

In Deutsche marks	.	.	U.S. $180m.
,, French francs	.	.	,, 100m.
,, Netherlands guilders		.	,, 40m.
,, Belgian francs	.	.	,, 30m.
,, Japanese yen	.	.	,, 20m.
,, Canadian dollars	.	.	,, 15m.
,, Swedish kronor	.	.	,, 15m.
,, Italian lire	.	.	,, 5m.
Total under item (B)	.	.	,, 405m.

(C) Member currencies purchased for gold—

West Germany	.	.	U.S. $93m.
France	.	.	,, 63m.
Netherlands	.	.	,, 26m.
Belgium	.	.	,, 17m.
Japan	.	.	,, 14m.
Spain	.	.	,, 10m.
Canada	.	.	,, 9m.
Austria	.	.	,, 8m.
Sweden	.	.	,, 7m.
Italy	.	.	,, 3m.
Total under item (C)	.	.	,, 250m.

Total of items (A), (B) and (C) U.S. $1,000m.

The detailed comments are given to indicate the nature and extent of I.M.F. action at the time of critical pressure on a member's currency.

THE INTERNATIONAL BANK FOR RECONSTRUCTION AND DEVELOPMENT

The plan for the establishment of this institution was accepted concurrently by those countries which accepted membership of the International Monetary Fund. In due course, therefore, the Bank was constituted and commenced operations in 1947. Although its resources are provided by subscriptions of members to the shares of the capital stock of the Bank on a quota basis, on lines similar to those of the I.M.F., there is a great difference in the extent to which the respective quotas had to be taken up immediately. In the case of the I.M.F. all gold and dollar subscriptions of 25 per cent had to be paid up at once, and at the same time the remaining 75 per cent of the member's quota had to be provided in its own currency, either by an immediate credit to the account of the I.M.F. or by the issue of non-interest-bearing notes. In the case of the International Bank, however, the initial payments were limited to 2 per cent of the quota in gold or U.S. dollars and 18 per cent in the member country's currency. The remaining 80 per cent of each subscription is subject to call by the Bank only when required to meet obligations of the Bank for funds borrowed or on loans guaranteed by it. Payments on any such call may be made at the option of the member in gold, in U.S. dollars, or in the currency required to discharge the obligations of the Bank for which the call is made. For example, if a call of 10 per cent of the uncalled capital were to be made for the purpose of granting a cash loan to Belgium, Britain could effect payment of the call in gold or in U.S. dollars or in Belgian francs. In addition to its paid-up capital the Bank obtains further resources by selling its own bonds, not only in the U.S.A., but also in any member country whose Government is prepared to allow borrowing by the Bank in its domestic capital market.

In the same way that the resources of the I.M.F. were intended to be used to smooth out temporary balance of payments difficulties arising from *current* international transactions and not for the purpose of providing for capital investment, the resources of the International Bank were never intended to provide long-term capital for the restoration of war-shattered national economies. Under its constitution the Bank is only allowed to make or to guarantee loans which are made to member countries for the development of specific productive resources which will then in due course provide the increased production out of which the service of the loans can be met. Although the Bank is prepared to make loans to private enterprises as well as to Governments and Government agencies, it has so far insisted that where loans are not made directly to the

Government in whose territories the project to be financed is located, the loan must be guaranteed as to principal, interest and other charges by the Government or its central bank or a comparable agency of the Government acceptable to the Bank. Loans must be for productive purposes and those which the Fund considers cannot be justified on economic grounds are excluded. Further, the Bank will not make loans of a nature that it considers the borrower could obtain in the private capital market on reasonable terms. One of the objectives of the Bank is to promote private investment and not to compete with it, so that it will not undertake business which private investors are willing to transact on a reasonable basis. Loans by the Bank are normally limited to financing the foreign exchange costs of a project. The internal costs must be met by the country concerned out of its own resources. The Bank may supervise the disposition of the loans but it may not impose conditions as to the countries in which the materials required for the project are obtained. Interest and commission are charged on all loans and the interest rate is based on the current estimated cost of money to the Bank.

The International Bank has certainly been able to operate more actively than the I.M.F., and it has been responsible for the emergence of development projects for which finance could not otherwise have been found. It has issued loans to borrowing countries, mainly of course in U.S. dollars, but also in comparatively small amounts in fourteen other currencies, at varying interest rates, with repayments usually spread over a period of not more than twenty-five years, though there have been instances of repayments spread to a final redemption thirty or thirty-five years from the initial grant. During 1969, the International Bank made 84 loans to a value of $1,399 millions and its affiliate, the International Development Association agreed 38 credits to a value of $385 millions.

The Organization for Economic Co-operation and Development (O.E.C.D.)

This international body came into existence officially on 30th September, 1961, to replace the Organization for European Economic Co-operation (O.E.E.C.) which had played an outstanding role in the deployment of economic resources, and in related financing in Western Europe for some thirteen years, many of which had been critical. To understand the nature and purpose of O.E.C.D. it is therefore necessary first to examine the history of the O.E.E.C. which it replaced.

O.E.E.C. came into being as a result of American plans to assist in the reconstruction and rehabilitation of Western Europe. The broad plan was conceived by Mr. Marshall, who was then United States Secretary of State, and announced by him to the world in a speech at Harvard University in June, 1947. By the Foreign Assistance Act of 1948 the American nation committed itself to the supply of goods and cash to Europe to a total value of £1,263,750,000 during the fifteen months from the end of March, 1948, to the end of June, 1949. Various conditions were naturally attached to this colossal gift, and its distribution was supervised by an authority entitled the Economic Co-operation Administration (E.C.A.), which was centred in Washington but which had supervising missions in each of the participating countries. For their part these countries established their own supervising authority, which was entitled the Organization for European Economic Co-operation (O.E.E.C.) and which was set up on 16th April, 1948, by the following countries—

Austria	Western Germany	Netherlands	Trieste
Belgium	Greece	Norway	Turkey
Denmark	Iceland	Portugal	United Kingdom
Eire	Italy	Sweden	
France	Luxembourg	Switzerland	

Whilst the United States of America and Canada were not full members in a formal manner, they were very closely associated with O.E.E.C. right from the start and throughout its existence, and they became full members of O.E.C.D. in 1961.

These countries bound themselves to the co-ordination of their economic endeavours, to agreement on the best possible use of their national resources and commercial capabilities, and to the increase of productivity. They undertook to develop and modernize their industrial and agricultural equipment, to reduce trade obstacles progressively, to strive for full employment and to restore or maintain economic stability and confidence in their national currencies. Finally, they agreed to work towards world freedom of trade and complete convertibility.

The essential function of the O.E.E.C. was to provide the machinery for putting this far-reaching programme into effect; and in fact it was designed structurally to deal effectively with the tasks entrusted to it. At its head was the Council, which met either on ministerial level or on that of high government officials. It took decisions binding member governments in their economic policies and approved the necessary measures for the smooth running of the Organization. In this task it was assisted by the Executive Committee, which consisted of seven members, elected annually, and which carried out a preliminary examination of all questions submitted to the Council.

A number of Technical Committees, set up to deal with the Organization's extensive tasks, took upon themselves much of the responsibility for carrying out studies and putting forward proposals for action. Some of these Committees devoted themselves to the general study of economic problems, for example the Economic Committee and the Trade Committee. The remainder specialized more narrowly in the study of a particular aspect of economic activity, as in the case of the Coal Committee, the Iron and Steel Committee, the Food and Agriculture Committee, the Machinery Committee, the Textiles Committee, etc.

The American plan for aid to Europe was known as the European Recovery Programme (E.R.P.) and participants were required to submit detailed statements of their minimum requirements, giving the approximate cost and the proposed sources of supply, to the O.E.E.C. by whom they were screened and then passed to the E.C.A. for final approval. This approval resulted in the allocation of a specified sum in U.S. dollars to the participant concerned for expenditure over a stated period in specified forms. As and when a participant desired actually to make purchases out of its allocation, it made a specific detailed application to O.E.E.C. who, if satisfied, passed it to the E.C.A. for the final "authorization."

One of the conditions attached to the allocation of E.C.A. dollars was that an equivalent in the currency of the participating country should be placed to the credit of a special account with the central bank and that the balances on these accounts should eventually be used only for the redemption of internal debt or for some other purpose approved by E.C.A. The equivalent in local currency of dollar aid received, or to be received, which was credited to these special accounts was officially known as "counterpart funds," and a rather complicated system of accountancy had to be adopted. The E.C.A. was eventually superseded by the Mutual Security Agency (M.S.A.), but the basic requirements and practices under the original E.R.P. were continued.

In addition to the commercial side of E.R.P., the E.C.A. and the O.E.E.C. were also concerned at the serious situation of unbalance in inter-European payments. An agreement was eventually signed in Paris on 16th October, 1948, which brought into force a kind of inter-European Clearing scheme. American aid in providing initial support to those countries which were prepared to extend credits to their weaker neighbours was forthcoming, and the scheme worked reasonably well for over two years. The experience gained during this period, however, showed clearly the need for some more elaborate and better-equipped organization to cope with the monetary settlements involved by the steadily increasing volume of European trade, and another new international body was established.

This was the European Payments Union (E.P.U.) set up in 1950 to provide a better mechanism for the settlement of inter-European debts, and to provide extra reserves to enable members to tide over temporary adverse balances. The E.P.U. adopted its own unit of account, equivalent to the U.S. dollar, and a quota of such units was accorded to each member based on estimated trade requirements. Certain of the members became clearing agents for their currency areas, which was particularly important in the case of the United Kingdom as agent for all the Scheduled Territories. The E.P.U. scheme was renewed annually until 1955 when moves were made to replace it by the European Monetary Agreement (E.M.A.).

The terms of this Agreement were drawn up in 1955 as a result of pressure from some of the member countries of the O.E.E.C., particularly West Germany, for an early return to convertibility of currencies, even if this were to be only for external purposes. It was specifically designed to replace the E.P.U. arrangements which would become unworkable if several of the leading members gave external convertibility to their currencies, and also to tighten up the rules in regard to the granting of credit facilities so as to render it more difficult for debtors to accumulate unwieldy deficits. The Agreement was kept in cold storage for over three years but, following the granting of external convertibility to their currencies by several leading European countries as from 28th December, 1958, it was actually put into operation on that date and, simultaneously, the former E.P.U. arrangements were suspended pending the complete dissolution of the Union. The system comprises two complementary parts, one dealing with credit facilities to be granted by a new Organization known as the "European Fund," and the other dealing with intra-European payments which is known as the "Multilateral System for Settlements." All the members participating in O.E.E.C. and E.P.U. subscribed to the Agreement and the system eventually came into operation quite smoothly and efficiently.

The European Fund assumed the credit duties of the E.P.U. and took over from that Organization the residue of its capital of about $271½m. which originally derived from American sources. It also received subscriptions in gold or dollars from its member countries on an agreed quota basis amounting to a total of about $328½m., which gave it initial assets of $600m. The whole of this was not, however, called up immediately and the Fund commenced operations with assets of about $148m., consisting of $113m. received in gold from the E.P.U. and claims on Norway and Turkey of $35m. also transferred to it by E.P.U.

The former automatic credit facilities of E.P.U. were withdrawn as the basic purpose of the Fund is not to iron out monthly shortages but to grant short-term credits to members who may be in temporary difficulties with their balance of payments. Credits will only be granted when the applicant has satisfied the Fund that its difficulties are temporary, that it is endeavouring to carry out any recommendations in regard to trade, financial and economic policies which have been made to it by the O.E.E.C., and that unless it receives assistance it will be compelled to retract a certain degree of its current liberalization of trade with other members. Credits are granted in gold for a maximum term of two years and interest has to be paid on drawings at a rate determined by the O.E.E.C., while a service charge is imposed on any portion of the credit which is not utilized. This has made it much less easy for weaker countries to run into debt than was the case under the E.P.U. arrangements. The accounts of the Fund are kept in terms of a unit defined on a gold basis and which is the equivalent of one U.S. dollar at $35 per fine ounce of gold. Under the Agreement the Organization has the power to modify the gold content of the unit of account, which would make possible a simultaneous multilateral devaluation or revaluation of all member currencies against gold and dollars, but it is probably merely a precautionary clause of which advantage may never be taken. Within the first six months of its existence, the operations of the Fund were very small and amounted only to the equivalent of a few million dollars, showing that the exchange markets of Europe were quite capable of absorbing surpluses or meeting deficits by arbitrage operations.

THE MULTILATERAL SYSTEM FOR SETTLEMENTS

Drastic changes were made in the former E.P.U. payments arrangements. There is still a monthly settlement through the Bank for International Settlements, but the valuation of debtor and creditor currencies is no longer carried out on the parity value. It was provided that each member must, at the outset, declare to the European Fund margins beyond which it would not allow the value of its currency in terms of a given standard to fluctuate and which were to remain valid until further notice. This obligation, however, did not apply to any member country whose currency was not quoted on the market of any other member country. These official exchange dealing margins were fixed on either side of the declared parity of the currency concerned, or on either side of a central fixed point if no official parity had been declared, and the exchange rates were fixed in relation to gold or the U.S. dollar. There was a provision that these rates could also be fixed in relation to some other convertible currency or in relation to all convertible currencies, but the exact value of the currency concerned in terms of the U.S. dollar had always to be capable of determination. It was the intention of all participating countries that the official margins to be adopted should be as moderate and as stable as possible and, although each country was given the sole right to determine its own official margins, an undertaking was given that where necessary the margins would be fixed after consultation with the I.M.F. This was done to prevent the overall spread of official dealing margins from becoming excessive and, although several countries have not fixed official margins for their exchange rates with other members, the respective Central Banks operate effectively to hold current market rates within not more than $1\frac{1}{2}$ per cent[1] on either side of the central figure by means of direct intervention or by arbitrage through other centres.

The monthly settlements are carried out in terms of U.S. dollars and there are provisions determining the exchange rates for the conversion into dollars of the currencies of members who may be in debit or credit. Each Central Bank keeps accounts with every other in terms of the respective currencies and has the option of bringing surplus balances into the monthly settlements or, alternatively, can carry them forward to a future settlement. The major change in the basis of calculation was that, instead of the value of each member currency being calculated at a fixed parity with the settlement unit (as was the case under E.P.U. arrangements), any debtor can now buy back its own currency from its creditors in exchange for U.S. dollars at its official *selling* rate for U.S. dollars. This removed a certain hardship which the E.P.U. arrangements placed on debtors. For example, if Britain was in deficit at any E.P.U. monthly settlement at a time when the current market rate for U.S. dollars against sterling was only, say, $2 \cdot 78\frac{1}{2}$, the rules of E.P.U. required her to take further surplus sterling balances held by other members at an exchange rate of $2 \cdot 80$. She was thus, in effect, giving her creditors a bonus of $1\frac{1}{2}$ U.S. cents. Under the E.M.A. rules, however, she would have been required only to redeem surplus sterling for U.S.

---

[1] Against Swiss francs the margins had to be fixed at about $2\frac{1}{2}$ per cent on either side of parity because of the wide dealing "spread" for the U.S. dollar in Switzerland.

dollars at her official selling rate for that currency which would have been 2·78.

As mentioned previously, the E.M.A. does not provide for any automatic credit facilities of even a temporary nature to be granted by the European Fund to debtor members, and to meet such temporary requirements the Agreement contains arrangements for what is called "Interim Finance" to be granted by one Central Bank to another in case of need. Each member has undertaken to provide such "Interim Finance" to all other members by making its currency available, within certain agreed limits, to any other member requesting such a facility. These limits were fixed by negotiations between members, and the facility takes the form of advances granted by one Central Bank to another either by way of an overdraft—in which case the lender has the right to demand a deposit in the borrower's currency of the equivalent of the advance and to charge interest for the period during which the advance is made—or by way of a "swap" of the lender's currency against the borrower's, in which case an interest charge is allowed for in the "swap" margin. All such overdrafts must be repaid, or "swaps" fixed to mature at or before the next monthly settlement, so that the system is very definitely short-term finance. If an overdraft is repaid or a "swap" matures before the next monthly settlement, the borrower can repay in terms of the lender's currency, which is, of course, the currency in which the facility was provided. If, however, repayment is delayed until the next monthly settlement, it must be made in U.S. dollars on the basis of the lender's *buying* rate for dollars in terms of its own currency. For example, if the Bank of Norway borrows sterling from the Bank of England for two or three weeks, she can repay in sterling before the end-month settlement and can purchase the sterling in any exchange market against her own or any other currency which she may have at the prevailing market rate. This will probably be not very far from the parity rate with sterling of 17·1428 kroner per £. If, however, she had not effected repayment by the date of the monthly settlement, her sterling deficit would have to be met by a payment in U.S. dollars at the Bank of England's official *buying* rate for that currency against sterling, which is 2·42. This is a further inducement to borrowers to keep their requirements down to an extremely short-term basis, and during the majority of the time of the operation of these arrangements this has actually been the case.

The re-adaptation of O.E.E.C., which caused its replacement in the guise of O.E.C.D., is mainly due to two causes. The first was the attribute of "convertibility" given to many of the currencies of the countries concerned, in the sense that they are convertible in the hands of non-resident holders, as explained in Chapter XIV, and free arbitrage is permissible. The second was the trend towards political and economic integration which many European statesmen held to be an important long-term objective. This had much to do with the emergence of the European Economic Community (the "Common Market," otherwise known as "The Six") and the trading area of seven countries known as E.F.T.A., dealt with in Chapter XV. Of these two causes, the major influence causing O.E.E.C. to be re-adapted was probably the formation of these two blocs.

The aims of O.E.C.D. are defined in Article 1 of the Convention as follows—

(*a*) to achieve the highest sustainable economic growth and employment and a rising standard of living in member countries, while maintaining financial stability, and thus contribute to the development of the world economy;

(*b*) to contribute to sound economic expansion in member as well as non-member countries in the process of economic development; and

(*c*) to contribute to the expansion of world trade on a multilateral non-discriminatory basis in accordance with international obligations.

O.E.C.D. operates through various specialized committees. If one could be picked out as being of major importance, it is the Development Assistance Committee, consisting of a group of nine industrialized countries who are net exporters of capital, plus Japan, whose objective is the co-ordination of economic aid for capital-hungry countries, many of which are former colonies of the United Kingdom and various other European powers.

Co-operation between Central Banks

The importance of reasonable exchange stability is now so generally recognized that measures to counteract exceptional influences, such as sudden movements of "hot" money, waves of speculation and crises of confidence in a currency, are now being taken increasingly by the leading Central Banks and Monetary Authorities acting in concert. When the U.S. dollar was under severe pressure in the latter part of 1960, with substantial gold losses on the part of the U.S. Treasury, and the price of gold in the free markets rose well above the possible shipment points, the European Central Banks came to a tacit agreement with the American authorities that they would refrain from taking advantage of the profit thus shown by converting their dollar balances into gold at the expense of the

U.S. holdings and selling it on the open market. Instead, they absorbed very large amounts of the dollars offered on the exchange markets and allowed their dollar balances to rise much above normal, thus helping to preserve the existing limits on fluctuations in the dollar exchange rates. Again in March, 1961, when sterling was under speculative pressure and the reserves were losing heavily, the major European Central Banks agreed to allow their sterling balances to rise much above normal. This arrangement was made in the course of the annual meeting of the B.I.S. in Basle, and is known as the "Basle Agreement." This was, however, a short-term measure and in July, 1961, Britain borrowed the equivalent of £535m. from the I.M.F. in nine different currencies and redeemed the surplus sterling holdings of her Continental friends. Further developments in Central Bank co-operation are taking place all the time, as witness the rescue operations in the sterling crisis during the winter of 1964-5 referred to earlier in this chapter.

Whilst, no doubt, this co-operation between Central Banks will be maintained there will always be advocates for different systems of exchange rates which would diminish the importance of such cooperation. Some economists claim that freely floating exchange rates would ensure that a currency would continually find its correct level in relation to the currency of any other country. It is further claimed that this system would provide an almost immediate regulator to obviate the remedial action at present necessary to counteract balance of payment deficits or surpluses. Arguments for and against now appear very frequently in both technical publications and the national press. These arguments pursue a variety of aspects but there is no doubt that freely floating exchange rates have a distinct disadvantage in that traders would be unable to fix even near-future prices for their goods in terms of another currency. In order to avoid this other economists suggest that future rates may be determined with a reasonable degree of certainty by adopting a system of controlled alteration to rates of exchange at specific intervals. This system is known as the adjustable, crawling or moving peg. A major argument of the critics of the crawling peg is that speculators would be unwilling to abstain from their actions because the creation of a crawling peg amounts to an admission that there is a disequilibrium in existence which could become aggravated and result in a more significant devaluation or revaluation.

CHAPTER XV

INTERNATIONAL ACTION FOR TRADE AND CURRENCY LIBERALIZATION

The General Agreement on Tariffs and Trade; Currency Convertibility and Steps towards that End

AN eminent British economist once said that the full industrial potential and consuming power of the world would not reach saturation point until the last Hottentot was driving his Rolls Royce. This is another way of saying that the potential of world output for the satisfaction of the wants of mankind is almost limitless. It is rather a paradox that a growing appreciation of long-term world problems is developing side by side with an increasing spread of nationalism in the less-developed countries, notably in Asia. The almost incredible discoveries of modern science have enormous possibilities for good as well as for evil, and the next generation will undoubtedly see a revolution in the production of energy and in many industrial processes. These factors need not necessarily cause a redundancy of labour, however, as the benefits resulting from them should be divided between greater output per man-hour with shorter working hours. This is one of the long-term problems, and another is that of the inevitable increase in world population. Looking into the distant future one can almost see such an increase in world population as to give "standing room only!" It is clear already that in the older countries the use of land for factories, private dwellings, public buildings, etc., is steadily encroaching on the acreage available for agriculture and the production of the primary products so necessary to the life of man. In time this situation will develop by degrees in the younger countries, and this gives rise to the problem of how to increase the fertility of land under cultivation or to decrease the fertility of mankind, or something of both. There must be general agreement, however, that the objective of all Governments should be to promote the well-being of their peoples by an expansion of the markets in which they can dispose of their own products and in which they can satisfy their wants, while at the same time making the means of payment for such transactions as easy and as unrestricted as possible.

Restraint of International Trade

Wars and rumours of wars, industrial and political unrest, intense nationalism aiming at the self-sufficiency of the national economy, natural disasters such as floods, droughts and earthquakes, all militate against the ideal of complete freedom between communities for the exchange of goods and services and the movement of capital. Hindrances to trade imposed by Governments take many forms and arise from many causes. The failure of crops in a primary producing country, or even over-production of a staple product, may affect the external balance of payments of the country concerned so adversely that steps have to be taken for the artificial restraint of trade. Similar steps may also be taken in cases where the balance of payments has moved adversely through over-importing or through a fall in the world price for the staple exports. It may be said therefore that, in general, official measures which operate in restraint of international trade are taken to correct an adverse balance of payments. The most usual measures of this nature are as follow—

TARIFFS AND EXPORT BOUNTIES

Since any reduction in imports or any increase in exports tends to move the balance of payments in favour of the country concerned, one of the most obvious methods by which a Government can intervene to correct an unfavourable balance of payments is to impose restrictive or even prohibitive duties on the import of certain goods and/or to offer subsidies, bounties or "drawbacks" or "rebates" to exporters of certain staple home products. Since the external selling price of any commodity is its internal price combined with the exchange value of the home currency in terms of others, the normal tendency is for a world level of prices to be reached by adjustments in either internal prices or exchange rates. Where import duties are imposed or export bounties granted, this equilibrium is disturbed. In the former case, either the eventual selling price of the foreign goods taxed becomes so high in the home country as to discourage altogether purchases of those commodities—which means a definite loss to the total trade of the world—or such selling price is perforce raised above the level at which home producers can supply a similar article—which means a diversion of world trade from the foreign to the home country, but probably with a small reduction in volume owing to the higher price. In the latter case the home exporter is subsidized at the expense of his own taxpayers; he can probably sell more goods abroad through the reduction in his selling price which the bounty should render possible, but this merely means a diversion of world trade. Further, this very diversion means a loss of trade to some foreign producer of similar goods which can only contract his potential consuming power while the home taxpayer must necessarily contract his consuming power in other directions in order to provide for the further taxation out of his current income.

The whole effect of import tariffs (including surcharges) and export bounties is therefore restrictive and constrictive but, as with armaments, each nation is afraid to be the first to deprive itself of weapons, and instead of the common woes of the world having induced a desire for common action, there seems to have been during the post-war years a deplorable spread of a nationalistic rather than an internationalistic spirit amongst those responsible for the destinies of nations.

It is temporarily possible, however, for a country to provide itself with a favourable balance of payments sufficient to meet its obligations on debt account by means of tariffs and bounties. The ultimate diversion of and reduction in world trade must, in the end, react unfavourably on all and at best can result only in constant amendments and adjustments which of themselves prove a disturbing element in the general progress of the world.

QUOTAS AND LICENCES

In cases where a country's balance of payments still remains adverse even after the operation of a system of tariffs and/or bounties (which often happens when too heavy a deadweight of unproductive debt has been incurred) more drastic steps may be taken to control trade by means of "quotas" and/or licensing systems for permission to import or export certain classes of goods. Under the "quota" system the Government, as it were, rations the country as to the quantity of any specified commodity which shall be imported. Recognized importers of that commodity are allowed to clear through the Customs only a fixed proportion of their normal imports, taken over a basic period, e.g. for January, 1970, each importer might be allowed to clear only 60 per cent of his average monthly clearances over the twelve months ended June, 1969. The "quota" system can be used as a weapon for international trade warfare as can tariffs. The system can be elaborated to permit of a reduced total of imports of a given commodity being spread disproportionately over the countries of origin according to the concessions granted by those countries to the home country. For instance, a reduction in the total imports to 60 per cent of an earlier volume may be so arranged that the most friendly or closely-allied of the countries of origin, or the one forming the best customer for

17

the products of the home country, is given preference by instructing home importers that, of the reduced total, 80 per cent, say, may be taken from the most favoured country of origin, and of the balance 10 per cent may be taken from the next best customer or ally, 5 per cent from another, and 2½ per cent each from two others, leaving other possible producers of the commodity without a share in the market. Again, the effect is restrictive and constrictive. Potential consumers can become buyers only after their own produce has been sold and purchasing power thus acquired. A seller deprived of the opportunity of selling becomes a buyer without the means of purchase.

The method of permitting the import and export of specified goods only under licence operates in very much the same way. In order to limit demands for foreign exchange on the part of importers, the Government will require application to be made to an official department for permission to import certain classes of goods. Permission is signified by the issue of a licence which acts as authority for the importer to clear his goods through the Customs. Obviously, complete discrimination on the part of the officials is possible. Certain importers may be favoured over others; the total quantity of the commodity allowed to be imported can be rigidly controlled, the countries of origin can be favoured according to the needs of the Government or the whims of the officials, etc. The whole process is objectionable, not only because of the hindrance to trade, but also because of the possibilities of abuse and corruption which present themselves.

CURRENCY RESTRICTIONS

Any measures which prevent the free movement of funds between countries also act in restraint of trade. For example, when sterling was convertible and freely exchangeable between foreign holders, it was possible for a Brazilian merchant to buy sardines from Portugal, to have them packed in tins made from tin-plate bought from South Wales and then packed in wooden cases made from timber bought in Sweden and, finally, to ship the goods from Portugal to Brazil in a Greek vessel, against payment in sterling for all these various commodities and services. As a result sterling was an international currency which any seller of goods or services was ready to accept because he knew that other sellers from whom he wished to obtain goods or services would similarly accept sterling in payment. The existence of such an international medium of exchange therefore acted directly to the benefit of the volume of international trade. When, however, the exigencies of war involved the creation of so many bilateral types of sterling which were only interchangeable with official permission, the loss of a universally recognized international means of payment acted as a severe deterrent to the volume of international trade. Over the past few years it has become more and more generally accepted that, while the abandonment, or at least the reduction, of tariffs, quotas, export subsidies and other artificial restraints on trade is a main objective, it must be accompanied by a corresponding abandonment or reduction of restrictions on the free international movement of funds, particularly for the settlement of *current* commercial and financial transactions. It is also agreed that capital should be allowed to move freely about the world but it is recognized that this freedom will take longer to achieve while the internal re-equipment and development of national economies demands the retention of most of the available local capital within those economies. Amongst the non-Communist countries economic co-operation is growing steadily and, like the mutual efforts to finance trade and development which have been made throughout the I.M.F., the International Bank and the E.M.A., other efforts have been and are being devoted towards a mutually beneficial international trade policy.

The General Agreement on Tariffs and Trade

The Bretton Woods Conference of 1944, to which reference was made earlier, not only considered international financial problems and their solution but also discussed problems of international trade and employment. After a good deal of preparatory work a Conference of twenty-three nations assembled at Geneva in April, 1947, and drew up a General Agreement on Tariffs and Trade, which summarized the results of certain tariff negotiations arranged on a multilateral basis between the members of the Conference and also laid down certain general rules covering other aspects of trade relations between the members. On American initiative the Conference also drew up a document designated as "The Charter of the International Trade Organization." The Charter aimed at raising standards of living all round, at ensuring full employment and at developing the full use of the resources of the world by "reciprocal and mutually advantageous arrangements directed to the substantial reduction of tariffs and other barriers to trade and the elimination of discriminatory treatment in international commerce." The terms of the Charter were again considered by a full Conference of United Nations delegations held at Havana in March, 1948, which revised the original draft in a manner that caused several countries, including the United Kingdom, to make their eventual acceptance subject to certain reservations. Further discussions and negotiations took place over the next three years, but the final draft which commanded the acceptance of a majority of nations was not in accordance with American views and, although she was primarily responsible for the project, America announced her formal withdrawal from the proposed International Trade Organization in 1951. This, of course, frustrated the whole idea which since then has remained, if not stone dead, at least in a very low state of health!

Meanwhile, however, the General Agreement on Tariffs and Trade (G.A.T.T.) was commanding more and more support. A second Conference had been held at Annecy in 1949 and a third at Torquay in September, 1950, which was on a much larger scale than the two previous Conferences and produced much more important results. This last Conference continued for over six months, and its Final Act adopted a very large number of further tariff concessions made between the contracting parties and affirmed the general rules for the conduct of international trade relations. Further meetings have since been held at Geneva, and special committees sit regularly. There have, of course, been dissensions of a more or less serious nature, principally in regard to the system of "Imperial Preferences" adopted by the British Commonwealth and Empire is a result of the Ottawa Conference in 1934 which other nations, particularly America, would like to see broken down, and latterly in regard to the admission of Japan as a full contracting party to the Agreement. There can be no doubt, however, that international trade and the amity of nations have derived great benefit from the G.A.T.T. discussions and negotiations as they offer a forum for the expression of national views by representatives addressing each other personally.

The general rules of G.A.T.T. can be summarized briefly as follows—

(a) Members undertake to concert together to achieve a mutual reduction of tariff barriers and preferences and the greatest possible development of mutual trade.

(b) The principle of "general most-favoured-nation treatment" is accepted, and Members undertake that any concessions granted to any one Member country shall immediately and unconditionally be granted to all the others.

(c) Discrimination by means of tariffs against foreign products which compete with home products shall be avoided in the future, and any existing discrimination of this nature shall be reduced and eventually abolished as soon as possible.

(d) "Quantitative controls" shall also be abolished as quickly as circumstances permit, both externally and internally, and existing systems of import licensing shall be reduced to a minimum and the greatest possible freedom be given to the international exchange of goods and services.

(e) Existing restrictions imposed by exchange controls shall be removed as quickly and as completely as may be practicable, but only in regard to current trading transactions and ancillary services such as freights, insurances, bunkering, port dues, etc.

There are other minor provisions, but it will be seen that in general these rules follow the principles laid down at Bretton Woods for the International Monetary Fund. It will also be noted that several of these rules have been given practical application in the liberalization of trade which has taken place between the Member countries of the European Monetary Agreement. By June, 1954, an average of 85 per cent of all intra-European trade conducted by private enterprise had been freed from all import restrictions and, as a result of the G.A.T.T. Conferences, many of the goods concerned had been made subject to mutually reduced tariffs and in some cases had even been made duty free. The objectives must remain a counsel of perfection as long as national production has to be devoted in greater or lesser degree to re-armament programmes, and while capital investment has still largely to be concerned with unproductive new construction, reconstruction and re-equipment. Only when national production can everywhere be devoted to the capital development of industry and to the provision of capital and consumer goods which are free for sale on the home and export markets, will it be possible for any really large strides to be made towards the goal set by G.A.T.T.

THE EUROPEAN ECONOMIC COMMUNITY

This is basically a political conception directed towards the creation of a United States of Europe. Such a scheme was first disclosed when the European Coal and Steel Community was established in July, 1952, by Belgium, France, Germany, Italy, Luxembourg and the Netherlands. Further discussions on economic integration took place between representatives of these six countries at Messina in June, 1955, and the subject was then taken up by the O.E.E.C. The six "Messina" countries proceeded to draw up a definite plan to set up between themselves what became known as a "European Common Market," but other members of O.E.E.C. felt strongly that this would introduce discrimination in trade between members and non-members of such a group. For over two years innumerable discussions took place on the possibility of promoting what was called a "Free Trade Area," in which the other seventeen members of O.E.E.C. would join and which would be closely associated with the Common Market. While a certain measure of agreement was reached on the question of progressive tariff reductions between all O.E.E.C. members, there were certain aspects of the Common Market proposals which were quite unacceptable to the other countries. The six Common Market countries, however, steadily developed their plan in detail and on the 25th March, 1957, they signed a Treaty in Rome under which a European Economic Community, comprising the six countries, came into being on 1st January, 1958. The original plans for an associated "Free Trade Area" died for want of support and no practical proposals for any other form of association with the E.E.C. and their Common Market have yet been put forward.

The terms of the Rome Treaty provided for a transition period of twelve to fifteen years, during which the Common Market was to be established and a considerable degree of political integration carried out. The time-table for the eventual complete Customs Union can be summarized thus—

(a) *Removal of internal tariffs and quotas and the setting up of common external tariffs.* As from 1st January, 1959, all duties levied on 1st January, 1957, by any member against all or any of the other five were reduced by 10 per cent, and all bilateral quotas previously existing between members were extended to all members and increased by 20 per cent in total value and by at least 10 per cent for each individual product. Further reductions of 5 per cent of original tariffs and 10 per cent of total Customs rates were to be made at intervals of eighteen months, and by the end of the first four years all basic duties were to have been reduced by 25 per cent. Quotas were to be increased by 20 per cent in total value at yearly intervals, and by the end of the fourth year no quota was to be less than 5 per cent of the national output of each product.

As regards a common external tariff, it was based on the arithmetical average of the tariffs in force within the Community as at 1st January, 1957, and at the end of the fourth year all existing external tariffs were to be replaced by this arithmetical average where the tariff then current was above or below that average, unless it varied by more than 15 per cent from the average, in which case it was at once to be reduced by 30 per cent. This erection of a common tariff wall by the Community against all other countries, and the extension of quotas inside but not outside the Community, were matters which aroused serious misgivings in other countries.

(b) *Competition between the Community members to be made*

completely free. Legislation must be introduced (if not already in existence) to forbid cartels and all restrictions which might arise through agreements on price-fixing, market sharing, output, or any other restrictive practices. Differing rates on road, rail and inland waterways were to be removed, and frontier fees were to be reduced. Any restrictions on the rights of companies and individuals to engage in business ventures anywhere within the Community were to be progressively abolished. Existing restrictions on capital movements to be gradually removed and any movements of capital between member states and outside countries were to be reported.

(*c*) *On the political side,* each member undertook to pursue economic policies necessary to ensure a balance in its international payments and to maintain confidence in its currency. Rules were to be established which would permit workers to accept jobs anywhere in the Common Market area and a common policy was to be worked out regarding overtime and other wage problems (such as equal pay for men and women), social security, industrial hygiene, labour legislation in general and collective bargaining. The ultimate objective was the harmonization of economic conditions within the Community.

(*d*) *A European Investment Bank* was set up to assist under-developed regions and to modernize or convert businesses where the harmonization process had produced redundancy or uneconomic working. Its capital was eventually to be the equivalent of $1,000m. subscribed in varying proportions by the member countries. There was also a European Fund to retrain and move workers who had been displaced by the general reorganization of industry. The controlling powers to be an Assembly of one hundred and forty-two, a Court of Justice of seven members, and, as the executive power and supranational authority, a Council of six members and a Commission of nine members.

In the years after 1959, the progressive steps towards the removal of internal tariffs were in fact taken, on some occasions ahead of schedule. At the same time, freer movements of capital and labour were progressively achieved, though the objective of a common agricultural policy could not go so far or so fast because of clashes between the national policies of the various states.

Progress towards monetary union has been slow but increased attention is now being given to this goal. In December, 1969, a special committee was appointed to draw up a plan for complete economic and monetary integration by 1978–80. An initial report by the committee has suggested that the first stage would be the setting of economic guidelines for each country indicating expected growth rates and harmonizing further the different tax systems. Meanwhile, an agreement has been reached between the six Ministers of Finance that the existing margins allowed in dealings between their currencies will not be widened even if such action should be officially permitted by the International Monetary Fund. In the second stage the member countries would co-ordinate their economic and monetary policies more tightly and begin to reduce their exchange rate margins for dealing in each other's currencies. Finally, the move towards full economic and monetary union would require the introduction of a common currency or, what is tantamount to that, agreement that the existing parities between the individual currencies should be irrevocably fixed.

THE EUROPEAN FREE TRADE AREA (E.F.T.A.)

In response to the establishment of E.E.C. by a mere six countries, other O.E.C.D. states, which had been left out by the six themselves, established the European Free Trade Area comprising originally Austria, Denmark, Norway, Portugal, Sweden, Switzerland and the United Kingdom. They are commonly called "the Seven" to distinguish them from "the Six" of E.E.C., though this is something of a misnomer because Finland subsequently became associated with E.F.T.A.

E.F.T.A. was established by the Convention of Stockholm very early in 1960 with the following objectives—

(a) To promote in the area of the Association and in each member state, a sustained expansion of economic activity, full employment, increased productivity and the rational use of resources, financial stability and continuous improvement in living standards.

(b) To secure that trade between member states takes place in conditions of fair competition.

(c) To avoid significant disparity between member states in the conditions of supply of raw materials produced within the area of the Association.

(d) To contribute to the harmonious development and expansion of world trade and to the progressive removal of barriers to it.

On the practical side, members agreed to reduce duties by progressive steps until the end of 1965, and thereafter to eliminate them. The definition of the goods which qualify for reducing duties is necessarily complicated. The underlying intention is to grant the benefit where the goods are wholly produced in the exporting member's territory, or incorporate not more than fifty per cent of materials, components or labour costs of an origin outside the area of the Association.

There have been negotiations since E.F.T.A. was set up with a view to the United Kingdom becoming a member of E.E.C., notably in January, 1963, when French *intransigeance* provided a stumbling block. Further negotiations have now been entered into on the basis that the logical place of the United Kingdom is geographically, commercially and politically in a European context. Meanwhile, since 1963, the "low-tariff club"—as E.F.T.A. has been called—has pushed ahead with renewed vigour, resulting in a much larger flow of trade between members than had been generally anticipated. By January, 1964, the tariffs were 60 per cent lower than in 1959, with a further cut of 10 per cent on 1st January, 1965.

There are at the time of writing a number of important directions in which developments can be looked for, or hoped for. Some of these are connected with the breaking down or weakening of the division between "the Six" and "the Seven"—the so-called "economic schism." Probably the E.F.T.A. members are keener than those of E.E.C. to get the whole integrated into one area of unity, or at least free-trade unity. The greater likelihood is that the two blocs will come together for many matters of mutual interest. Thus, it seems fairly certain that they will get very close to working out a European Patent Convention and to sorting out differences between rival claimants to fishing rights, whilst the G.A.T.T. negotiations also offer many opportunities for collaboration of a type which, by bringing the two sides into harmony, could indicate scope for closer working in other spheres.

Currency Convertibility and Steps towards that End

The generally accepted definition of the attribute of "convertibility" as applied to a currency is simply that the holder of such a currency can transform it at will into gold or any other currency and that the use of such gold or foreign currency is not in any way controlled or hindered by the Authorities of the country whose currency is being so converted. This definition was adopted in a report by the Managing Board of the European Payments Union issued in May, 1954, dealing with the problems which would arise in connexion with a more or less general return to currency convertibility. The inclusion of the right of conversion into gold is very important because it is not difficult to conceive a world situation in which a seller would be unwilling to hold currency, whether in the form of liquid bank balances or balances in the hands of an agent, or whether in his own or in a foreign currency. In such circumstances a seller would consider himself safe only if he received payment in, or had the right immediately and freely to obtain, some medium of exchange which would command universal acceptance and which had an intrinsic and stable value of its own. This universally accepted medium is, of course, gold, and absolute convertibility of a currency requires that it should be capable of being transformed into gold as well as into any other quoted currency. This implies, therefore, that a currency which possessed absolute convertibility shall be on some form of gold standard, which in turn requires the fulfilment of the following conditions—

(a) Official buying and selling prices for gold in unlimited amounts are fixed by the Government, and these are supplemented by a free gold market in which gold can be bought and sold at prices fluctuating between the official limits.

(b) Any holder of the currency, whether native or foreign, must have the unfettered right to convert that currency into gold either by purchase from the State financial authority or in the free market; conversely, any native or foreigner must have the unfettered right to import gold into the country and to sell it in exchange for local currency either to the State authority or in the free gold market.

(c) The egress and ingress of gold must be unhindered by any system of export or import licences so that gold can move freely between the country concerned and any foreign centre.

A lesser degree of absolute convertibility is where a currency is firmly linked with the currency of some other country in which the above-mentioned three conditions prevail. This would place the first currency on a "gold exchange standard," but it would be essential that there should be officially fixed buying and selling exchange rates for the currency in terms of the gold currency, that the conversion of either currency into the other should be possible freely and without formality and that a free exchange market operating between the official upper and lower limits should exist. While such a system enables the country adopting it to dispense with a costly and unproductive gold reserve and only to maintain adequate reserves of the currency to which its own is linked, it has certain drawbacks. The economy of the country adopting it will necessarily be affected by changes in economic conditions in the gold currency country. Economic or political events in that country might cause an alteration in its current money price for gold, i.e. a devaluation or revaluation of the currency, or even a complete suspension of gold payments without warning. Unless, therefore, the economic ties between the two countries are normally so strong as to give them almost a joint economic policy, both internally and externally, the system can be dangerous. The British Commonwealth and Empire is an outstanding example of a group of countries with common economic interests and policies. The currencies of the independent Commonwealth countries (except, of course, Canada) and those of the Colonies have always been linked to sterling whether or not the British pound has been convertible. While Britain was on a gold specie standard prior to the 1914 war, and again while she was on a gold bullion standard for a period between the wars, the currencies of the Commonwealth countries were on a gold exchange standard because, through their link with sterling, they could be exchanged into gold. Even then, however, temporary economic disturbances or misfortunes caused restrictions to be placed on the exchange of local currencies for sterling, as was the case with Australia between 1927 and 1931 when her adverse external balance of payments became so acute that she had to ration supplies of sterling to her importers and other residents wishing to make payments abroad, and eventually in 1931 had to declare the suspension of official control over the exchange rate for the Australian pound with sterling so that the local currency became inconvertible.

The report of the Managing Board of the E.P.U. (see page 238), after adopting the orthodox definition of convertibility, introduced two concepts of this definition which it described as "full" and "limited" convertibility. Having regard to the varying strength and weakness of the balance of payments of every country in the world, it was recognized that while all the major countries wished to restore convertibility to their currencies in conjunction with a general liberalization of trade, some were in a better position than others to introduce what would be tantamount to absolute convertibility. The concept of "limited" convertibility was therefore designed for those countries whose balance of payments position forced them to proceed only by stages towards absolute convertibility.

Under "full" convertibility no limitations whatever would be placed on any transactions between residents and non-residents. There would be no quantitative import restrictions maintained for balance-of-payments reasons, and there would be no exchange control, either on current or on capital transactions. Further, and importantly, no distinction would be made between residents and non-residents as regards the convertibility of assets held by them *regardless of the date on which they were acquired*. This means, of course, that convertibility would not only apply to the settlement of transactions entered into and of capital invested *after* its introduction, but that it would be retrospective and would apply to all outstanding debts and *existing* capital investments as at the time of its introduction. Countries adopting "full" convertibility would also have to maintain fixed par values for the rates of exchange between their currencies and those of other countries, and/or fixed buying and selling prices for gold. It is admitted that even under "full" convertibility some countries might wish to maintain certain quantitative import restrictions, not for balance-of-payments reasons but as a means of protecting local industry in preference or in addition to other methods of protection such as tariffs. Such restrictions, however, would necessarily have to be strictly limited if the system were to deserve to be called "full" convertibility.

The term "limited" convertibility is used to describe an intermediate stage of convertibility under which a wide degree of freedom is given to non-resident holders of the currency, but control is still maintained over the foreign exchange dealings of residents and over the external trade of the country. Under such a system the following conditions would exist—

(a) All of the currency acquired by non-residents *after* the date of the introduction of the system would be freely convertible into gold, dollars or any other currency, and the use of such gold or foreign currency would not be in any way controlled or hindered by the country adopting the system.

(b) All payments permitted to be made to the account of a non-resident in discharge of current commercial or financial obligations would become immediately convertible, whether made to the account of a central bank, a commercial bank or a private holder.

(c) Capital movements, both in to and out of the country, would continue to be controlled so as to prevent an inflow of undesired, e.g. speculative, capital or a flight of non-resident or resident capital from the country.

(d) The country would continue to maintain foreign exchange controls over the transactions of its residents and could also continue to apply quantitative restrictions on imports and controls over current invisible transactions in accordance with internationally agreed rules.

(e) The country would retain the right to allow the rates of exchange for its own currency in terms of others to vary according to its estimate of the current needs of the country but in conformity with any obligations it may have undertaken to such organizations as the I.M.F. and the E.M.A.

The advantage of this system is that it gives complete transferability and convertibility of currency deriving from current commercial and financial transactions *to all non-residents*, thus making the currency international in scope while, at the same time, preserving control over the trading and foreign exchange operations of residents pending the time when the balance of payments situation will permit the introduction of "full" convertibility.

The discussions on currency convertibility raised the question as to whether fluctuations in exchange rates should be controlled or uncontrolled. Some quarters hold the view that a "free" or "floating" exchange rate for a currency should accompany convertibility. It is argued that only by allowing exchange rates to fluctuate in accordance with world demand for and supply of the currency will its true international value be ascertained, and that the arbitrary fixation of a parity exchange value with gold for the currency, with fluctuations restrained by official intervention or by the existence of fixed gold prices, may cause distortions in the external economy by over-valuing the currency in some directions and under-valuing it in others. The example of Canada is quoted as a country which successfully allowed a "free" exchange rate to operate for three years during which time her economy, both internally and externally, displayed marked strength. This example cannot, however, be taken as typical. Canada is still a young and developing country into which foreign capital has been poured in considerable volume but whose currency is not used internationally as a medium of exchange. The British pound sterling is the unit of account for a number of countries with very large external interests and it is also an international currency in terms of which a large proportion of the trade of the world is conducted. A comparison of the two economies in this way would, therefore, be on a most unequal basis.

Against these views it is correctly argued that a free exchange rate is capable of manipulation. It can be depressed at will by the Government so as to become, in effect, an export subsidy, and it can be raised equally artificially during any period of seasonal buying so as to cheapen the cost of imports. Equally importantly, a free exchange rate offers an attractive medium to the speculator, and a concerted "bull" or "bear" attack on the currency by outside speculators would cause most undesirable and unjustifiably adverse effects on the trade of the country concerned. The opponents of a free or floating rate also argue, again correctly, that such a system is contrary to the objectives of convertibility. If a currency is made convertible into gold and/or dollars, it is because gold is universally acceptable as a medium of exchange and because dollars or any other convertible currency are capable of being converted into gold at a fixed price. It is this ultimate convertibility into gold at a fixed price that gives the dollar and other gold standard currencies a stable value for exchange purposes, and one of the chief objectives of convertibility is to give the currency such stability of exchange value. Only by this means can world confidence in the currency be promoted so that other countries will be willing to acquire it and to hold it indefinitely because of its stability of exchange value. In addition, there are the twin points of the obligations to the I.M.F. by its members and of the consistent and rigid attitude of America towards stable exchange rates and an unchanged dollar price for gold. Members of the I.M.F. must undertake to confine the fluctuations in the exchange value of their currencies to a maximum movement of 1 per cent on either side of their declared official parity, which allows an overall fluctuation of only 2 per cent.

In spite of various currency crises and business recessions, progress towards economic stability continued to be made by most of the European countries. Over the week-end preceding Monday, 28th December, 1958, several leading European countries, headed by Britain, announced that thenceforth their currencies would be given limited convertibility and would become freely exchangeable for other currencies, including U.S. dollars, or for gold. Limited convertibility for sterling took the form of the merging of the previous types of foreign-owned sterling current accounts into one type of "external account" sterling, to which reference has already been made. This does not give full convertibility to sterling as residents of Britain and the other Sterling Area countries are still not free to use "resident sterling" to purchase any foreign currency, or gold, for whatever purpose they choose, whether for commercial or financial transactions or for private or business travel.

Full convertibility will only be attained when the same free use of sterling can be granted to residents as is now enjoyed by foreigners. This will involve—

(a) The removal of restrictions on the export of capital, whether this represents new capital to be invested abroad by residents or the withdrawal by foreigners of capital already invested here.

(b) The removal of all restrictions against the free import of goods and services, regardless of their nature or of their country of origin, and the granting of permission for payment for such imports to be made to any other country according to the desires of seller and buyer.

(c) The granting of permission to residents to purchase and to hold privately gold in any form purchased either here or abroad, and to import and export the metal without formality or hindrance.

In view of the heavy holdings of sterling assets by foreigners, it is most unlikely that the state of the central reserves and of the balance of payments of the Sterling Area will justify the removal of the restrictions on capital exports for some years to come. For the same reason, purchases and holdings of gold by residents cannot at present be permitted, but discriminatory barriers to trade are being steadily dismantled.

APPENDIX

SPECIFIED CURRENCIES

THE following is a current list of foreign currencies which have been specified by order of H.M. Treasury for the purpose of Section 2 of the Exchange Control Act, 1947, and which must be offered for sale by residents of the United Kingdom to an Authorized Dealer—

> Austrian schillings
> Belgian francs
> Canadian dollars
> Danish kroner
> Deutschmarks
> French francs
> Italian lire
> Japanese yen
> Netherlands guilders
> Norwegian kroner
> Portuguese escudos
> Spanish peseta
> Swedish kronor
> Swiss francs
> United States dollars

INDEX

30/-

2011773